The World of the Policy Analyst

The World of the Policy Analyst
Rationality, Values, and Politics

THIRD EDITION

Robert A. Heineman
Alfred University

William T. Bluhm
University of Rochester

Steven A. Peterson
Pennsylvania State University, Harrisburg

Edward N. Kearny
Western Kentucky University

CHATHAM HOUSE PUBLISHERS
SEVEN BRIDGES PRESS, LLC

NEW YORK · LONDON

Seven Bridges Press, LLC
135 Fifth Avenue, New York, NY 10010-7101

Copyright © 2001 by Chatham House Publishers
of Seven Bridges Press, LLC

Publisher: Ted Bolen
Managing Editor: Katharine Miller
Production Services: Sarah Evans
Cover Design: Stefan Killen Design
Cover Art: PhotoDisc, Inc.
Printing and Binding: Victor Graphics, Inc.

Library of Congress Cataloging-in-Publication Data
The world of the policy analyst : rationality, values, and politics /
Robert A. Heineman ... [et al.].— 3rd ed..
     p. cm.
  Includes bibliographical references and index.
  ISBN 1-889119-35-0 (pbk.)
  1. Policy sciences. I. Heineman, Robert A.
H97 .W68 2001
320'.6—dc211
                                      00-012246

Manufactured in the United States of America
10 9 8 7 6 5 4 3 2 1

Contents

Preface to the Third Edition

IT IS A PRIVILEGE for the authors to be able to offer a third edition of this text, and we extend our gratitude to the readers who have supported our effort and shared their thoughts with us. We believe that for the most part political events since the last edition have substantiated our analysis of the policy process and the analyst's role therein. Continuing fragmentation and conflict within the American system provide abundant evidence that negotiating the twists and turns of the policy process remains challenging. We hope that this volume will remain a useful guide for the working analyst and the student of American politics.

Changes in the current edition have focused on updating the analyses of the previous edition. Examples that were no longer timely or appropriate have been deleted and new ones have been provided. Additionally, the discussions of such topics as ethical issues raised by technological change, electoral trends, the budgetary process, and environmental policy have been made current.

We wish to thank our trusty secretary Karen Mix and able editor Sarah Evans for their assistance. Last but by no means least, we must record our heartfelt appreciation to the late Ed Artinian, who started us on this journey into the policy process and who, as a trusted adviser, editor, and friend, accompanied us much of the way.

Introduction

IN RECENT YEARS, policy analysis, as both an academic pursuit and a vocation, has grown in number of practitioners and in reputation. Major universities have instituted curricula centered on policy analysis, and a large amount of literature applying analytical techniques to social problems has been published. At all levels of government and at every stage of the policy process, analytical studies of problems and evaluations of programs have become commonplace. Yet despite the development of sophisticated methods of inquiry, policy analysis has not had a major substantive impact on policymakers. Policy analysts have remained distant from the power centers where policy decisions are made.

Concern about the limited influence of rational analysis in the policy process has raised fundamental questions about the orientation and role of policy analysis. It now seems clear that to be politically influential, policy analysis must be practiced as an integral part of its broader cultural context. It is not, and cannot be, a separate "scientific" endeavor inherently entitled to the deference of politicians and citizens. Its practitioners must understand that they are both in and of a particular kind of political world and that to maximize their policy effectiveness they must acknowledge the characteristics of that world—that its decentralized, poorly coordinated political institutions enshrine and implement the values of a paradoxical political culture. This book is about these institutional and cultural contexts of policy analysis. We have tried to provide students of the policymaking process and future decision makers (policy analysts, administrators, legislators, judges) with a perspective for grasping the manifold dimensions of the world in which policy analysis takes place.

This work is not intended as a how-to-do-it book. Instead, it is a detailed analysis of the situation of the policy analyst. Our intent is to help the analyst become more sensitive to the salient factors that influence the way he or she conceives and executes the task at hand. The goal of the book is therefore to illustrate the elements of scientific rationality in the enterprise of policy analysis, the ways in which ultimate values and conceptions of moral right and wrong are intertwined with this approach, and the influence of decentralized institutions of political authority on attempts to implement rational moral purpose. The reader may find here suggestive clues about ways to become a more rigorous policy analyst. But our focus is not on how to practice that vocation. Instead, we examine the difficult and complex context that practitioners must understand to be as effective as they can be.

The book has two primary purposes: (1) to contribute to a more realistic understanding of policy analysis in the policy process by examining the normative assumptions that permeate policy analysis; and (2) to explain the essential elements of the political process with which analysts must be prepared to work if they expect their efforts to be influential. At a minimum, this perspective should make policy analysis a more self-conscious process by encouraging analysts to be aware of the values behind the numbers and how these values necessarily shape the outcomes of both policy analysis and the policy process.

Over the past several decades, analyses of democratic culture and political processes in America have questioned whether contemporary conditions permit the constructive resolution of social problems. With *The End of Liberalism* in 1969, Theodore J. Lowi was one of the first to provide a thorough critique of the corrosive effects of "interest group liberalism" on the democratic policy process.[1] Lowi, a political scientist, argued that the dominance of interest groups in the policy process had diluted the legitimacy of formal norms and procedures and had undermined the proper role of governmental authority. Government was rapidly becoming little more than an arena for the negotiation of interest-group demands. He concluded that in this context, neither rational planning nor meaningful standards of right and wrong were possible and that the nation was approaching a crisis in public authority. Others have concurred with Lowi's analysis.

Taking a broader perspective, Mancur Olson, an economist, contended that in democracies, freedom of association inevitably leads to economic stagnation. Groups soon discover that manipulation of the government is easier and more profitable than competition in the open market. The scramble to use governmental powers and favors for narrow advantage engenders "an unending process of loophole discoveries and closures with the complexity and cost of regulation continually increasing."[2] Those successful in obtaining governmental protection become vested interests who resist change and stifle open competition in their areas. Adeptness at political manipulation—as opposed to efficient, competitive production and marketing—becomes the route to economic success.

A number of commentators have suggested that interest-group dominance in the policy process has led to a pervasive value relativism. In *After Virtue,* Alasdair MacIntyre, a student of ethics, contended that society and government are enmeshed in the claims of "emotivism," the belief that all moral judgments "are *nothing but* expressions of preference, expressions of attitude or feeling, insofar as they are moral or evaluative in character."[3] According to MacIntyre, our pluralist culture "possesses no method of weighing, no rational criterion for deciding between claims based on legitimate entitlement against claims based on need."4 He was particularly harsh on assertions that social science expertise can provide the knowledge and means for social change. In a statement perhaps more prescient than he intended, MacIntyre argued that the most effective bureaucrat "is the best actor."5 In his view, dexterity in manipulating images and beliefs about science and government, rather than specialized knowledge of policy expertise, are the tools of effective power.

The implications of these assessments of the policy process have to be disturbing to any policy analyst, no matter how intrepid he or she may be. According to these assessments, interest-group power has elevated informal relationships and understandings to a level of influence and complexity that threatens to swamp the formal boundaries and procedures of constitutional government. Samuel P. Huntington's comment that in America "effective power is unnoticed power; power observed is power devalued" speaks directly to this point.6 Under such conditions, the claims of those relying on rational analysis carry little weight when confronting interests adept at working within the interstices of the system. With no widely accepted sources of official or normative legitimacy, values (rational or irrational) become dependent on those with sufficient power to impose their definitions of morality. Group theorists did not cause the fragmentation of the American policy process, but, as thinkers like Lowi have recognized, their failure to provide a more comprehensive model of politics has contributed significantly to the diminution of expectations for American democracy once held by devotees of policy analysis, as well as by the public at large. In the words of Hugh Heclo, "At all levels of government, the political culture of hyperdemocracy encourages citizens to behave like spoiled children, demanding that government 'meet my needs,' and alternating between sullen withdrawal and boisterous whining."7

Not surprisingly, many studies of American politics in recent decades have been pessimistic in tone. Olson found himself hoping and "searching for a happy ending."8 Huntington concluded his survey of American political culture with the suggestion that America is not a failure but a "disappointment."9 And Heclo warned that "things *can* keep going from bad to worse."10

Studies dealing directly with the mechanics of the policy process have taken a similar tack. At the beginning of his analysis of the implementation process, Eugene Bardach warned the unwary reader that "this is not an optimistic book."11 In their treatment of implementation, Jeffrey Pressman and Aaron Wildavsky noted that "the remarkable thing is that new programs work at all."12 And in his text on the policy process, Thomas R. Dye asked, "Does government really know what it is doing?" His answer was, "Generally speaking, no."13 G. Calvin Mackenzie asserted, "Our government does not work well. It cannot perform with any consistency or reliability the simple functions of democracy."14 Kevin Phillips echoed this view: "From the White House to Capitol

Hill, the critical weakness of American politics and governance is becoming woefully apparent: a frightening inability to defuse and debate emerging problems. For the moment the political culture appears to be brain-dead."[15]

Perhaps stimulated by these rather pessimistic assessments, some recent work has taken a broader perspective on the position of government in the nation. These analyses contend that effective government is linked to the social and cultural conditions of a nation. Much of this analysis was stimulated by Robert Putnam's article "Bowling Alone," in which he suggested that the social associations important to democratic values and practices in America were disappearing—that the civic fabric was unraveling.[16] Putnam's analysis and conclusions have been the targets of some telling criticism,[17] but he deserves credit for broadening the discussion of what constitutes the components of effective democratic government. In a similar vein, Francis Fukuyama's *Trust* examined the importance of reliable social relationships to stable government and the growth of capitalism.[18] Our intent in this book—to encourage policy analysts to broaden their focus to encompass the context in which analytical work occurs—is in keeping with the orientation of these scholars. A broader comprehension of the position of policy analysis in relation to the problems facing American democracy may facilitate understanding and, perhaps, mitigation of these problems.

The question of normative perspectives and assumptions deserves brief preliminary treatment. A number of commentators have noted the absence of discussion about fundamental values in policy analysis literature and curricula.[19] In a sense, such criticisms are inaccurate, for numerous works have examined ethical issues from a philosophical perspective. The problem has been that these discussions, although helping to clarify and stimulate, have tended to be of marginal applied use to the practicing policy analyst. Their exposition of ethical difficulties has far too often concentrated on logical rigor, not on the conflicting, changing, and often irrational values that influence political decisions. Used carefully, however, they can demonstrate the limitations of purely utilitarian calculations. An example of this approach that has achieved some fame is the "trolley problem" stated by Judith Jarvis Thomson.[20]

In the trolley problem, Thomson hypothesized a runaway trolley headed down a track with a spur. If the trolley remains on the main track, it will hit and probably kill five people. If the driver or a bystander diverts it to the spur, it will kill but one person. Elaborating on this hypothetical situation, Thomson postulated a variety of details and modifications from which she tried to extract moral lessons or generalizations. Models of this sort have important pedagogical uses in the appropriate context but are only tenuously linked to real life. Their fundamental danger is not so much their isolation from the real world as their tendency to suggest to students imbued with the virtues of analytical precision that values can be defined and approached with similar rigor. Unfortunately, the policy process already contains too many individuals who in their zealous pursuit of particular goals operate with cognitive blinders in their approaches to issues and problems. Far more important to the policy analyst is an understanding of the fundamental, culturally determined normative expectations of those who will respond to or be affected by his or her suggestions. In this respect, the policy analyst needs to recognize that contradictory beliefs and irrational positions are not aberrations but inherent facts of the political system that have to be confronted with both flexibility and persuasion.

In the discussions that follow, we use the term *values* to describe beliefs and attitudes that guide individual behavior in the policy process. These beliefs and attitudes can be divided into three general categories ranging from broad cultural forces to orientations that are specific to individuals. The least definable and articulate of these categories includes cultural norms and expectations that have deep roots in American culture and that are usually uncritically accepted as valid. Closely related to and originating from this category are ideological positions that provide rationalizations for particular policy views. A reasonably distinct and different set of values can be identified as those positions formed by one's role in the policy process. Agencies, legislative bodies, courts, and interest groups have all developed norms and expectations about goals and appropriate forms of behavior. Policy actors will naturally tend to respond to issues within the framework of the norms and expectations of the institution or organization with which they are affiliated. Although these norms and expectations may appear peripheral to substantive policy issues, they frequently determine policy decisions. Finally, at the most specific level are personal beliefs and attitudes that vary from individual to individual. These would include desire for power or fame, concern for integrity, and pursuit of wealth or security. As used in this work, the term *values* refers to one of the three categories just described, and in each instance the context should make clear which of these concepts is being considered.

This book assumes a broad definition of policy analysis. It recognizes that analysis relevant to understanding the policy process and to policy decisions may be undertaken from a number of useful viewpoints. When working to provide input to policy decisions, physicians, attorneys, or chemists could be seen as doing policy analysis.[21] The very concept of analysis, of course, presupposes the importance of rational argument and rigorous methodology, and in this respect, policy analysis must be differentiated from approaches to the policy process that do not meet, or make minimal use of, these criteria. At the same time, it is essential that analysts recognize the limitations of their rigorous standards in the workaday world. This seems to be the major point of James C. Scott's *Seeing like a State*. In his study of government projects in other nations, Scott has emphasized the importance of flexibly meshing a government's goals and procedures with those of the society in which it exists. Too often, this does not happen. In

Scott's words, "The utopian, immanent, and continually frustrated goal of the modern state is to reduce the chaotic, disorderly, constantly changing social reality beneath it to something more closely resembling the administrative grid of its observations."[22]

While there is general agreement on the importance of analytical rigor as a criterion for legitimate policy analysis, there remains considerable diversity of opinion as to what should constitute a discipline of policy analysis. Duncan MacRae Jr. argued that policy analysis should be seen as an "applied discipline." From his perspective, policy analysis is concerned with "the constructive analysis of concrete policy choices through research and effective policy advice."[23] William D. Coplin, asserting that his use of the term *policy studies* was the same as MacRae's use of *policy analysis,* viewed policy studies as "the application of the social sciences to societal problems."[24] Another, broader view of policy analysis was offered by Thomas R. Dye, who saw policy analysis as more concerned with understanding and explaining policy issues. According to Dye, policy analysts should strive for generally applicable explanations, or theories, of policy issues because "developing scientific knowledge about the forces shaping public policy and the consequences of public policy is itself a socially relevant activity."[25] We conceive of policy analysis in the larger sense of encompassing the application of analytical techniques to social issues for the purpose of both enhanced understanding of and improved input into the policy process. In this respect, our concept is close to the broad view first suggested by Yehezkel Dror.[26]

At this stage in the development of approaches to policy analysis, restrictive delineation of what legitimately constitutes policy analysis can easily be more harmful than helpful. For example, efforts to distinguish between policy analysis and evaluation research do not at this time seem to be sustainable. Policy analysis requires evaluation as an integral part of the continuing cycle of input into policy decisions. But more important, those trained outside the usual disciplines that contribute to schools of policy analysis should be encouraged also to see themselves as analytic contributors to public policy and should have available to them the means for gaining a better understanding of and perspective on their position. Policy analysis as a field of endeavor, whether applied or theoretical, is developing techniques and models that may give it a more specific identity and expertise. But the perspective being urged here should be useful and comprehensible to anyone who expects to provide analytical input into the decision-making process.

The reader will discover that this book moves from the general, broad issues raised by the emergence of policy analysis to the particulars of the policy process itself. First, we examine the American cultural roots of the ideal of rational social analysis. This is followed by a discussion of some of the important techniques of policy analysis in terms of essential, although often unarticulated, assumptions about them and in terms of their relationship to decision making. Next, we analyze leading American values with reference to their historical development, their present paradoxical character, and the way they fit into recent efforts to analyze systematically the ethical dilemmas in policy analysis. We then illustrate the importance of norms and their effects on political behavior by examining recent trends in the electorate. This discussion moves naturally into the problems that fragmented policymaking institutions pose for policy recommendations. The courts are treated separately because they differ in important respects from the elected branches in their response to policy analysis and policy issues. In conclusion, we examine proposals for structural reform of the policy process and present tentative suggestions about how policy analysis might be made more effective in the policy process and how analysts might integrate normative considerations into the specifics of their work.

Obviously, students are free to pick and choose as they see fit from the ideas offered, but the intent is to provide a broad cultural understanding of the American policy process that will produce a more comprehensive and realistic conception of policy studies than the specialized treatments that dominate the field. Our aim is not to denigrate the need for rigorous analysis of social problems but to enhance understanding of the capabilities and limits of policy analysis by placing it in the context in which it functions.

CHAPTER 1

The Emergence of a Field

A COMMITMENT TO science and its methods as the most important source of progress has permeated scholarly assumptions about the possibility of a social science. This view and the cultural heritage of American social science have both been exceptionally important influences on the development of policy analysis. Yet today policy analysts find themselves confronting a policy process that is unable to utilize effectively the sophisticated methodologies and related technology that have been developed to examine social issues. Except during rare periods of national crisis, policy analysts have seen recommendations that they have justified on the basis of rational merit submerged in a policy process marked by the proliferation of organized interests and by the growth of institutional complexity and fragmentation. In this environment, the values of analytical rigor and logic have given way to political necessities.

THE HISTORICAL BACKGROUND

In most important respects, the origins of the anomalous position of policy analysis can be traced to intellectual and social developments that first became salient and began to affect political thinking during the latter part of the nineteenth century. The emergence of increased concern for greater analytical rigor in the study of individual and social behavior provides one of the important sources of contemporary ideas about social science. These ideas in turn have engendered policy analysis as an identifiable endeavor. Basic to these changes was the belief that rational, scientific methods could be applied to the improvement of social conditions. The growth of large industrial organizations led to efforts to control human behavior in the interests of increased efficiency and profit; Frederick W. Taylor remains famous for his formulation of the principles of scientific management around the turn of the century. In addition, new views of science, which were influenced heavily by Charles Darwin and which emphasized change and evolving concepts of truth, were used by philosophers and social scientists to buttress their efforts at social reform. Scientific approaches began to be applied directly to social activity and were seen as particularly useful to efforts to improve society.

The Era of Reform

These views moved rather quickly into the realm of public policy and led to what Russell Hanson termed the "rationalization" of political discourse.[1] The criterion of efficiency was seen as equally applicable to industry and government, and it became fashionable to argue that administration in government should be separated from "politics." These ideas gave rise to the Progressive movement, which, although it did not establish extensive welfare programs, did contribute significantly to an increase in government regulatory efforts. Legislation creating such agencies as the Federal Reserve Board and the Federal Trade Commission, along with other major regulatory legislation, is a clear indication that the American public was willing to accept government intervention in the private sphere on a much larger scale than ever before. Of particular note was the public's willingness to make the regulatory agencies "independent" by insulating them from the political pressures faced by other agencies. Such an approach signaled a new deference to experts in the areas being regulated.

This period also marks the beginning of the professionalization of academic social science. The movement toward disciplinary rigor was linked closely to the actively reformist motivations of scholars dissatisfied with social conditions and confident in their ability to fashion improvements. Another contributing element was the influence of German ideas on American social scientists. Many Americans studied in Germany, where they saw firsthand the effects of Bismarck's welfare measures and were exposed to the power of the historical method in social analysis. Reflecting on his German educational experience, William Graham Sumner, himself a critic of reform, asserted that the German "method of study was nobly scientific, and was worthy to rank, both for its results and its discipline, with the best of the natural science methods."[2] As a result of these experiences, reform-minded students of society tended to be sympathetic to criticism of the limitations that the laissez-faire doctrines of Herbert Spencer and the classical economists imposed on government. Between 1886 and 1895, no less than six major social science journals were established to assist in the propagation of social science expertise, and by the early 1900s, major graduate schools in the United States had assumed the responsibility of preparing social scientists to assist in the formulation of governmental policy.[3]

Dewey's Influence

John Dewey was probably the single most influential source of intellectual support for the application of rational analysis to social problems. Noting that in the 1890s Dewey became America's intellectual spokesman for practical social reform, Richard Bernstein asserted that Dewey's ideas constituted a "distinctive intellectual expression of American culture."[4] Dewey argued that no useful metaphysical absolutes exist. Philosophy and science contribute to truth and progress only as they are applied to changing human conditions. Social scientists must not hesitate to apply the experimental method to social problems, The criteria of truth are grounded in the feelings of individuals in society, and the validity of ideas and social institutions is properly judged by the degree to which they contribute to the improvement of oppressive conditions.

In works like *The Public and Its Problems*, Dewey expressed a tremendous amount of faith in the ability of organized social interests to articulate public values and to effect social reform.[5] For him, government was simply a larger form of organized public interest and as such was subject to the limits and demands made on it by the citizenry. Dewey's support of democratic processes, his application of the scientific perspective to social issues, and his focus on immediate, practical problems appealed to Americans generally and provided philosophical legitimacy for the efforts of social scientists.

One of the most important works for understanding the intellectual lineage of the modern policy analyst in more rigorous social science and for grasping the political effects of the ideas that Dewey fostered is Arthur F. Bentley's *Process of Government*. Bentley disdained formalism and metaphysical concepts in favor of description of the dynamics of the political process. "We must deal with felt things, not with feelings, with intelligent life, not with idea ghosts."[6] The source of facts, the bedrock of usable data, was group activity. Human behavior was describable and definable only in terms of activity: "There is no idea which is not a reflection of social activity,"[7] and that activity is group activity. Thus, Bentley wrote, "When the groups are stated, everything is adequately stated,"[8] and he proceeded to describe the political scene of his time in these terms.

Bentley's group approach did not come into vogue among political scientists until after World War II, with the rise to prominence of pluralist interpretations of the political process. But his treatment of politics is important for the insight that it provides into the wide influence of Dewey's ideas during the early twentieth century and for its reflection of contemporary thinking about the contours of scientific social analysis. Dewey's impact is especially apparent in Bentley's rejection of any form of metaphysical absolutes, or "idea ghosts," and in his choice of group activity as the essential datum of human life. More important, perhaps, for an understanding of the development of policy analysis is Bentley's stance of normative neutrality. Unlike Dewey, Bentley was simply interested in the facts. He made no judgments as to the worth or lack thereof of group activities. He tried to remove himself from any hint of social activism or reform. For him, science demanded no less.

Of more immediate impact on public policy was Dewey's influence on judicial thinking. In particular, Dewey's advocacy of experimental social planning translated readily into Roscoe Pound's concept of social engineering. Pound, dean of Harvard Law School and a major legal thinker, argued that judges should be aware that "continual changes in the circumstances of social life demand continual adjustments to the pressure of social interests."[9] Following Dewey's approach, Pound insisted that judges should move from behind the facade of formal, abstract legal logic and make judicial policy that deals accurately with the social facts involved in a particular case. Additionally, he urged that judges enlist social scientists in their efforts to work social reform through judicial decisions.

Value Neutrality

Although social science arose in the context of reform, by the early twentieth century it had withdrawn from advocacy of social reform into a more comfortable posture of scientific objectivity, or "value neutrality." The reasons for this were various and the consequences profound for both democratic society and its students. Many social scientists sincerely felt that their proper role in analysis was that of objective technician. In important respects, their position was bolstered by Dewey, who, even though he was concerned about social reform, consistently refused in his extensive writings to articulate any substantive normative positions. Although not value neutral in the broadest sense, the Progressive movement, while supporting specific reforms, tended toward nonpartisanship in its emphasis on efficiency in government. Robert Scott and Arnold Shore noted, for example, that Herbert Hoover, who as president was more supportive of the concept of scientific social analysis than any chief executive before or since, maintained a strict nonpartisan stance right up to the eve of the 1928 party nominating conventions.[10]

Mary Furner has argued persuasively that in addition to these general cultural currents, academic social scientists advocating social reform were hard hit by challenges to their positions and academic freedom made by corporate interests and their allies in higher education during the late nineteenth century.[11] The tribulations suffered by some of these leading activist social scientists made plain to their academic brethren that social advocacy carried with it the potential for direct personal hardship. Although exceptions to the general rule occurred throughout the twentieth century, by World War I social activism and objective social analysis were generally seen as incompatible. Scholars served in many official and advisory capacities in government at this time, but the accepted view was that the scientific element in social science required the linkage of rigorous analysis with the avoidance of overt partisanship.

Unfortunately for the pursuit of policy analysis and the health of democratic processes, the move toward scientific objectivity spawned a denigration of the importance of values. Whether social scientists articulated them or not, values remained embedded in their methodological techniques as well as in the policy process. Their unwillingness to confront the normative aspects of their fields of study created a misleading conception of political reality and led to such artificial distinctions as the separation of administration from politics. The result was that social scientists rendered their work less relevant for those moving the levers of the policy process and by default contributed to the emergence of a political system that became increasingly subservient to the narrow demands of organized interests. Social scientists were in effect left tiptoeing along the edges of the moral claims of reform and the practicalities of politics, refusing to recognize the importance of either.

The New Deal

After the Progressive era, the New Deal was the next instance of major governmental reform, and it confirmed the propensity of reform efforts to fit comfortably within the instrumentalist ideas articulated by Dewey. Raymond Moley, Rexford Tugwell, and Adolf A. Berle Jr., members of Franklin Roosevelt's Brain Trust, came to the administration from Columbia University, where Dewey was now teaching, having moved there from the University of Chicago in 1904. These advisers to FDR embraced the importance of organizational activity for dealing with economic problems. This approach to reform closely followed Dewey's suggestion that interest organization in society should be encouraged. By integrating this idea in major legislation, New Deal leaders moved it beyond the private sector and in effect gave official recognition to the group interpretation of American politics.[12] The National Industrial Recovery Act, the Agricultural Adjustment Act, and the National Labor Relations Act all encouraged organization among economic interests in an effort to improve their positions by making them more effective in both the policy process and their particular spheres of private activity. In these and other programs, social scientists played important roles as technicians and advisers, but as foot soldiers in the effort at economic recovery, they remained removed from advocacy positions and attachment to normative goals.

The New Deal program has often been characterized as a pragmatic reaction to specific economic problems, rather than as the implementation of a coherent theory. In this respect, it demonstrated both the strengths and weaknesses of the narrowed focus encouraged by many social scientists. On the positive side, the New Deal reconfirmed the ability of Americans to act decisively and effectively in dealing with immediate problems. On the negative side, any commitment to long-range planning and goals that existed foundered on the power of special interests that encouraged the proliferation of programs that overlapped and occasionally conflicted with one another.[13]

FROM TECHNIQUE TO POLICY ANALYSIS

In the post–World War II era, a number of developments combined to give policy analysis greater status. At perhaps the most general and fundamental level, the movement of scientific issues onto the national policy agenda created a climate in which analytical approaches to policy problems became increasingly important. These approaches were integrated into the formal policy process by new policy initiatives, especially those fostered by the Johnson administration. Within higher education, the social science disciplines began to focus on dealing with social problems and on describing the policy process itself more objectively. But their perceived inability to be effective in the changing policy environment stimulated the emergence of policy studies as a distinct field of study that drew on contributions from a variety of disciplines. Within the general framework of this policy studies approach, the importance of rigorous analysis to improved understanding of the policy process and better decision making became recognized.

The Impact of Science

Efforts at social reform and attempts of social scientists to formulate value-free models of the public policy process have not been the only sources of support for policy analysis in recent decades. After World War II, advances in the natural sciences caused significant modifications in governmental structure and in policy goals and processes. Jurgen Schmandt and James Everett Katz contended that during this period, Americans experienced a transition from an administrative welfare state to a scientific state.[14] Today, national policymakers must cope with an agenda heavily loaded with difficult scientific issues. These include exceedingly complex questions about nuclear and nonnuclear weapons systems, environmental protection, technology and the economy, space research, and energy resources.

The salience of scientific issues on the national agenda has influenced how policymakers frame their goals, as well as their methods for approaching them. Schmandt and Katz predicted that in the age of the scientific state, "we can expect scientific and technological thoughtways to slowly permeate the language, culture, and conceptual processes of at least middle-level policymakers, if not the highest echelons of governmental leadership."[15] The language and conceptual apparatus of science encourage policymakers to think in terms of quantifiable goals and to give greater consideration to rigorous analytical arguments: "The tools of science—the evidence and the methods of research—become parts of the policy battles. The use of advisers and panels, reports and studies, research findings and data analyses are and increasingly will be important weapons in policy battles."[16] Finally, the concern with scientific questions has led to changes in institutional structures. The national government now has a number of agencies created for the specific purpose of making science policy, and throughout that bureaucracy, other agencies have added units for research and development and program evaluation. Today, the wonders of technology and the importance of environmental issues have been embraced by important political leaders from both political parties. Speaker of the House Newt Gingrich was a vigorous proponent of new-wave technology, and one of his first acts as Speaker was to oversee the activation of the Thomas.loc.gov web site. Similarly, as vice president, Albert Gore advocated widespread access to computer technology and data and continually voiced concern about global warming and other perceived threats to the environment.

Policy analysis has historical roots in the development of the social sciences, but the emergence of the physical sciences as an important part of the public agenda has created a policy environment in which rigorous analysis of problems is required and demanded. This does not mean that the additional impetus behind policy analysis will enhance its articulation with policy decisions. Schmandt and Katz cautioned: "Of particular concern here is the extent to which the technical functions of assessment and analysis become substitutes for decision making, feeding a demand for ever more research and analysis while the decision point continues to recede."[17] Despite the growing hegemony of a scientific perspective in the policy arena, coordination of democratic processes with the contributions, methods, and challenges of the sciences remains an essential task for social scientists and policymakers.

Analysis and Policy

World War II stimulated the development of techniques that remain important to policy analysis. Chief among these was operations research, which was later tied into the broader analytical perspective of systems analysis. Operations research tended to be heavily quantitative and focused on narrow, specific problems, such as the optimum deployment of weaponry, men, and materials. Working within a framework of normative consensus, analysts could concentrate on the technical aspects of problems and were able to produce noteworthy results. The improvement of computer technology and the development of additional tools (e.g., linear programming) have made operations research an even more powerful analytical approach. In times of peace, however, normative consensus weakens, and analysts must contend with the controversy and conflict that characterize democratic politics.

The relevance of social analysis for public policy was brought to public attention in dramatic fashion in the Supreme Court's decision in *Brown* v. *Board of Education* (1954).[18] In arriving at its decision to rule racial segregation in public education unconstitutional, the Court had commissioned social science studies of the effects of racial segregation on children and on society at large. In his opinion, Chief Justice Earl Warren drew on these and previous studies, and in doing so seemed to be accepting the idea, advanced earlier by Pound, Dewey, and others, that courts should use the social sciences to implement reforms. Whether social science analysis persuaded the Court to overturn segregation, or whether it merely served the more symbolic role of bolstering an already determined decision, remains a nice question. In any case, the Court's apparent reliance on social science brought its practitioners public notoriety. Social scientists were criticized by segregationists led by a rampaging Governor George Wallace, who was to make "pointy-headed professors" the focus of many of his attacks. In contrast, those hoping to use analytical expertise in the cause of continued social reform were encouraged by the Court's recognition of their efforts.

The 1960s appear to be the next crucial period in the development of policy analysis. Particularly important at this time was the movement of Robert McNamara and his "whiz kids" into leadership positions in the Defense Department. Impressed by the contribution of analytical techniques to better decision making, these officials introduced a wide range of methods into the analysis of management and policy issues in the military.[19] These included cost-benefit analysis; operations and systems research; linear programming; and the Planning, Programming, Budgeting System (PPBS). The latter so impressed President Lyndon Johnson with its potential for better management control that in August 1965 he ordered it implemented throughout the federal government. This directive was stymied by unenthusiastic budget officers and the difficulty in applying the concept on a large scale to domestic programs, and it was finally voided by President Richard Nixon.[20] Despite opposition both within and outside the Defense Department to the application of analytical methods to problems, the McNamara people clearly established that there was a body of knowledge constituting policy analysis and gave it the legitimacy of official recognition.[21]

While the McNamara approach was in many ways a key breakthrough toward public recognition and acceptance of policy analysis, relevant disciplines in the social sciences had since World War II also been the focus of debates and changes that moved them closer to becoming contributors to policy analysis. In sociology, an applied orientation to the study of society was being implemented by scholars like Paul Lazarsfeld, who demonstrated that analytical techniques, especially those utilizing survey research, had uses in private industry and public policy.[22] Lazarsfeld's activities provoked debate between sociologists favoring a more theoretical stance for their discipline and those wishing to see sociological ideas and analyses applied in society, an argument that in many ways reiterated issues that had been contested at the turn of the century. Political scientists until well into the 1960s found themselves struggling with a "behavioral revolution" that focused attention on the application of quantitative techniques to empirical political data, a movement to which Lazarsfeld's work in voting studies contributed. But political scientists also began to feel the tug of "relevance." In his 1969 presidential address to the American Political Science Association, David Easton called for a "post-behavioral" approach that crossed disciplinary boundaries and moved toward dealing with social problems.[23]

Economics, however, rapidly outdistanced other social science disciplines as an important source of ideas and methodologies for public policy. John Maynard Keynes's ideas had provided economic theory with coherence and what has been termed a "robustness" that enabled it to retain applicability in the uncertain conditions of the real world. Additionally, within the framework of their general theories, economists were successful in innovating quantitative techniques, such as cost-benefit analysis, that delimited alternative approaches to problems. The discipline had in fact gained official stature with the establishment of the Council of Economic Advisers in the Employment Act of 1946.

By the time of the Johnson administration, scholars in the social sciences had begun to germinate the concept of a broader policy perspective. Political scientists, for example, found the narrow focus of behavioralism not very useful in anticipating developments like the civil rights movement or the Vietnam War and began to look toward more inclusive paradigms. Harold Lasswell was especially active in moving the social sciences toward a policy focus, and in a 1951 article on the subject, he appears to have coined the term "policy sciences."[24]

It was Yehezkel Dror, however, who at an early stage in the increased concern with policy suggested a role for policy analysis specifically. Dror in the late 1960s was concerned about the degree to which the techniques and assumptions of economists had become part of the analyses upon which public officials depended.[25] He pointed out that there was need for a perspective broader than that provided by the prevailing systems analysis approach. Moving beyond the application of technical analysis to specific problems, a policy analysis orientation would include consideration of intangible cultural factors, political problems, and organizational variables that should make studies more useful to policymakers. Finally, from 1967 through 1970, with the assistance of major private foundations, graduate programs in public policy were initiated at Harvard, Berkeley, Carnegie-Mellon, the Rand Graduate Institute, and the Universities of Michigan, Pennsylvania, Minnesota, and Texas.[26] In the next decade, at least thirteen journals in policy studies and policy analysis were begun. This period also saw the founding of the Policy Studies Organization and the Association for Public Policy Analysis and Management.

Policy analysis came of age during the days of the Great Society, and, as with many maturing processes, this change carried with it both frustration and wisdom gained from experience. The administration's efforts at large-scale social intervention engendered an enormous increase in employment opportunities for social scientists, and its funding of higher education provided a stimulus for the establishment of graduate programs in policy analysis, or policy studies.[27] At the same time, the Great Society acted on the basis of interpretations of society and politics that suffered from unwarranted faith in scientific rationality. The advocates of analytical prowess were soon brought face to face with the realities of political power. As one commentator has noted, "In the Johnson years the policies of all those brilliant apostles of rationality gradually lost sight of the most elementary common sense,"[28] with the result that their noses were badly bloodied in some instances. Of more fundamental importance and long-term significance was the lack of attention given to normative goals and assumptions about American society. In essence, policy analysis found itself in harness with goals often no more tangible than those of "good intentions." The consequences of inattention to cultural and political expectations were sufficiently disastrous to place the proponents of government-sponsored social reform on the defensive for at least the next two decades.

Analysis and Ideology

Belief in the efficacy of social science knowledge was deeply embedded in the assumptions of the architects of the Great Society programs. Even before the Kennedy administration, the Ford Foundation had funded efforts to apply social science knowledge to designated "gray areas" in cities in an attempt to prevent these marginally blighted urban enclaves from deteriorating into slums.[29] The Kennedy administration accepted the need for greater governmental intervention and made some movement in that direction, but it was President Johnson who was given the historic opportunity to flex the resources of the national government to their maximum on behalf of social reform.

The Great Society planners were particularly impressed by the ability of organized interests to work successfully in the policy process. Some of this attitude may have stemmed from their knowledge of New Deal programs, especially those fostering labor organization. Additionally, group interpretations of politics indicated that agencies and legislators responded most sympathetically to organized interests. Equally important, no doubt, was the experience of President Johnson's assistants with the influence that organization had brought to the civil rights movement. Thus, it was natural for the Johnson administration to assume that the route to greater political effectiveness and more social justice for the disadvantaged lay through organization that would enable them to compete with other groups in the policy process. The result was a conscious attempt through the War on Poverty to use government programs to organize the poor in what has been described as "a distinctive managerial kind of politics" directed by the White House.[30] These efforts were exemplified by requirements for citizen participation at the local level in the allocation of funds for most programs, whatever the socioeconomic status of their recipients.

Faith in the effectiveness of social science as a support for reform reflected assumptions that had been part of what might be termed the "culture" of social science throughout the twentieth century. To their discomfort, the Johnson people were soon to learn that analysis of social conditions and policy need not necessarily result in findings sustaining the merits of their approach to social change. First, they had the unpleasant experience of having their own policy people criticize their programs. In the words of Carol Hirschon Weiss, "The news was dismaying. Nothing seemed to be working as expected. The programs launched with such great hopes and fanfare did not appear to be attaining their objectives to alter poor people's lives."[31] Then, they were subjected to the equally difficult experience of having the tools of social analysis turned on them by their ideological opponents. Edward Banfield's *Unheavenly City* was a broad attack on programs of federal social intervention,[32] and the establishment of the *Public Interest* provided neoconservatives with a continuing forum for their views.

The Johnson administration could perhaps have weathered the critiques of their own analysts better if their programs had developed stronger political affiliations. But President Johnson had tried to move beyond incremental change by formulating many of his programs outside the usual policy process.[33] By relying heavily on task groups external to the bureaucracy, Johnson was able to obtain new ideas, but at the cost of political support. Subsequently, the old-line agencies chosen to implement these new programs had little attachment to their success, and similar sentiments existed in Congress. Meanwhile, the burgeoning interest in policy studies had given rise to an increased application of program evaluation, which when applied to the Great Society initiatives uncovered numerous shortcomings and a lack of tangible results.[34] In a context of strong political programmatic support, these findings could have been used to improve programs. But in this instance, the initial failure to maximize political support rendered the Great Society efforts particularly vulnerable to political attack. Instead of assisting in the improvement of social reform, the conclusions of policy analysts tended to give greater credence to the suspicions of already uneasy politicians.

Attacks by the conservatives and neoconservatives were even more devastating than those of occasional supporters of the Great Society because they combined the use of analytical techniques with criticism of the unexamined assumptions about society that had accompanied reform efforts throughout the twentieth century. The conservative reaction to active government had been growing since World War II, and think tanks like the Heritage Foundation and the American Enterprise Institute provided scholars with additional bases from which to formulate their criticisms of reformist government. Conservatively inclined thinkers, such as Edward Banfield, Daniel Patrick Moynihan, and James Q. Wilson, demonstrated conclusively that policy analysis was not solely the province of social engineers. Banfield's widely read *Unheavenly City*, for example, drew on social science findings relating to poverty, race, health, education, housing, employment, and crime in attacking most of the Great Society's programs. But the really telling element in the positions of these scholars and their colleagues was not their use of analysis but their insistence on examining the assumptions about human nature and behavior that seemed to be the basis for reform efforts. These thinkers directly challenged the egalitarian optimism that had suffused reform, and in doing so, they served notice that in the United States, policy analysis could no longer be considered the exclusive resource of any particular ideology.

The focus on philosophical and sociological assumptions raised reservations about the accuracy of the group-oriented, or—in social scientist terms—"pluralist," model of politics that had become prominent in both scholarly discussion and official policy. Much of the intellectual basis for this model can be traced to David B. Truman's *Governmental Process*,[35] whose publication in 1951 revived the interpretation of American politics first offered by Bentley. Although

Truman suggested that interest-group competition could incapacitate governmental policy, he gave far more attention to the merits of group activity. He argued that democratic processes would be protected from extremes of group conflict by the existence of latent, unorganized groups that would spring into being if one interest became too powerful or threatened the "rules of the game." Protection was also to be found in overlapping group memberships by individuals, which had the effect of limiting the demands and activities of group leaders. Questions about this perspective came from both the ideological left and right. In both instances, they raised normative issues that Truman's posture of value neutrality avoided. The left tended to be concerned that a pluralist model of politics gave de facto legitimacy to organized interests over those unable to organize. The right was more concerned that a pluralist conception of politics moved moral judgment to the status of political compromise. These debates were accompanied by the somber spectacle of a government rendered increasingly impotent by the ability of organized interests to overcome the constitutional authority of institutional processes.

The interest-group interpretation illustrated another facet of the unwillingness of the social sciences to look beyond tangible, measurable activity. That this stance had ramifications for understanding of the public policy process generally was demonstrated by Charles Lindblom's article "The Science of 'Muddling Through.'"[36] Written in 1959, Lindblom's essay has become something of a classic for its statement and defense of incremental decision making. Less noted has been the extent to which Lindblom drew on the group perspective in this seminal piece. Like the group theorists, Lindblom grounded values in the behavior of particular political actors. It made good sense, he argued, for administrators to eschew long-range goals in favor of immediate problems. In dealing with short-term goals, the official can more easily identify and operationalize the values conducive to the result to be achieved. The pluralistic system, he asserted, will ensure that interests are not ignored in this process: "Almost every interest has its watchdog. . . . It can be argued that our system often can assure a more comprehensive regard for the values of the whole society than any attempt at intellectual comprehensiveness."[37] In fact, it is wrongheaded to conceive of only long-term planning as rational: "Even partisanship and narrowness, to use pejorative terms, will sometimes be assets to rational decision making, for they can doubly insure that what one agency neglects, another will not."[38] In "The Science of 'Muddling Through,'" Lindblom raised to a level of rational legitimacy the fragmented, halting, incremental approach to decision making characteristic of the American policy process and in doing so relied heavily on arguments previously made by the group theorists.

What was not apparent to either economists or policy analysts in the postwar years was the degree to which the Keynesian economic model also reflected the dominant ideological positions of its time. Noting the pervasive influence of this approach, Robert Heilbroner and William Milberg concluded that "what seems ultimately of crucial importance is the capacity of a consensual model to embody the sociopolitical values and the historical prospects of the period in question."[39] In a more detailed analysis, Karen Orren and Stephen Skowronek characterized Keynesianism as a political regime that was "a governing formula as essential for political management as it was for economic management."[40]

By the late 1960s, as American culture became more ideologically polarized, the Keynesian paradigm no longer permeated economic thinking in the United States. Yet policy analysts continued to work within its framework, primarily, it seems, because no alternative model of comparable policy power emerged. The decades since then have witnessed continued theoretical disarray among economists. In this rather chaotic climate, many policy analysts have adopted the rational-choice approach from the economists' pantry of goods; however, at the macro level of economics and policy modeling, the rational-choice position has not attained the degree of acceptance once enjoyed by Keynesian theory. Heilbroner and Milberg pointed out that among economists, the "econometric practices of the various rational-choice theoretics have encountered a barrage of criticisms,"[41] and serious attacks on this school have also been forthcoming in the other social sciences. Thus, economics, which had served as a conceptual refuge for many policy analysts, has experienced a "period of prolonged intellectual disagreement" characterized by Heilbroner and Milberg as unique "in the history of economic thought."[42]

At the same time that policy analysts have found their theoretical moorings threatened, advances in information processing have presented them with technological tools of unparalleled analytical power. Through computer systems, policy analysts have at their disposal huge amounts of data and a wide range of systems models for the processing and analysis of these data. The policy analyst can draw on data banks on a particular problem (e.g., poverty, crime, education) and can utilize statistical packages, decision formats, and formal models to interpret the information. While the results of this integration of data and analytical tools can be impressive, they can also be misleading. First, due care must be exercised to assure the reliability of the data used and the application of appropriate interpretive tools. Second, and perhaps most important, the analyst must retain sufficient perspective to be able to stand outside the decision-support models and to understand that these humanly conceived and constructed systems in turn contain particular assumptions.

Science and Truth

The programs of the Great Society provided the context within which policy studies and policy analysis became endeavors in which the national government invested both great hope and copious resources. Political scientists and sociologists moved to follow the lead of the economists in the hope that they, too, could become more relevant to decision making by applying their methodologies to the analysis of important social issues. As the grand plans of the initiators of the Great Society foundered on the shoals of political reaction and bureaucratic fragmentation, reliance on rational, analytic methods could not provide policy analysts with sufficient status or power to cope with political interests.

Social scientists and, more recently, policy analysts have often assumed that the objective, scientific quality of their analyses would carry weight in the policy process and protect them from the effects of political partisanship. Because it rests on a superficial view of the scientific enterprise and a faulty conception of the policy process, such a posture can lead to considerable frustration for the practitioner of policy analysis. While policy analysis can contribute significantly to the improvement of political decisions, critics from a broad range of disciplines have shown that analytical methodologies cannot provide scientific, objective answers to policy issues. Unfortunately, in important respects, policy analysis has suffered unfairly from expectations about its policy role and scientific capabilities, and it is therefore essential that today's policy analyst have an understanding of prevailing interpretations of scientific endeavor and the political components of the policy process.

Although the knowledge may not be essential to their day-to-day work, students of policy analysis should have at least an awareness of critiques of the physical sciences as a source of objective truth. Thomas Kuhn, in particular, had an enormous impact on ideas about science and its methods with his argument that science advances not through careful attention to the experimental method, but through new ideas introduced during periods of fundamental cultural change.[43] These cultural upheavals cause paradigmatic changes in how science is viewed and thus lead to major discoveries. Kuhn, in effect, suggested that the physical sciences, which have since Newton stood as the ultimate test of truth in the Western world, are more culturally and historically conditioned than was previously recognized.

Paralleling this intellectual controversy have been attacks on positivism that have damaged its claims, probably irreparably. By defining meaningful statements as those that have tangible referents or are statements of mathematical or formal logic, positivists believed that they could construct a form of truth that encompassed all areas of human life. But despite herculean, and procrustean, efforts toward this goal, the positivists could not overcome the diversities of human life and the reality of intangibles as causes of human behavior. In 1984, Douglas J. Amy asserted that

> positivist methodologies continue to dominate in policy analysis, despite the fact that their intellectual foundations were undermined at least a decade ago. Positivism survives because it limits, in a way that is politically convenient, the kinds of questions that analysis can in-

vestigate. Moreover, the aura of science and objectivity that surrounds positivist policy analysis adds to the image of the policy analyst as an apolitical technocrat.[44]

Whether they have bothered to think the issues through thoroughly or not, policy analysts obviously obtain some benefit from the persistence of outmoded preconceptions about what they are doing. As is becoming increasingly apparent, however, the price being paid for this lack of perspective has been serious confusion about the proper role of the analyst in the policy process and American political culture at large.

THE ANALYST IN THE POLICY PROCESS

Before working through conceptions of the role of the policy analyst in contemporary America, it may be helpful to relate the activities of the policy analyst to the complex of considerations that enter into democratic policy decisions. In broad terms—and certainly there are some who would argue for a much narrower definition—one might describe the working analyst's duties as including the collection and organization of data, application of appropriate analytical techniques, clarification of the issues involved, and formulation of alternatives for resolution of a problem, with perhaps a recommendation as to the best way to go. These are important tasks, and each of them involves some judgment on the analyst's part. But the bottom line in a pluralistic society is that for the policymaker, the rational methodology of analysis constitutes only one kind of approach to a problem, and often not the most persuasive one. As Rosemarie Tong has observed, in the political process there are other, equally legitimate forms of argument than the logical-rational mode of policy analysis.[45]

The Environment of Policy Decisions

Policymakers draw on a variety of considerations in reaching decisions. While some of those lacking analytical rigor may be deplored, others make perfectly good sense from a democratic perspective. A policymaker may respond to the intensity of particular interests, as, for example, with the abortion issue or gun control. He or she may defer to the intuitive grasp of a situation by an experienced adviser or friend, as President Harry Truman did in moving the United States to support the creation of Israel, or to the input of a spouse, as in the case of Hillary Rodham Clinton's attachment to health-care reform. In other instances, programs like Head Start and Women, Infants and Children (WIC) may have such strong emotional appeal that regardless of findings about their effectiveness, a policymaker will refuse to change them. Also, many policy decisions are the result of compromise among a number of officials representing different personal and political perspectives. Indeed, Douglas Yates Jr. contended that a failure to recognize these political facets of the policy process can convert the policy analyst into a "source of rigidity in the give and take of conflict resolution."[46] Many tradeoffs and sources of influence enter into policy decisions, and policy analysis is merely one among them. Definitions of the public interest come in many sizes and shapes, and the analyst must remain aware that it is the very essence of democratic policymaking to draw on a range of sources in constructing the public interest on a particular issue.

A number of factors inherent in the nature of policy analysis also help ensure that it will remain but one form of input, although an increasingly important one, into the making of pluralistic, democratic policy. Of prime importance, perhaps, are the clear elitist implications of deferring heavily to the opinions of experts. Descriptions of the physical world, whether by physical scientists or social scientists, cannot by themselves produce normative standards. No matter how skilled an individual is in an area, he or she will remain democratically incompetent to impose value positions on the public.[47] At the same time, it is important to recognize that the methodologies used by analysts carry with them necessary normative choices in terms of assumptions involved in identifying problems and goals.[48] Indeed, Laurence Tribe went so far as to assert that policy analysis has an atomistic ethic that is utilitarian, liberal, democratic, and egalitarian.[49] Not surprisingly, policymakers may feel that efficiency and equity are not the only goals worthy of attention in a particular situation.

In addition to having to deal with the tactical and normative considerations involved in applying a methodology to a problem, the analyst invariably suffers from more practical limitations. These revolve around money and time, as does much of life. Rarely do analysts have sufficient time or funds to collect enough information and analyze it as thoroughly as they would wish, although in recent decades computer technology has vastly increased their data-collection capabilities. Occasionally, when the focus of the problem is narrow and specific and time is of the essence, as with the use of operations research during World War II, policy analysis may well determine the final decision. But in the course of the normal policy process, it will likely continue to receive heavy competition from many other directions.

The expectation, or hope, harbored by some social scientists that it is but a matter of time until the policy world conforms to the canons of logical structure is badly misplaced. The dislocations between the methods of the policy analyst and those of the politician, bureaucrat, or judge must remain because the two approaches begin from fundamentally different premises and often strive for different goals. To deal with this dichotomy constructively, the politically effective policy analyst will combine technical skill with an understanding of the political and normative contexts of the issues being considered. The chapters that follow have as a common goal the enhancement of that understanding.

The Role of the Analyst

For the policy analyst, organizational affiliation and issue orientation can be fairly closely interrelated. Obviously, analysts working within a public-interest group (e.g., the Sierra Club) or a private-interest group (e.g., the U.S. Chamber of Commerce) will evince a greater degree of activism than those operating in the middle echelons of the New York State Department of Education or the National Institute of Standards and Technology. But at times, the organizational climate of even the most established agencies can transform passive analysts into advocates.

Analysts working within the bowels of the bureaucracy tend to identify eventually with their agency's ideology, and when that agency's turf or mission is threatened, they may well be drawn into the controversies and conflicts generated in the effort to maintain agency status. This protectiveness operates within an agency as well. Martha Feldman has made this point:

> Analysts from the policy office will . . . be concerned with the consistency of the report with general policies of the department; analysts from the General Counsel's office will be concerned with the legality of what is in the report and the consistency with current legal actions the department is involved in. [Those] from offices dealing with the production of statistical information will be concerned about the proper use of this information. Analysts from offices dealing with environmental or economic impacts will make sure that facts and concerns relevant to these interests are included in the paper.[50]

At times, such differences in focus can, from the perspective of those affected, become far more intense than conflicts generated by differences over substantive issues of more general public interest.

An assumption that should form the basis for any legitimate conception of policy analysis as a profession is that the analyst is a person of professional integrity. In his study of policy analysts in the federal bureaucracy, Arnold J. Meltsner rightly concluded that integrity is a fundamental standard: "To be politically sensitive does not mean to be insensitive to ethics or morality. . . . Those who are dishonest, distort their work, and deliberately lie should have no place in the analytic fraternity."[51] Drawing on discussions of professional ethics generally, Tong supported this view with her argument that analysts should demonstrate the attributes of honesty, candor, competence, diligence, loyalty, and discretion as components of trustworthiness.[52] Although no serious student of the policy process would disagree with the merit of these qualities, discussions limited to integrity are of little more help to the analyst dealing daily with a variety of complex issues than the Boy Scout code would be. In a more practical vein, Robert D. Behn has suggested that doing "policy analysis well requires intellectual honesty, political creativity, a respect for a diversity of values, the ability to deflate phoniness, and some scientific rigor."[53]

At this point, it is probably advisable to sound a cautionary note against the tendency of scholars to move quickly to worst-possible-case scenarios when discussing ethics and the professional policy analyst. While these hypothetical cases provide opportunities for classroom discussions, it really is difficult to see their day-to-day relevance for the working analyst. Fortunately, it is exceptionally rare that an analyst is in a position where he or she sees clients sending people to their deaths or causing widespread disease or pestilence. In these instances, one would expect an analyst, simply as a decent human being, to speak out, just as one would expect anyone aware of a serious wrong to act to correct it. Much of this kind of discussion derives from the powerful perspective offered by post hoc analysis. It is, of course, easier to point to what should have been than to make the correct decision at the time. But it is not helpful to an understanding of the policy process to be too eager to ascribe sinister or criminal motives to those who have made decisions that have had unfortunate consequences. The point is that these issues involve disputes in which reasonable persons can and do differ. That is the virtue, and sometimes the defect, of the democratic process.

Attempts to categorize the styles and perspectives of policy analysts tend to make a basic distinction between analysts who see themselves as politically non-involved technicians and those who take a more activist role. Both Meltsner and Hank C. Jenkins-Smith,[54] for example, saw the technician as a rudimentary policy analyst type. Both also posited the more politically involved analyst as a contrasting type. However, they described this second type differently. Jenkins-Smith, who framed his discussion in terms of organizational context, believed that issue advocates (e.g., those working for causes) and client advocates (e.g., those working for congressmen) are accurate ways of depicting the more activist analysts; Meltsner, who limited his study to the bureaucracy and adopted a perspective drawing on the analyst's self-image, thought of activist analysts in terms of entrepreneurs and politicians. In Meltsner's typology, the politician, the most removed from day-to-day technical analysis, possesses the instincts of a high-level political bureaucrat and is dedicated to advancing the interests of his or her supervisor or political leader. The entrepreneur, in contrast, is technically skilled but wants a greater voice in policy decisions.

Both Meltsner and Jenkins-Smith indicated that the technician posture is the one most widely assumed by policy analysts. Organizationally, one would expect to find analysts with a technician orientation most numerous in the middle and lower echelons of bureaucratic hierarchies, where they have some insulation from political pressures, and, to some extent, in think tanks or academic settings. The technician simply wants to "get on with the job" and values insulation from political pressure as an advantage of the job. Beyond the question of personal orientation, however, is the possibility that the technician stance is a response to the policy environment. Scott and Shore asserted, for example, that narrowly focused, technical studies are the kind of input that policymakers value. In their view, administrators are most receptive to succinct analysis that provides them with usable data. In this regard, the technician may simply be responding to the demands of his or her supervisors.[55] Additionally, the neutral, objective aura of expertise projected by the technician may convey an author-itative image that enhances his or her status.

The questions that emanate from the technician perspective do not in any way draw into question the analytical skills or the integrity of the analyst. They relate instead to the personal satisfaction that can be derived from such a lim-ited perspective and to the degree to which narrowly focused analysis can be effective in the policy process. In Meltsner's view, the technician believes that he or she is objective and scientific.[56] But analysis of any kind is immersed in cul-tural assumptions and tactical normative judgments relative to the methodology used, and these condition the range of alternatives that can be considered in any specific study. In other words, whether they acknowledge it or not, technicians must make value judgments. Jenkins-Smith saw these kinds of issues as leading to increasing criticism of the technician perspective.[57] In terms of immediate effect on the policy process, one of the most important questions raised by the technician self-image rests on its apolitical claims, for as one of Meltsner's entre-preneurs argued, "Only analysts who use political considerations will do relevant and influential analysis."[58] In contrast, Scott and Shore concluded that bureau-crats are receptive to narrow, technical analysis because it enables them to imple-ment programs more easily.

Each individual is, of course, free to choose the image he or she wants to convey and work within. But those articulating the technician view must accept the consequences of narrowness and superficiality or be prepared to operate in an activist manner behind the technician facade. While the technician's work in a textbook sense may be very skilled, without more, it must be politically flawed. And in the democratic policy process, that is often a fatal attribute in terms of influence. However, the choices need not be between technical narrowness and a politically activist position. It seems feasible for an analyst to take great satis-faction in technical work and yet develop the awareness and interpersonal skills to make that work attractive to decision makers.

The Challenge of Activism

The closer the policy analyst becomes tied to issue advocacy, the more likely it is that questions will be raised about adherence to professional standards and the effect of untoward pressures on the analyst. On reflection, however, there appears to be no logical objection to the existence of professional analytical integrity and partisanship in the same unit, be it policy study institute, congressional committee, or administrative agency. The argument here seems reasonably straightforward. From both the perspective of the analyst's standards and that of the client's need to be fully informed, the analyst owes the client the best analysis of which he or she is capable. The client, of course, then remains free to accept or reject the alternatives put forth. In the current literature, differences between the policy analyst and the policymaker are often stretched to raise fundamental ethical issues.

Unfortunately, the discussion of fundamental moral differences tends to obscure the essential distinctions between policy analysis and the factors involved in making political decisions. As discussed above, there is no inherent reason why the policy analyst's views should make better public policy than the opinions implemented by decision makers. The move of the Justice Department under Attorney General Edwin Meese to diminish job protections for those with acquired immune deficiency syndrome (AIDS) provides an example. There is little question that the Justice Department's position ran counter to the views of many experts on AIDS, who saw minimal danger from the employment of AIDS victims. Nonetheless, in its policy position, the Justice Department exploited the degree of uncertainty involved in knowledge about transmission of the disease. The issue here is not whether the decision was wise or unwise. Clearly, the Justice Department was moving toward different goals and responding to different constituencies from those influencing many experts in the field. While Justice personnel may have recognized that their approach carried the risk that expert opinion might eventually have considerable weight with the courts or the electorate, they believed they had the right to act as they did. Obviously, an analyst may become so outraged by a policy decision that he or she chooses to resign, but such a decision is a personal moral act and should not be confused with the fact that there are inherent differences between policy analysis and democratic decision making.[59] To argue otherwise is to slip into the error of assuming that policy analysis is in fact an objective, scientific form of endeavor that results in unbiased truth. In a given situation, policy analysis may result in suggestions that to outside observers appear far more reasonable than the public policy promulgated, but such differences are an essential characteristic of democracies.

This is not to argue that the analyst should be unconcerned about values in his or her work. Quite the contrary. Understanding and examining the various normative issues involved in a problem are the most difficult tasks an analyst faces in the attempt to provide really useful material for the policy process. We examine the intricacies involved in integrating normative perspectives into analysis in detail later. But here it is important to note that the retreat into claims of objectivity and science is too easy an approach to invariably complex policy issues. Policy analysis that moves beyond the assertions of objectivity and efficiency is one route toward analysis that speaks more comprehensively to social concerns.

Because policy analysts have not been able to influence the policy process to a great extent, some have urged a greater degree of advocacy on the part of the analyst.[60] While advocacy in itself is a perfectly legitimate form of activity for the analyst, as it is for most other citizens, it may tempt the analyst to try to gain advantage through the manipulation of data and findings. That some should succumb to this temptation is not surprising in view of the emotions and reputations that may be at stake. Even the natural sciences, in which the standards of research are perhaps more rigorous (but the rewards far more prestigious and profitable), have experienced notorious cases of fudged data and findings.[61] The ramifications of such behavior for a scientist or policy analyst can be disastrous for the individual personally and damaging to the profession involved.

In a pluralistic society, it is simply expecting too much for analysis to go unchallenged. Meltsner, who once served as editor of Policy Analysis, emphasized that studies are vulnerable to a wide range of criticisms: "Analysts and researchers are shot down for wrong assumptions, for too circumscribed or biased a view of the problem, for bad research design, for faulty and misleading statistics, for lack of causal connection between hypotheses and findings, for simpleminded hypotheses, and for alternatives involving conflicting objectives."[62] Such attacks do their share to heighten controversy over public policy issues, but they, too, are part of the process. The introduction of deliberately distorted analyses into the cause of partisanship, however, converts policy analysis from an approach that can make very real contributions to clarifying issues and suggesting alternatives into simply another manipulative tactic in the already confused arena of interest-group politics. Although policy analysis has not provided the steady guide to public policy that many have hoped, it clearly has been an asset to that process, and it is a happy circumstance that standards of integrity have stood as the overriding rule.

Policy analysts have the capability to continue to provide useful input to the policy process in an era when American society increasingly faces problems so complex that they are beyond the layperson's comprehension and yet so pervasive that they touch everyone's fundamental beliefs. Advanced means for controlling the reproductive process through genetic planning, improvement of life-sustaining technology for severely handicapped newborn infants and the comatose elderly, and the development of increasingly sophisticated devices for monitoring every moment and movement of one's privacy are but a few of the inevitable changes that must raise serious questions for policymakers. No doubt, new methodologies and techniques will also be devised to improve analytical prowess. But more important to the status of policy analysis will be the degree to which its practitioners are able to combine technical skills with a certain humility about their use, a mature sense of the vicissitudes of politics, and a recognition of the necessity and difficulty of reconciling normative concerns.

CHAPTER 2

Rationality and Decision Making

POLICY ANALYSIS: A THUMBNAIL SKETCH

THIS CHAPTER EXAMINES policy analysts as actors in the policy process. In particular, it discusses the normative factors that influence the techniques often used by analysts and that emerge as important determinants of decision making in the policy process. In both activities, values serve as important contextual constraints on the use of analytical findings. The kind of policy analysis performed by working analysts might be termed prescriptive in that it normally results in recommendations of some sort. Other forms of policy analysis focus on studying the policy process and are not geared toward making specific recommendations. Some studies, for example, trace proposals through the various stages of the policy process, while others examine the origins and effects of policies in particular areas. Whether or not they generate recommendations, all three approaches to policy analysis share common characteristics. They strive to improve government decisions and provide information that can be used to enhance the quality of life, and they proceed on the assumption that one can analytically study policies, their causes, and their consequences. Nonetheless, policy analysis that produces recommendations (prescriptive analysis) raises the most interesting and practical questions about how values affect analysis and how analysis, in turn, affects policy decisions.

Since the early efforts of the great philosophical system builders of the seventeenth century, students of society have been attracted by the possibility of constructing models of social behavior that have the rigor and predictive power of those in the physical sciences. These attempts persist, and it is easy for the student to confuse the meanings of *science* as used in the physical sciences with its often rather loose and diverse use in the social sciences. Science has had tremendous status in the Western world, and appropriation of that label has been seen as a way of providing legitimacy to a number of different fields of activity.

In the seventeenth and eighteenth centuries, claims were made that a truly scientific model of society was possible. Usually, these models were based on the principles of deductive reasoning. Through an incisive argument, as yet essentially unanswered, David Hume discredited those ambitious notions. Hume asserted that only in the constructs of mathematics and logic can necessary relationships be established by deductive reason. In society and the physical world, cause-and-effect relationships are only inferences drawn from observing the high correlation of certain events. One cannot *prove* that a second event is caused by the first. Finally, Hume pointed out that what had been seen as universal rational truths, such as the value of private property or individual liberty, were in fact only conventions that societies had found useful or agreeable. In short, deductive reason utilizing logically necessary relationships could not provide the basis for a science of society.

In the aftermath of Hume's attack, thinkers continued to argue on other grounds that a scientific model of society was possible. In the nineteenth century, Charles Darwin's evolutionary ideas were appropriated as a basis for a science of society. The twentieth century saw the rise of logical positivism, an important movement encouraging the idea of a science of society. As noted in chapter 1, positivists tried unsuccessfully to define all meaningful statements either as representations of tangible phenomena or as logical formulations. Nonetheless, social scientists became heavily influenced by the idea that their disciplines could become more scientific by eliminating metaphysical values and assumptions and dealing directly with human behavior. Because of the insistence by logical positivists and social scientists on the need for empirical referents, their analyses tended to be confined to empirical description. When applied to policy analysis, this orientation can favor the immediately useful in policy outcomes.

Yet the philosophical basis for a narrow analytical focus that precluded the incorporation of intangibles like perceptions and values was rapidly eroding. Taking a different perspective on the scientific enterprise, Karl Popper, an eminent philosopher of science, maintained that no scientific conclusions are certain. They have a tentative validity that lasts only until they are found deficient in some manner. In fact, to be scientific, a statement or hypothesis must be falsifiable. If Popper's position is sound, narrowing the focus of social science to achieve a certainty believed to exist in the physical sciences is self-defeating. Popper's ideas on the scientific method also addressed the limitations of schools of social science that attempt to exclude values from their studies. Addressing the inductive approach to scientific research, Popper demonstrated that before any data collection can start, the researcher must have some idea of where and how to begin.[1] In the social sciences, this speaks directly to the *fact* that research must begin with assumptions about what is worth investigating. Carried far enough, this line of reasoning must lead one to the researcher's basic value assumptions and interests.

In the last edition of this work, we suggested that while many students of policy analysis asserted the importance of values in the analysis of policy problems, there was actually very little discussion of how normative considerations are to be made part of this process. Increasingly, however, scholars are working to integrate normative considerations into their analytical work. Frank Fischer, for example, explicitly wed the standard quantitative methodology of policy analysis with normative concerns. He urged two-tiered analysis, adopting Jurgen Habermas's discursive orientation. In Fischer's view, "The theorists of practical discourse or deliberation [such as Habermas] have challenged the positivist contention that normative argumentation is irrational. For these writers, normative deliberation about goals and values is not inferior to scientific discourse; rather it is only different."[2]

Fischer then explained his approach to linking the normative and the scientific. The first level is what he termed "first-order evaluation," which begins with "technical-analytic discourse." Technical-analytic discourse is simply the standard social scientific analysis of programs to see if they are fulfilling their stated goals and objectives. After this is completed, the task of "contextual discourse" must be undertaken. Here, the policy analyst steps back from the narrow analysis characterizing the first stage and examines whether the program's objectives have effectively targeted the problems for which the program was originally established. "Second-order" evaluation then moves to examination of broader social questions framing the program being analyzed. The preliminary phase of this is "systems discourse: societal vindication." It addresses the question, "Does the policy goal have instrumental or contributing value for the society as a whole?" Finally, at the highest level of "ideological discourse," normative questions of social choice enter the equation. The guiding question becomes, "Do the fundamental ideals (or ideology) that organize the accepted social order provide a basis for the legitimate resolution of conflicting judgments?"[3]

Fischer's approach is an attempt to tie the scientific discourse of program evaluation to a normative discourse providing a broad normative and ideological context within which this analysis should be understood to exist. Obviously, not all policy analysts are engaged in program evaluation work, but they all can profit from the wider perspective on their work that Fischer's model offers.

This model exemplifies what has come to be called the *postpositivist* approach in policy analysis—and in policy studies more generally. Fischer defines the postpositivist position as "a contemporary school of social science that attempts to combine the discourse of social and political theory with the rigor of modern science. It calls for a marriage of scientific knowledge with interpretive and philosophical knowledge about norms and values."[4] The greater visibility that this perspective has been gaining appears to vindicate previous editions of this book by explicitly building values and democratic processes into the world of the policy analyst. Indeed, a special symposium in *Policy Studies Journal*, one of the flagship journals in policy analysis, recently focused on postpositivism as an alternative to the more traditional and more narrowly defined quantitative and positivist approaches to policy analysis.[5]

In a related vein, several recent books on policy design have stressed the necessity of considering democratic values in the work of policy analysis. The authors of these works see technically proficient analyses that are not informed by democratic values as falling short of the status of sophisticated, constructive analysis. Davis Bobrow and John Dryzek provided a template for examining policy design within an explicit value framework.[6] Peter deLeon, John Dryzek, and Anne Schneider and Helen Ingram have all emphasized that policy design and analysis must be thoroughly informed by democratic values and processes.[7] The works of critical theory and the discourse theory associated with Jurgen Habermas have heavily influenced these works and thus have contributed importantly to the developing maturity of the field of policy analysis.

In this chapter, we attempt to integrate a normative viewpoint into the consideration of policy analysis. We examine some important techniques of policy analysis, values underlying these techniques, and the use of analysis by decision makers. In a broader context, we also consider the role of policy analysts in the policy process and the critical—and sometimes ignored—impact of values on that process.

IDEOLOGY AND POLICY ANALYSIS

In a pluralistic society like the United States, variety in belief systems is a natural consequence of differences in backgrounds and aspirations. To the extent that they provide reasonably comprehensive rationales for expectations about how government should act, belief systems can be said to constitute ideologies. Although they may be neither rational in structure nor cognitively salient, ideological beliefs are especially influential normative frameworks for both policy analysts and decision makers. In this section, we examine welfare liberalism, utilitarianism, social conservatism, and support for the institutional status quo as ideologies that in the past several decades have significantly influenced many of those active in the policy process. In contrast to the more amorphous and general ideological views held by the electorate, these belief systems can be fairly directly linked to policy positions.

Dewey and Welfare Liberalism

John Dewey's ideas have provided the most comprehensive philosophical support for welfare liberalism, an ideology supporting an activist government and social reform through scientific analysis. Dewey was an early advocate of the idea of a "positive state" that would take responsibility for acting to redress social grievances. For him, this was the essence of modern liberalism. In his words:

> The many who call themselves liberals today are committed to the
> principle that organized society must use its powers to establish the

conditions under which the mass of individuals can possess actual as distinct from merely legal liberty. They define their liberalism in the concrete in the terms of a program of measures moving toward this end. They believe that a conception of the state which limits the activities of the latter to keeping order as between individuals and to securing redress for one person when another person infringes the liberty existing law has given him, is in effect simply a justification of the brutalities and inequities of the existing order.[8]

In urging a pragmatic approach to dealing with social problems, Dewey emphasized the importance of results—what worked best was best. Government should try different policies in the spirit of working hypotheses for approaching solutions to problems.

The need to adopt the experimental method in applying "organized intelligence" to the cause of social reform was a consistent theme throughout Dewey's extensive writings. He saw this as the means by which government could become more "scientific" in the formulation of policy. Scientists and experts from other fields would provide data for policymakers. "Their expertness is not shown in framing and executing policies, but in discovering and making known the facts upon which the former depend. They are technical experts in the sense that scientific investigators and artists manifest expertise."[9] In his efforts to have government apply organized intelligence to social problems, Dewey seemed to be calling for the creation of a profession much like policy analysis. Harold Lasswell commented on the importance of Dewey in this respect, noting that the policy sciences "are a contemporary adaptation of the general approach to public policy that was recommended by John Dewey and his colleagues in the development of American pragmatism."[10]

Dewey was a spokesman for the welfare liberal ideology of social reform through government social intervention, a perspective that has formed the presuppositions of many policy analysts. Critics of Dewey have pointed out that his pragmatic approach provided strong support for analysis of social problems but few guidelines as to what constituted acceptable solutions. Analysts whose work is informed by welfare liberalism may discover that careful analysis of issues cannot overcome the normative power of competing ideological positions held by decision makers. In these instances, the practical use of their recommendations may be minimal.

Utilitarianism

A bias toward the value of efficiency is inherent in the methods of policy analysis, and utilitarianism has been the ideological position most forthrightly incorporating this standard as a central value. Laurence H. Tribe, following the analysis of John Rawls, argued that the heavy reliance of policy analysis on economic concepts and methods had fostered a "wants" orientation toward public choices, in which "wants" are defined simply as what individuals happen to desire.[11] Alternatives are weighted in terms of self-interest, usually measured in monetary terms. Public policies that do well by this standard are deemed to be efficient and therefore "good." Tribe contended that public policy should be based on values and principles larger than quantifiable costs and benefits, and his critique focused on one of the ironies, and limitations, of policy analysis performed within a utilitarian framework—namely, that this approach incorporates efficiency as a basic value while maintaining a posture of being "value free."

Obviously, any methodology undertaken in social analysis will include value judgments. Policy analysis from utilitarian assumptions, however, carries the ever-present danger that values unacceptable to the public will be surreptitiously promoted under the guise of "objective" analysis. Utilitarianism has provided firm ideological support for many of the methods of policy analysis, but unlike Dewey's pragmatic welfare liberalism, it does not necessarily promote social reform by activist government. In fact, at least one important American school of utilitarian thought supports limited government and greater market freedom for private activity as the most efficient form of public policy.

The basic belief of utilitarianism is that laws, customs, and institutions should be evaluated in terms of their social utility. Jeremy Bentham, the intellectual father of utilitarianism, declared that

> by the principle of utility is meant that principle which approves or disapproves of every action whatsoever; according to the tendency which it appears to have to augment or diminish the happiness of the party whose interest is in question. . . . I say of every action whatsoever; and therefore not only of every action of a private individual, but of every measure of government.[12]

From this perspective, the idea of human good becomes equated with preference. The guiding criterion for policy is the greatest good for society, quantitatively defined. But contemporary utilitarians, primarily economists and theorists of public choice, like Bentham, still have no principle for distributing this social good according to manifest principles of equity. "One dollar, one vote" is not on the face of it an acceptable principle.

The basic difficulty with both Dewey's liberalism and utilitarianism is that public policy is left without any firm normative foundations on which to act. That is, if the focus of decision makers is on making things better for people through application of the pragmatic or utilitarian approach, it remains unclear what level of wants deserves attention. In a pluralistic society, can utilitarianism establish a consensual hierarchy of wants? Which is more important, a policy that establishes a universal legal right to a decent minimum of health care (national health insurance) or one that contains growing public health-care costs? How are the opposed values of environmental integrity and full employment to be reconciled? The effort to satisfy people's wants can also deflect attention away from the processes by which decisions are made. If an authoritarian government is most efficient *(reductio ad absurdum)*, then is not that the best form of government? Mussolini, after all, made the trains run on time.[13]

Social Conservatism

In recent years, social conservatism has emerged as an ideology with substantive, if somewhat amorphous, content and with implications for public policy. With its concern for family and religious values, this ideology has popular appeal and provides the background for opposition to abortion, support for school prayer, proposals for aid to parochial schools, and similar positions. Historically, social analysis in America has claimed to provide value-free rationales for social reform. The social conservatives, however, make no pretensions of being without value positions and have shown flexibility in applying analytical techniques in support of their policy proposals. Charles Murray's *Losing Ground,* which extensively criticizes liberal welfare policies, is an example of this approach.[14] Much of this research has been supported by conservatively oriented think tanks and thus has origins independent of academe or government.

Institutional Status Quo Orientation

To the extent that policy analysts are part of an ongoing government agency, they may become so closely tied to their agency's programs that their analyses will not suggest radical changes from the status quo. Anthony Downs noted the tendency of bureaucrats to adopt the values of their agency and to come to defend that agency's "turf."[15] Applying this to policy analysts, Arnold Meltsner noted that the analyst "cannot escape the preferences of his organization; and soon, rather than remaining a skeptical generalist, he, like other bureaucrats, becomes a defender of the faith."[16]

Some contend that policy analysts from outside an agency can avoid a status quo orientation and have some policy impact. Regulatory reform in the federal government under Ronald Reagan has been used as an example. Lawrence M. Mead concluded that "precisely because the outsiders were more academic, closer to the economic paradigm of the free market [as compared with the analysts in the bureaucracy], their thinking was *more* effective in broad policy terms, not less."[17] Getting outside the status quo can, at least on occasion, actually *increase* the effectiveness of policy analysts—if their views are closer to those of powerful clients, such as the president, than are the perspectives of bureaucratically situated analysts. And, as discussed in chapter 7, think tanks (and the broader policy communities of which they are a part) provide a basis outside of government for ideologically inclined groups to try to influence policy. Policy analysts working through these organizations are freer to be critical of government programs, although they themselves will tend to adhere to the values of the organizational interests that they represent and from whom they receive financial support.

Non-Efficiency-Based Values

As already mentioned, a common value underlying policy analysis is economic efficiency, a component of what we refer to in chapter 3 as "the politics of interest." Taking other values into account may make the task of providing advice to clients even more complex for policy analysts, as these are frequently "soft" values that cannot readily be quantified. What value, for example, should be placed on human life, the beauty of a redwood forest, or preservation of the whales?

Charles Anderson argued that authority and justice must also be recognized as standards by which public policy is measured. He asserted that authority is "a necessary characteristic of any legitimate policy decision."[18] If a decision cannot be demonstrated to be a rightful exercise of government power, it is simply an act of coercion or domination. In short, "Good reasons have to be given for regarding a problem or project as appropriately the subject of public action."[19] With regard to the dimension of justice, the policy analyst should begin by treating like cases alike and dissimilar cases differently. The policy analyst who is sensitive to normative concerns should recognize that "any policy evaluation must include a justification of the categories of universal or differential treatment to be established."[20] For example, treating two individuals in essentially similar situations differently by providing an advantage to one or the other must be defensible. Anderson, then, contended that efficiency alone is not sufficient justification for a policy recommendation by an analyst. Authority and justice must also be considered, and as the following chapter indicates, principles of justice, in particular, may be various.

In chapters 3 and 4, we discuss in detail two separate wellsprings of values: interest and conscience, or the utilitarian perspective versus the deontological, or Kantian. Techniques of policy analysis are dominated by efficiency-based utilitarian criteria. The second set of values, which utilizes such ideas as equality, justice, the moral worth of each individual, and the common good and is clearly metaphysical and transcendent in nature, generally receives little consideration in the application of analytical techniques. But, as chapter 4 illustrates, ethicists have argued that this need not and *should not* be the case and have shown how different values can be tied into policy analysis.

How Policy Analysis Is Used

Studies in recent decades have indicated that policy analysis has at least two kinds of use: instrumental and enlightenment. While instrumental use is the most common way in which analysis is expected to have an impact, such expectations are frequently disappointed.

As reported by Grover Starling, interviews with 204 policymakers indicated a generally positive attitude toward policy analysis. Nevertheless, only 13 percent could name as many as five to ten instances of having used policy analyses, whereas 44 percent reported explicitly disregarding such information. Starling also noted that a 1976 General Accounting Office (GAO) study found that 30 percent of the federal units questioned said that policy analysis had accomplished nothing; 30 percent indicated some use of it; 40 percent suggested that it may have had an impact but that sorting out the independent effects of policy analysis as compared with other inputs was very difficult.[21] Michael Quinn Patton's examination of twenty evaluations of federal programs also suggested little independent impact of analytical research on decision making. The effects tended to be a reinforcement of decision makers' preexisting views or the filling in of a few gaps in their knowledge. Overall, research seems to reduce uncertainty in decision situations. Patton concluded that utilization "is a diffuse and gradual process of reducing decision-makers' uncertainty within an existing social context."[22] Based on her work with analysts in the Department of Energy, Martha Feldman noted the general belief of analysts that analyses should be performed even though most thought that policymakers would never use their studies.[23]

David Whiteman explored congressional committees' use of research conducted by the Office of Technology Assessment (OTA). He found that use of information depended on the situation. Substantive impacts (i.e., helping committees outline a legislative position) occurred in the early stages of committee work. In later stages, the use was "strategic" (justifying, confirming, reinforcing an already preferred position). Overall, strategic use was more common.[24] Peter House and Roger Shull, two practitioners of policy analysis, found support for these findings. Using a series of case studies as a database, they concluded that "possibly the single most important lesson to be learned . . . is that no sophisticated or formal decision technique was really used in these decision processes in the sense that they [sic] were intended."[25]

There is a second, "sloppier" way in which analysis has an effect. Robert F. Rich's summary of agencies' use of a series of National Opinion Research Center (NORC) surveys of public opinion is somewhat more encouraging. Rich found two distinct patterns of use. First, information from research filters upward in a bureaucracy and is used to help solve very specific problems. Then, later on, those higher in an agency may use these results to formulate broader policy ideas that are transmitted down to lower levels to help structure future policy choices. His essay points toward a more diffuse impact of policy analysis.[26]

Carol Weiss suggested that policy analysis may be used more for "enlightenment" than for instrumental purposes, although these need *not* be mutually exclusive. She argued that clients of policy analysts may be less interested in analysis as a tool to arrive at a solution than as a means of orienting themselves to a problem. In her estimation, clients

> use research to help them think about issues and define the problematics of a situation, to gain new ideas and new perspectives. They use research to help *formulate* problems and to set the agenda for future policy actions. And much of this is not deliberate, direct, and targeted, but a result of long-term percolation of social science concepts, theories, and findings into the climate of informed opinion.[27]

Indeed, policymakers may not even be aware of where their ideas originate. They absorb bits and pieces of information from different sources, one of them being policy analysis. Weiss referred to this diffuse use as "enlightenment." In her study of the Department of Energy, Feldman came to similar conclusions about the eventual value of analytical studies. Even though their direct use is rare, studies provide "inventories" of interpretations of problems that are available within agencies for use by decision makers.[28]

A study of 155 mental health decision makers in the federal government indicated the possibility that they had used fifty actual research reports for enlightenment, even if they had made little instrumental use of the findings. Two distinct factors increased the odds of this diffuse use: a "truth" test and a "utility" test. The former refers to the quality of the research *and* to its conformity to clients' previous understandings, values, and experience. The latter refers to the ability of the research to help solve problems *and* to challenge the status quo. That is, if there is an interesting twist to the research that can help reorient thinking about a problem and if the research challenges dominant views, the findings can assist in redefining the original problem—even if specific recommendations are not used.[29]

In summary, instrumental use of policy analysis is not as widespread as analysts would like; however, there is a more diffuse use of policy analysis, which can be significant. This use for "enlightenment" is often underplayed in the literature on utilization of policy analysis. Its existence, though, should be taken into account by the policy analyst. If the analyst cannot easily shape a specific policy, his or her findings may still have an impact on the broader policy agenda, a not insignificant contribution.

POLICY ANALYSIS: TECHNIQUES, VALUES, AND EFFECTS

The tools available to policy analysts seem impressive. In this section, we examine four of them: cost-benefit analysis, decision-tree methods, simulations and models, and experiments. This scarcely exhausts the supply; other approaches include an array of forecasting techniques—for example, Delphi, linear programming, risk assessment, program evaluation review technique (PERT), and game theory.

No agreement exists as to which discipline provides the most valid foundation for policy analysis, but in practice the methods and assumptions of economics are central. Meltsner, for instance, found that a plurality of federal policy analysts have the greater part of their professional training in economics.[30] As chapter 1 makes clear, there are historical and theoretical reasons for the influence of economics.

Cost-Benefit Analysis

Cost-benefit analysis is one of the most basic methods of policy analysis. Its essence is deceptively simple. One adds up the costs of a program, then its benefits. Next, one subtracts costs from benefits. If several options are being considered, the one with the greatest *net* benefit should be selected. This axiom is referred to as the "Fundamental Rule" of cost-benefit analysis. A study of the effects of helicopter surveillance patrols on burglary rates in high-crime areas has illustrated the essential elements of this type of analysis.[31] Simply adding patrol cars to such areas had no apparent impact. Helicopter patrols, which enhance the ability of law enforcement officers to see wrongful acts, were introduced to see if they had a more significant impact on crime. The study indicated that the helicopter patrols did lead to a reduction in crime rates. The relevant question then became whether the reduction in crime was worth the program cost. Table 2.1 summarizes the basic data.

On a cost-per-day basis, helicopter patrols expended $126; benefits amounted to $333 per day (cost of burglaries during no-helicopter patrol period minus cost of burglaries during helicopter patrol period). The resulting ratio of benefits to costs was 2.6:1, indicating that under the logic of the Fundamental Rule, the program was justified.

As already noted, this method presents a number of difficulties. Some are obvious, such as the problem of putting dollar figures on intangibles like quality of life, value of a human life, or the benefits of beauty.[32] Such intangibles are, however, often assessed indirectly; for example, a value for human life can be cal-

Table 2.1. Helicopter Patrol Cost-Benefit Analysis

	DAILY
Cost of program	$126
Cost of burglaries during no-helicopter patrol period	$494
Cost of burglaries during helicopter patrol period	$161
Benefits	$333
Benefits-to-cost ratio: $333/$126 = 2.6	

culated from the rate of awards in wrongful death cases that go to trial. That the valuation of life remains problematic is clear from a comparison of government assumptions about the dollar benefits accruing when a life is saved; variation across agencies can be enormous, from $5 million at the Occupational Safety and Health Administration to $475,000 at the Environmental Protection Agency.[33] In our helicopter example, what is the cost to residents of the additional noise likely to be generated by helicopter patrols? This is not an easy question to answer in dollar-and-cent terms, even though studies have been carried out with surrogate prices when no market price exists for purposes of estimate.

Another clear obstacle to the use of quantitative measures is the uncertainty often associated with a social problem. More systematic treatment can be given to known than to unknown probabilities. It is not always clear what the facts really are; costs and benefits calculated under conditions in which probabilities are not known will surely not be as reliable as desired. Aaron Wildavsky observed that "the cost-benefit analyst must learn to live with uncertainty, for he can never know whether all relevant objectives have been included and what changes may occur in policy and in technology."[34] This is not a counsel of despair but an admonition of the need to be sensitive to uncertainty.

Also, the future can be an imponderable complicating the cost-benefit calculations of the analyst. In theory, through discounting, one can incorporate the future into cost-benefit analysis. In practice, important questions remain. First, and most apparent, the future is opaque and not easily predictable; hence, there is often built-in uncertainty in considering the future. Second, in actual practice, consequences are often not seriously weighted.

In their widely used text on analytical methods, Edith Stokey and Richard Zeckhauser asserted that their bias in public policy was toward the well being of individuals. In their view, "The objective of public policy should be to promote the welfare of society. Moreover, the welfare of society depends wholly on the welfare of individuals; it's people that count."[35] Superficially, this appears to be an incontestable position, but the present and future needs of individuals are difficult to assess in both their nature and their magnitude. When one includes the needs of future generations, the task of promoting human welfare becomes even more problematic. Almost two hundred years ago, Edmund Burke addressed this very point with his often quoted description of the proper way of conceiving of the social contract between the state and its constituents: "As the ends of such a partnership cannot be obtained in many generations, it becomes a partnership not only between those who are living, but between those who are living, those who are dead, and those who are to be born."[36]

With its emphasis on measurement and tangible factors, the cost-benefit form of analysis has enjoyed wide popularity among policy analysts. Yet these characteristics can also be viewed as limitations in the area of public policy. Obviously, in some ways, cost-benefit analysis can be a hindrance to long-range planning or commitment. This shortcoming stems as much from its insistence on quantifiable measures as from its inherently incremental bias. As used in the area of public policy, the cost-benefit approach usually stresses costs over benefits. One widely conceded reason for this is that many public programs—in such areas as health, education, and environmental protection—produce intangible benefits that are not quantifiable but whose dollar costs are readily calculated. The cost-benefit approach is politically debilitating in another, less widely recognized sense, for it tends to saddle leaders with the onus of costs when their actions may have averted major disasters. Citizens can feel the pinch of the costs of public measures designed to prevent serious misfortunes, such as a natural disaster, enemy attack, or economic depression, but they may experience no noticeable benefits if the measures taken are successful. In these instances, voters may in effect punish leaders for their foresight. At the same time, careful analysis of social problems remains an especially useful approach, and responsible public leaders would be well advised to consider its findings.

Basic values are built into the cost-benefit method despite its surface appearance as an objective, value-free technique. The Fundamental Rule demands that the most efficient alternative be selected. Maximization of goods or services in quantifiable terms, usually dollars, guides decisions under cost-benefit analysis. The many factors involved in the *process* by which decisions are made are deemphasized. There is little "independent concern for the *procedures* whereby those outcomes are produced or for the *history* out of which they evolve."[37] By deemphasizing these factors, utilitarian values tend to crowd out other concerns. Slighted in the process may be such values as equity or the welfare of unborn generations. Cost-benefit analysis is exceptionally valuable for clarifying and arranging alternative ways of approaching problems, but by no stretch of the imagination can it be considered "value free."

Decision Analysis

Decision analysis is used when "decisions must be undertaken sequentially and where uncertainty is a critical element."[38] A common technique used under these conditions is the decision tree. The choice between the cost per month of purchasing a new car and the cost per month of purchasing a used car provides a simple example of this approach (see fig. 2.1).

There are one *decision node* (two courses of action open to the decision maker); two *chance nodes* (the four uncertain events with their possible outcomes)—cost per month associated with purchase of a used (*a*) versus a new (*b*) car; *probabilities* (associated with each outcome); and *payoffs*, the consequences of each possible combination of choice and chance. The Expected Monetary Value (EMV) of buying a used car (EMV/*a*) is the average of the sum of each choice multiplied by the odds of the different choices. Simply, for a used car in this case, EMV/*a* = .5(1000) + .5(200) = $600. For a new car, EMV/*b* = .1(800)

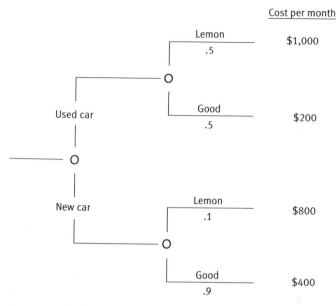

Figure 2.1 Decision Tree for Purchasing a Car

+ .9(400) = \$440. The better choice, then, would be to purchase a new car, since the expected monetary value (\$440)—in this case, cost—is *less* than that of acquiring a used car (\$600 per month).

One immediate question about this technique is the set of quantitative assumptions undergirding each decision choice. Probability estimates and the costs associated with the array of choices are straightforward in our example, but decision trees are often constructed when there is considerable uncertainty about root assumptions. In complex situations, branches representing various choices, or decisions, can be added at a geometric rate, making the final result dependent on a heavy amount of estimating. In the opinion of Susan Welch and John C. Comer, "Decision tree analysis seems more a useful heuristic device than a yardstick by which a final decision should be measured. Past experience with decision trees shows that failure rates of systems and other risks are often severely underestimated, thus making the whole payoff calculation pure fantasy."[39]

Related to these operational problems is the fact that it is not always easy to identify all relevant "branches" of the decision tree; some alternatives may simply be ignored, especially in complex situations. The Rasmussen Reactor Safety Study, for example, which utilized event-tree analysis and fault-tree analysis—methods similar to the decision-tree approach—cost \$4 million over three years. Despite the thoroughness with which the study was conducted, soon after its completion, numerous criticisms exposed flaws in its methodology and its assumptions, indicating, again, the need for any analyst to retain a critical posture in the application of analytical techniques.[40]

Values underlying the decision-tree method parallel those of cost-benefit analysis. The approach is outcome-oriented and hence reflects utilitarian values. While this tool is, on its face, more future-oriented than cost-benefit analysis, that appearance is misleading. Probability and cost estimates are essentially based on current understandings, and efficiency is a built-in value. Adopting this as a criterion embedded in a "value-free" technique may cause competing values to receive short shrift.

Simulations and Models

Simulations and models are techniques that represent attempts to create the equivalent of a laboratory setting to determine the likely outcomes of various policy choices. The result is a prediction in the following form: Given conditions X_1 through X_i, policy choices A_1 to A_i will have impacts Y_1 to Y_i. With this information, one would select the option that seems best—normally the most cost-effective option. The usual means of creating a simulation or model is through computers and software packages. The goal of these techniques is to develop more rational control over decisions and to increase the odds that the actual policy adopted will be an efficient choice. These approaches tend to be fairly abstract in that through the construction of hypothetical relationships, they attempt to encompass a broad range of individual behavior.

For instance, governments at the local level have increasingly purchased computer software models to try to rationalize the budget-making process. The computer models (in budgeting called Fiscal Impact Budgeting Systems, or FIBS) forecast government service needs and both expenditure and revenue needs over one year or several years. The database for projections includes previous expenditure and revenue levels, demographics, intergovernmental funding relationships, and predicted changes in each of these parameters. Kenneth L. Kraemer and William H. Dutton noted that

> FIBS are a classic management-science response to a fundamental policy problem—that of developing more rational control by elected officials and the general public over decisions that affect the fiscal position of government. They are promoted as leading to improvements in information processing, content, and flows, and as such, they represent a potential tool for managerial rationalism.[41]

Generically, such computer models produce predictions of the impact of different budgetary decisions. They are important tools in analyzing budget-making policy not only at the local level but at the national level as well; both the Office of Management and Budget and the Congressional Budget Office employ complex models to discern potential impacts of different budgetary strategies.

Like cost-benefit analysis, modeling draws heavily on ideas from economics, especially in areas involving budgeting. Some models, of course, may *not* be based on economic assumptions. Examples would be those utilizing engineering principles or dealing with problems in air pollution. Much of the concern over the issue of global warming stems from the use of these kinds of complex computer models. Many of the questions raised about this instrument of policy analysis are familiar. There is great uncertainty in decision situations, and computer simulations must necessarily oversimplify reality and be based on artificial assumptions. Thus, in a 1998 article in the *Proceedings of the National Academy of Sciences*, James Hansen, a leading climate modeler for the National Aeronautics and Space Administration who was among the first to raise concern about global warming, concluded that his model and others simply did not encompass sufficient variables to "assess accurately the effectiveness of policy options."[42]

Moreover, in application, other problems occur as well. To be manageable, the number of policy alternatives examined must be limited, but political bias frequently determines the boundaries of choice. Often, public officials specify that they want a choice between just A and B. If one of the options is obviously preferable to the other, this produces a prearranged, or "cooked," result. The temptation thus exists for the political preferences of public officials to encourage manipulation of this "scientific" technique. And, as the reader shall see in chapters 5 and 6, political pressures on elected officials produce short-term thinking that can overwhelm the results of policy analysis—or lead to skewing of analyses for political ends. With or without overt political concerns, the analyst must make initial choices in modeling. The essential point is that he or she remain aware of the ramifications of these choices for later policy decisions.

In fact, amenability to manipulation through control of the choice of alternatives to be considered renders all the techniques we have discussed thus far especially vulnerable in the policy process. Students of policy analysis, such as Stokey and Zeckhauser, are fully aware of the possibilities in this respect and caution that the legitimacy of policy analysis depends on everyone's playing by the rules. Speaking directly to this issue with regard to cost-benefit analysis, Stokey and Zeckhauser noted that outright deception can involve "submerged assumptions, unfairly chosen valuations, and purposeful misestimates"; they added the caveat that "any procedure for making policy choices, from divine guidance to computer algorithms, can be manipulated unfairly."[43]

Experimental Analysis

The final tool we examine here is social experimentation. Using this approach, the analyst examines results from quasi experiments or—ideally—true experiments to determine the best course of action. The true social experiment relies on random assignment of subjects to an experimental group receiving the services of the program being tested and a control group not receiving those services. Experiments are normally conducted with pilot or demonstration studies to see if the experimental programs should become general policy. If those assigned to the experimental group benefit more than those in control groups, that is considered evidence that the program has had a positive benefit (i.e., it "works"). In contrast, the quasi experiment proceeds without random assignment of subjects and is therefore less rigorous procedurally. This approach, while often the best available given the constraints of particular situations, usually cannot produce results with the same level of validity as those from the more rigorous experimental design. It attempts to apply the scientific method of the natural sciences through the social sciences (especially sociology and political science).

An impressive array of policy experiments has been carried out from the late 1960s through the present. Among them are various income maintenance (negative income tax or guaranteed annual income) experiments, housing allowance programs, voucher-type plans for educational expenses, and programs imposing federal penalties on any crime in which a gun is used. Ostensibly, the goal has been to use results from these pilot studies to help design better programs on a large scale. In these instances, the policy analyst can base policy recommendations on actual experiments carried out in a "real-world setting."

One negative income tax (NIT) experiment in metropolitan areas of New Jersey and Pennsylvania had as participants almost 1,400 low-income, male-headed families. They were randomly assigned to one of eight experimental groups or to the control group. Each experimental cohort was governed by a different NIT structure (different levels of guaranteed income and different tax rates). Every two weeks, a check was sent to experimental subjects. The amount of the checks was computed by a formula based on the family's income and the structure of the specific experimental NIT. Families were interviewed every three months over a three-year period to try to determine if a guaranteed income would create a work disincentive and how much such a program would cost if implemented on a larger scale.

This NIT experiment indicates why the impact of social experimentation has been minimal. Full experiments take much time to complete. Often, by the time results are made available, the program has become a "dead issue" for one reason or another. The policy cycle begins with public interest aroused about a specific problem. The government may then undertake experiments. But by the time results are in, the citizenry's interest has waned, and impetus for change has dissipated. When final results of the income maintenance experiments came in under the Nixon administration, political conditions were no longer ripe for enactment of such a policy. Furthermore, after the experiments were well under way, officials became interested in a "work for welfare" component; however, it was by then too late to include this critical element in the experiments. Not surprisingly, opponents of programs have seen the use of the experimental technique as a way of delaying action on a major commitment until it can be safely killed.

Basic technical problems abound with conducting experiments in a social setting. They include the sometimes difficult task of just getting enough participants, the resistance of prospective subjects to "being experimented on," the tendency of experimental programs to "drift" (i.e., to evolve over time and change) and thus render uncertain how the program actually affects people, and the question of external validity (i.e., the extent to which the results of a particular social experiment are generalizable to other settings).

In addition to technical problems in constructing a valid experimental design, there are serious normative limitations on how it can be used. For instance, to construct a "tight" experimental design, can one withhold services from some while supplying them to others? Ethical considerations prevent a wide variety of experiments on humans. When ethics are ignored, as in the Tuskegee quasi experiments of the 1930s, in which a group of more than 400 blacks went untreated for syphilis so that the disease's progress could be studied over decades, the results are grotesque and violate the subjects' basic rights.[44]

THE POLICY PROCESS

At its most basic level, policy analysis operates under the assumption that decision making ought to be a more rational process; analytic methods are assumed to enhance rationality in the policy process. Rationality does not describe very well how decisions are actually made, however. The very way in which humans think can cause their values to become more important in decision-making situations than purely rational conclusions based on policy analysis.[45] To understand policymaking, one must understand policymakers' values. Analysts may underestimate the significance of decision makers' values and overestimate the persuasive value of policy analysis. This is particularly true in high-risk and stress situations.

In addition, political considerations can elevate voters' values over policy analyses. Elected public officials must receive public support for reelection; consequently, mass values, even if not always sensible or coherent, can override policy analysis. As we shall see in later chapters, elected and unelected officials follow changes in public opinion. In this respect, the Clinton White House's reliance on weekly and even daily polling results provides a particularly clear illustration of one public official's sensitivity to what the public was thinking at any given moment. Within this kind of policy context, the swirling currents of politics can rather quickly sweep away purely "objective" analyses if they do not comport with the current direction of public beliefs.

Knowledge of the policy process—and the role of values in it—is important for the policy analyst. James Anderson has summarized the overall implications:

The policymaking process in the United States is an adversarial process, characterized by the clash of competing and conflicting viewpoints and interests rather than an impartial, disinterested, or "objective" search for "correct" solutions for policy problems. Public officials—legislators, administrators, and perhaps to a lesser extent, judges—do not stand impartially about the policy struggle. Rather, they have their own values and positions which they seek to advance and hence are often partisans in the policy struggle. Given this, policy analyses done by social scientists, for instance, may have little impact except as they provide support for the positions of particular participants in the policy process.[46]

The whole policy process is messy, replete with considerable randomness, but careful research can have an important impact—from agenda setting through the implementation stage. The policy analyst is in a position to add an element of rationality to this process and to increase the likelihood that programs will operate successfully. Although this impact may not be exactly what analysts have hoped for, it adds an important degree of enlightenment to the policy process that might not otherwise have been there.

To be understood properly, policy analysis must be examined within the context of the larger policy. Normally, the policy process is seen as a series of stages. Three of these steps—agenda setting, decision making, and implementation—are sufficiently critical to the policy analyst to warrant examination here. Agenda setting occurs when decision makers conclude that an issue must be considered in the policy process. Some problems are seen as worthy of debate; others are not. Decision making describes the process of formulating policies in response to issues that are on the agenda. Finally, these policies must be implemented, or actually put into effect.

The analyst must understand that the different values and perspectives brought to bear at each phase of the policy process can determine the definition of the issue at that point. Policy actors at each stage redefine the issue in terms relevant to their particular context. This can begin as early as the agenda-setting stage. For example, many may have seen the Equal Rights Amendment as a means of creating greater legal protection for women, but for others, it was important to have it on the agenda as a rallying point for keeping the feminist movement vibrant.

One problem for the policy analyst is that social problems tend to be what are called "wicked problems," on which there is no consensus whether a problem exists. Furthermore, even if there is some agreement that a problem exists, there is no agreement on its nature.[47] The issue of education provides an instance of this difficulty. One can argue that there are serious problems with education in the United States—or that the American educational system is doing quite well. By one indicator, for example, Americans are smarter than ever; they get more answers "right" on IQ tests each decade when compared with previous decades.[48] What is the problem? Is there in fact a problem? Such wicked problems render policy analysis that much more difficult from the earliest stages of the policy process, and this is one reason why Feldman, for example, contended that policy analyses should be viewed as forms of issue interpretation. Analysts from different political persuasions or different agencies can use the same data and emerge with radically different conclusions. Feldman concluded that this variety provides decision makers with an "inventory" of approaches to problems and that in this manner policy analysis, while unable to definitively solve many issues, remains exceptionally important to the policy process.[49]

As issues move into the legislative branch, a wide variety of concerns, at times with little relevance to the issue as the analyst has described it, come to bear. An instance of the intrusion of extraneous concerns into consideration of a policy issue occurred in the 1960s when, in an effort to aid the less-developed countries, some senators supported the export of powdered fish to these nations. Unfortunately, they labeled the substance "fish flour," thereby drawing the immediate and intense opposition of America's wheat farmers. These farmers might have opposed the export in any event, but use of the term *flour* served to intensify their opposition by making it appear that powdered fish was in direct competition with their product. Other examples of diversion from the original issue are frequent at this stage of policymaking.

The administrative and judicial sectors are not exceptions to the principle that issues can become hostages to the various contexts of the policy process. Administrators have their own interests to promote. Indeed, William Niskanen advanced a theory of bureaucracy that assumes that administrators are primarily interested in increased salaries and more prestige, power, and patronage.[50] Courts also have routines that can redefine issues as cases proceed through the judicial process, for instance, from trial to appellate review. Richard Richardson and Kenneth Vines noted, for example, how straightforward civil cases in the U.S. District Courts became redefined as civil rights cases as they moved up the appellate process.[51] Additionally, the power of judicial precedent and the configurations of an issue provided by opposing attorneys can greatly influence a court's views, as well as reshape the definition of the issue.

The politically astute analyst, then, will understand that his or her data and the recommendations carefully based on those data can easily become sidetracked by other considerations as the issue moves through the policy process. The label on the issue may remain the same, but the contents undergo continual change. As a consequence, policymakers who appear to be debating an issue as originally defined are actually often contesting other questions of more importance and personal interest to them.

Agenda Setting

The agenda reflects the basic power patterns of the policy process and is the crucial first step for any proposal. If no one wishes to discuss a proposal, obviously its supporters are nonplayers, and it is a nonissue in the policy process. While the process by which problems are placed on the agenda is tangled, there are nonetheless regularities. Three basic elements help to shape what gets on the governmental agenda: problems, politics, and visible participants.[52]

First, if a condition is not identified as a problem, it will not be placed on the agenda. Statistical indicators (e.g., the number of people living in poverty) may show that a condition is growing into a real problem. This may force government officials to place more emphasis on this issue. Natural disasters or national tragedies, such as the killings at Columbine High School in Littleton, Colorado, can focus attention on a particular condition and increase the odds that it will be put on the agenda. Getting officials to believe that there is a problem is a key first step in agenda setting, and at this point, analysts, within and outside government, can have significant influence by providing data and framing the dimensions of the problem.

A second set of factors that affect agenda setting is political. A kind of consensus may emerge that certain circumstances call for government consideration; this general agreement is often a product of bargaining, negotiation, and compromise among the multitude of actors.

Third, visible political actors are central in deciding what to decide about. Among them are the president, Congress, key high-level appointees, top administrators, media, parties, and interest groups. If few or none of the visible actors are in favor of placing a problem on the agenda, it is highly unlikely that it will be considered.

Values are key factors at this stage. One value having some impact is equity, the redress of imbalances or unfairness. Proposals can get onto the agenda if an existing policy is seen as unfair, even if proposed remedies are more inefficient. Equity as a value may thus override policy analysis based on efficiency criteria. The implementation of affirmative action plans, for example, may require adjustments in the interests of long-term fairness that cause considerable dislocation and inconvenience in the short term.

Even if the policy analyst does not have great overt impact on getting an issue put on the agenda, he or she can play a role in the agenda-setting process by helping identify conditions that *may* come to be seen as problems deserving of agenda placement. The analyst can also help develop the alternative proposals that "bubble up" through various policy communities (think tanks, academics, government employees, and others who have an interest in a particular policy area) and that become adopted by visible political actors. Finally, analysts can help frame discussion of an issue in a specialized language that places policy competitors at a disadvantage. Thus, in the 1960s, by structuring issues in terms of systems analysis, Secretary of Defense McNamara's "whiz kids" were able to gain increased leverage over the Joint Chiefs of Staff, who were less conversant in the argot of policy analysis.

Decision Making

When or whether policy alternatives get taken up seriously is partially a chance proposition. The process depends to some extent on unpredictable events, on political currents, and on the desires of visible political actors. Nevertheless, policy analysts play important, although less visible, roles in developing alternatives that can be considered once a condition is defined as a problem to be placed on the political agenda. These alternatives form a "policy stream" that flows parallel to the current of events. At some point, appropriate policy proposals that have been under tentative consideration may be coupled with the pressure to "do something" about a problem that events have propelled onto the agenda.

Formulation of policies or specification of policy alternatives is only one part of the actual decision-making portion of the policy process. Officials must then select one policy from the number of policies described by John Kingdon as "floating around."[53] Decision making ultimately means adopting a particular policy and providing at least some budgetary support for it. At the national level, key actors include the president, his advisers and top administrative appointees, Congress, interest groups, and interested agencies. Normally, to get approval of a policy, majority coalitions must be developed. This entails a process of negotiation and compromise among many of the parties with a stake in the policy. These decision makers will take into account the role of public opinion or the national mood. One common result is incremental decision making, with the new policy tending to be a tinkering with existing policies or a series of changes on the margins of the status quo. A final characteristic of the process as a result of these different considerations is a short-term perspective on decisions that coincides with the two-year election cycles of Congress.

Findings from psychology suggest that, in general, people who make decisions under conditions of uncertainty—quite common in the political world—use certain "rules of thumb," or "heuristics."[54] That is, when facts are not clear and when the context in which decisions are made is murky, people adopt nonrational shortcuts to facilitate making decisions. One frequent characteristic of decision making in such circumstances is the central importance of an individual policymaker's preexisting values and beliefs, often derived from past experiences. People interpret uncertain facts to comport with their values and beliefs; their preconceptions shape the types of information used in decision making. One common consequence is inappropriate use of historical events. Time and again, policymakers have succumbed to the temptation to interpret a current problem in terms of a controversy from their past when more objective examination would have uncovered important differences.

Values and decision-making shortcuts used by policymakers play a large role in determining which choices leaders will actually make under the conditions of uncertainty that commonly prevail. The use of personal values and beliefs as heuristic shortcuts to decisions has been especially noticeable in foreign policy. Foreign policy decision makers often develop "value screens" that influence their decisions. These images act as powerful filters and affect their perceptions and expectations. During the Eisenhower administration, Secretary of State John Foster Dulles seemed to ignore important information before the Suez Crisis in 1956. An operational code study has indicated that Dulles's belief system led him to interpret Soviet behavior as "bad" and British behavior as "good"—ignoring, as a result, obvious signs that Britain planned to join with France and Israel to attack Egypt. Apparently Dulles's belief that Britain would do nothing to harm American policy interests (one attribute of a "good" state) acted to screen out clear, nonconfirming evidence.[55]

On the domestic front, personal value priorities must also be taken into account. Surely, President Ronald Reagan's threefold tax and budget strategy, which he elaborated on during his 1980 presidential campaign (tax cuts plus increased defense spending plus a balanced budget), was constructed on his deeply held beliefs about the role of government and the primacy of a strong defense. The value screen was so strong that Reagan did not seem to hear David Stockman's continual warnings about a massive federal deficit and the likely ensuing economic difficulties. Similarly, when Howard Baker, known as a person adept at negotiation and compromise, became President Reagan's chief of staff, he soon learned that some of the president's positions were simply not open to discussion.

In short, policy analysis alone is not likely to provide the clear, unassailable data needed to cause decision makers to abandon or change their preexisting values and beliefs in policy situations. Because values and previous experiences are important in shaping the decisions political officials make, policy analysts must also take these factors into account.

Implementation

The central figures in implementation are administrators in the agencies charged with putting a paper policy into operation. But high-level officials in the executive branch or legislators can have an effect by serving as "fixers," prodding, if necessary, the bureaucracies in charge of implementation. Other actors can get involved, too. Interest groups with a stake in the specific program may have real influence; judges, through judicial review of agency regulations, can also be key players.

The major contribution of policy analysts to implementation would appear to occur at the stage of policy formulation. Policy analysts can have an impact on program administration by having the foresight to build into their analyses specifications that increase the odds of successful implementation later. A relevant example here is FDR's insistence that the Social Security program be enacted as an insurance program that covered most working Americans, thereby making it virtually immune from attack, as recent policy debates have demonstrated. Analysts can also have considerable influence through their evaluation of the effectiveness of a program, especially if they conclude that implementation procedures are hampering a program.

Personal values play an important role in aiding or hindering implementation. Because administrators often have considerable discretion in how they implement policy, their attitudes toward a program are important. If their values differ from those of the decision makers who formulated the policy, they are in a position to shape the program to fit their own views more closely. As an example, the opposition of the Office of Education to the goals of Title I of the 1965 Education Act and to the National Teacher Corps contained in the same act reshaped both programs dramatically after they were enacted into law.[56] This potential for slippage between decision and implementation is a particularly important consideration for the analyst when formulating approaches to dealing with a problem. It is especially critical when, as under much of the Clinton administration, the presidency and Congress are at opposite ends of the ideological and political spectrums.

POLICY ANALYSIS AND THE POLICY PROCESS

Policy analysts have accumulated and developed numerous sophisticated and powerful techniques to provide data, analyze relationships, and clarify alternatives. Yet the use of analysts' work in the policy process remains limited, a problem that can be traced to its vulnerability to other forces.

First, decision makers often are faced with information overload. Especially when highly controversial issues are being considered, congressmen, administrators, and even judges can be deluged with studies and recommendations from many contending sources. The result can easily be that all information becomes diluted in persuasiveness, and the decision maker ends by relying on less rationally defensible but more comfortable and personally satisfying modes of reaching a solution.

Second, the use of analysis primarily for reinforcement of choices already made seems to be a common feature of political reality. Patton found that political considerations affected use of evaluation research in fifteen of the twenty cases he studied.[57] Whiteman, in his study of Congress's OTA, found that political and strategic use of analytical findings was greatest in the most controversial, contested, and visible cases. These post hoc uses may serve to protect individual members of Congress from electoral retribution.[58]

A third problem is the politicization of research. An agency's analyses may be countered by studies carried out by opposing researchers hired by interest groups and other political actors. This can lead people to see research as a commodity to be bought and sold, devoid of any intrinsic value. Cynicism about the usefulness of "scientific" findings can easily result. If some research suggests that acid rain comes from midwestern manufacturing plants and is devastating eastern forests and lakes, one can easily predict that there will emerge countervailing analyses from representatives of the accused economic interests.

A fourth problem is overtly political: policy analysts often lack an independent power base or political acumen. Many times, to have influence, the analyst has to link up with a client who possesses power. Meltsner asserted that the agency policy analyst "does not have a constituency to support him when he is in trouble; and like the *staff* person who relies on the holder of a position, the analyst is dependent on his client."[59] Sometimes, analysts may be politically innocent, not understanding the importance of political considerations. As Feldman has cautioned, effective analysts "have to have ideas about the interests of their organizations and what the officials in the organization consider to be the appropriate grounds for concurrence or nonconcurrence."[60] Part of the analytical naiveté that continues in some areas may result from the economics background common to many analysts. This can facilitate narrow, technically proficient analysis of a problem without adequate regard for the administrative or political process, an approach characteristic of the analyst operating in the technician role described earlier. Clearly, however, in addition to taking technical validity and efficiency into account, elected officials in particular must consider many other factors, such as the attractiveness of the policy to voters and the implications of a decision for personal career goals. Another value taken seriously by policymakers, and less seriously by some analysts, is equity, since the public finds fairness an important criterion for policy.

Fifth, policy analysts may provide useful information about a particular policy and yet give very little guidance on how the policy should be implemented. Meltsner noted that analysts should move beyond defining policy to considering how it can be put into effect.[61] Policy analysts ought to put a higher priority on implementation issues, such as how the program can best be put into operation and administered, than they currently do. More concrete consideration of the "how-to-do-it issues" would increase the instrumental use of policy analysis. This suggests the importance to policy analysts of linking their analysis more closely to the broader policy process within which it is embedded. Given the indirect "enlightenment" impact of policy analysis, this becomes an important tactical consideration.

A final factor that cannot be overemphasized is the importance of the values of the participants—from policy analysts to policymakers to the general public—in the policy process. For the policy analyst to maximize his or her role as adviser, this basic but often ignored reality must be fully appreciated. Rational-scientific analysis *can* assist in approaching social life, but it can neither supplant nor entirely explain its normative core. As discussed earlier, Frank

Fischer noted the importance of going back and forth from the concrete pro-gram to the larger social setting, including basic values. He wrote, "A policy to introduce a multicultural curriculum in a particular university should not only indicate specific course offerings but should also address the larger requirements of a pluralist society, such as the need for a set of common integrating values capable of holding the social system together."[62] Thus, the world of the policy analyst is circumscribed by values—whether individualistic, narrowly held by special interests, or widely and fundamentally accepted by many throughout society. The next two chapters explore in more detail how values can be incor-porated in the analysis of policy issues.

CHAPTER 3

The Cultural Setting of Policy Analysis

THE LAST TWO chapters examined the values implicit in the concept of policy analysis, in the roles the analyst plays, and in the techniques the analyst employs in his or her work. Also mentioned was the importance of the values the analyst brings to the workplace, as a citizen and as a person. These values are mirrored in or contradicted by the values of clients and in the ways in which the policy issues are defined for the analyst. They also find their way into the studies an analyst produces.

An examination of those values indicates that they reflect the complexity of American society and its past. They are a paradoxical set of notions put together under the name "American political culture." Sometimes they appear to be a mere potpourri, but there is an underlying order to them, the structure of which can be delineated.[1] This takes the form of a patterned political culture and systematic ethical systems that mirror that culture.

Gilbert and Sullivan sang that "everyone who's born into this world a-live is either a little *lib*-er-al, or else a Con-ser-va-*tive*." Today, the choices in America are more varied: old-fashioned welfare liberal, cultural conservative, economic conservative, Yuppie libertarian, neoconservative, left-leaning liberal, communitarian, various brands of Marxist persuasion, and more. One of the more remarkable things about this motley array of ideological positions is that they all tend to contain more or less the same vocabulary, although the various theories do differ in how they nuance and position the words, weight them, and combine them. Also, when one moves away from that small group of intellectuals whose chief employment is to define and defend ideological positions and from political and economic leadership circles into the general public, it becomes difficult to discover groups of people who subscribe to thought-out, coherent ideological positions and to find ideological groups that are stable over time.

Whatever combination of values an analyst brings to his or her desk, it will be, in part, a mixture attributable to a number of environmental influences. They include having been born in a family with a particular tradition, having a particular social status, hailing from a particular region of the country, having been raised during a particular period of time, and being employed by a particular agency. But the analyst's value ideas will also have uniqueness; they will be the values of a particular person who has had unique experiences. In this chapter, however, we concentrate on general themes and concepts—on the cultural materials out of which individuals in the United States fashion their worldviews and arrive at their ethical judgments.

LIBERTY AND EQUALITY: THE POLITICS OF CONSCIENCE AND THE POLITICS OF INTEREST

Two concepts form the core of American political culture: liberty and equality. Each has been variously defined over the years, sometimes in ways that support one another, other times in antagonistic fashion. Both have focused on the individual and have been expressed in terms of individual rights. Each has also played a role in two sets of ideas and attitudes that have dominated American thought over the years: a politics of conscience and a politics of interest.

The politics of conscience manifested itself for the first time in American life in the Puritan "New Jerusalem" of colonial Massachusetts, a "city built upon a hill." In this society whose structure mirrored in salient ways the theocentric organicism of premodern Europe, the good of the individual was realized in fulfilling God's law, which was identified with the common good. Service of this objective good was also declared the substance of civil liberty. This was a liberty "to that only which is good, just, and honest . . . exercised in a subjection to authority."[2] With this view of liberty was paired a concept of the equal worth of all men and women in the eyes of God. Ralph Barton Perry has called this a "generic equality" and explained it as "the idea that beneath the clothes they wear, and the status or occupation which organized society has bestowed upon them, all men are men, with the same faculties, the same needs and aspirations, the same destiny, and similar potentialities of development. . . . No one will deny it, once the question is raised in this form."[3]

The politics of conscience in Puritan times also displayed a concept of individual liberty rather different from the one just characterized, a concept that has frequently come into conflict with the notion that liberty must be defined in relation to a publicly sanctioned standard of morality. It was represented in the antinomian stance of Anne Hutchinson, who asserted that God's will can be revealed directly to the individual, not just through authoritative interpretations of Scripture by church ministers supported by public authority. Her insistence on personal autonomy eventuated in Anne Hutchinson's persecution by the leaders of the Bay Colony and ultimately led to her banishment. The pluralist society of today has worked out the antinomian conception of freedom in great secular detail and embodied it in laws that give wide protection to individual freedom of choice in lifestyle. A patient's autonomy in the face of a physician's paternal authority reflects this conception of freedom, as do disputes about a woman's right to control her body.

The politics of interest has also been part of American political culture from the earliest days. But in this frame of reference, liberty and equality receive a very different definition and are differently related to one another. In the politics of interest, liberty is understood as security and as the right to accumulate private property. It is a politics of material well-being. Its terms of reference were fashioned in the seventeenth century out of the rising commercial culture of that time. An eminent figure in giving voice to them was James Harrington, a classical republican political theorist schooled in the egoistic political philosophy of Niccolò Machiavelli.[4] It was not Machiavelli of *The Prince*, however, but the republican enthusiast of the *Discourses* upon whom Harrington drew for inspiration. Politics in this framework is conceived as a realm of strategic maneuver and rational calculation among self-interested individuals who wish to win in the great game of life. As a republican theory, it envisages the competition of individuals taking place within a system of rules that break up concentrations of power and limit exercise of power through institutional balance. Harrington saw economic self-interest rather than generalized selfishness as the dominant human motive. In his study, C.B. Macpherson pointed to evidence of Harrington's "awareness of and acceptance of market motivations and relationships."[5] With his observation that property is gained by industry, not by mere ambition, Harrington also united the work ethic, which Puritanism had bred deeply into American life, with the freedom to acquire. In addition, he recognized that commercial and urban society is tremendously productive and that it is the "natural operation of a law of supply and demand . . . that brings the secondary growth."[6] Harrington's philosophy expresses the optimistic individualism of the middle-class settlers of seventeenth-century America, and his constitutional prescriptions for the defense of liberty are found written large on many colonial charters.

CONSCIENCE AND INTEREST IN ETHICAL THEORY

Over the past two decades, academic courses on ethics in developing public policy programs have proliferated. This has resulted in part from an awareness that traditional standards do not furnish ethical models for a score of new ethical problems spawned by the growth of technology. It is also a fruit of change in American political culture, and in particular of a change in the balance between authoritative norms of moral respectability and a rapid increase in claims of individual liberty. Ethicists have responded by adapting their formal ethical systems to the analysis of the public policy dilemmas that confront analysts and decision makers.

When ethicists have been bred in the same moral culture as most Americans, it is not surprising that the systems they employ bear a remarkable resemblance to the politics of conscience and interest under discussion here. Deontological, or Kantian, ethics places special value on the rights and dignity of every person because of the individual's freedom and rationality. This school of thought grounds the special worth of the individual in his or her ability to understand principles of right and to respond to them freely, rather than to the dictates of desire. Utilitarianism, by contrast, is concerned with the social good, quantitatively considered. Its fundamental rule is that public policy should aim at maximizing the utilities of society as a whole. Like the adherents of the politics of interest, most utilitarians assume that the sole legitimate basis of social good is what individuals happen to value. And they view the process of social choice as an aggregative one, in which individual preferences are added to one another in arriving at decisions on the substance of social welfare. Utilitarians, however, have no principle for distributing social values. Their criterion of judgment is the criterion of maximum social product: efficiency.

THE POLITICS OF CONSCIENCE TODAY

The notions of liberty as grounded in obedience to moral law and of equality as referring to fundamental worth are still powerful forces in American life. The importance of morality, especially in the models of character that leaders present to the general public for their emulation, has been highlighted in reactions to scandals involving public figures. In a 1987 national telephone survey, 74 percent of the sample lamented the failure of leaders to set good examples. "Ethics, often dismissed as a prissy Sunday School word, is now at the center of a new national debate. . . . Has the mindless materialism of the '80s left in its wake a values vacuum?" asked a writer for *Time* magazine.[7] Another writer in the same issue observed that the "good idea" on which America was founded "combines a commitment to man's inalienable rights with the Calvinist belief in an ultimate moral right and sinful man's obligation to do good."[8]

The most recent manifestation of concern for absolute moral principles in American public life has been the politics of moral regeneration championed by the Christian Right. The latest battle in this war raged around the Clinton presidency, culminating in an effort to remove Clinton from office following his impeachment. Especially striking was the rhetoric of the House managers in presenting their case to the Senate. While the legal charges against the president consisted of allegations of perjury and obstruction of justice, in the background was the question of sexual misconduct extending over a period of years. Liberal opponents of impeachment claimed that even if proven, such acts were private and did not rise to the level of "high crimes and misdemeanors," nor did they constitute abuse of public authority. In contrast, in the tradition of Cotton

Mather and John Winthrop, many of the proponents of impeachment refused to make such a private-public distinction; they maintained that the criminal charges against the president justified his removal. In the end, both charges against the president failed to obtain the support of even a majority of the Senate, although the obstruction of justice charge resulted in a 50-50 tie, far short of the two-thirds needed for removal. According to polls, the Christian Right was able to mobilize only one-third of the public for removal of the president. The discrepancy between the Senate and the House in this matter may be attributable to the power of an entrenched conservative minority in control of key positions in the House. In any case, it seems fair to conclude that in this highly publicized and weighty constitutional matter, the libertarian view of individual freedom triumphed over the absolute moral principles emanating from a divided politics of conscience.

Significantly, with the failure of their efforts to remove the president through impeachment, a number of leaders of the Christian Right announced their intention to withdraw from the political defense of morality and to focus on social and cultural regeneration. Much of this effort clearly will be directed toward inculcating moral principles through the educational systems of the nation.

The Right to Equal Opportunity

A good deal of work has been done on the idea of equality as a salient concept of American political culture. In 1976, Jennifer Hochschild, a professor of political science, conducted a particularly significant study that entailed open-ended interviews with twenty-eight working adults in New Haven, Connecticut. The respondents were chosen at random from the lowest-income and highest-income neighborhoods of the city. The book that resulted from this experience is a splendid qualitative description of attitudes toward equality defined in a variety of ways. Remarkably, Hochschild found an extraordinary agreement across social and economic lines in both affirmation and rejection of the value of equality. She also found ambivalence toward equality, as well as tensions and psychological conflicts, that cut across social groups. The book was in part an update and extension of Robert Lane's pioneering study of 1962, *Political Ideology: Why the American Common Man Believes What He Does.*[9]

Hochschild found that rich and poor alike strongly supported the principle of equality in "the socializing domain—the arena of home, family, school, and neighborhood" (p. 44). In summarizing the beliefs of one respondent, she remarked that "the fact of equal human worth and the obligation it imposes on socializing agencies to seek equal well-being for all—these principles matter more than any specific normative claim" (p. 106). Here is a value squarely in the tradition of the politics of conscience. One respondent thought a community is obliged to equalize its members' chances to succeed and be happy; the needy ought to be subsidized to be sure "everybody [has] a fair shot at a happy life." The talented can take care of themselves (p. 105). All of this seems to fit under the heading of a broad agreement on social obligation to ensure equality of opportunity.

Survey research statistically bears out the results of Hochschild's qualitative study in a single urban area. These findings coexist with the fact that American life has displayed rampant racial, ethnic, and religious prejudices and discrimination over the generations. Injustices to blacks and Native Americans are blatant facts of U.S. history, along with ill treatment of newly arrived immigrants of minority ethnic origin. Ethnocentrism has been an American tradition that contradicts its cultural egalitarianism. But it appears that the civil rights movement of the 1960s and 1970s severely eroded such prejudice. Political leaders now avoid making statements that suggest racial prejudice. As early as 1978, a survey found that only 15 percent of white respondents expressed the belief that blacks are inferior to whites. Although almost 50 percent of Americans polled in the 1950s agreed that "like fine race horses, some classes of people are just naturally better than others," only 30 percent were of that opinion in the early 1980s. Most Americans, however, acknowledged that *individuals* may differ in talent and capacity.[10]

Political Equality and Community: The Idea of "the People"

Although the franchise was limited to property holders in the eighteenth century, it had become a prerogative of all white males by the Jacksonian period. It included both an equal right to vote and an equal right to hold office. The process of constitutional amendment later served to broaden the franchise to include blacks and, much later, women. In James Prothro and Charles Grigg's study of American values in the late 1950s, 95 percent of the sample affirmed that "every citizen should have an equal chance to influence government policy."[11] Data from 1958 and 1978–79 show that a substantial majority of the general public and an even larger majority of influential persons also favored equal voting rights for adult citizens, "regardless of how ignorant they may be" and "even if they can't vote intelligently."[12] The idea of equal franchise has evidently been closely tied to the idea of the equal moral worth of all human beings.

Derivative of the attribution of equal dignity to all persons is the concept of the moral and political infallibility of "the People," the concept of the egalitarian community. As far back as the 1830s, Alexis de Tocqueville wrote that "the people reign in the American political world as the Deity does in the Universe. They are the cause and the aim of all things, everything comes from them and everything is absorbed in them."[13] Not many years later, one finds Walt Whitman asserting that "the life of the common people is the life of God."[14] In the emotional attachment of Americans to the idea of "the People," there is an affective ground for the ideal of community. Though lacking in specific moral connotations, the idea of "the People" represents united virtue, and in the language of the politics of conscience, it is counterposed to the idea of "the interests," who are understood as special groups that either enjoy or seek special place and privilege without any moral claim to it. This language is found in the rhetoric of both major political parties from generation to generation. Interests are self-seeking and manipulative partial groups; "the People" are, by contrast, the moral force of the community. It is probably not too much to say that in a pluralistic and secularizing time, the idea of "the People" fills the role played by "the Church" in Puritan times; it is the community of the saints, the elect. The idea developed at the same moment that Emersonian transcendentalism supplanted Puritan theology as the major language of the American politics of conscience. Just as liberty and the moral commands of the holy community are in perfect harmony in the thought of John Winthrop, so are they fused and harmonized in the thought of Walt Whitman. As Vernon Parrington has paraphrased Whitman's idea, "Not in distinction but in oneness with the whole we find the good life, for in fellowship is love and in the whole is freedom; and love and freedom are the law and the prophets."[15]

THE POLITICS OF INTEREST

In the American politics of interest, equality does not support liberty. The two are squarely pitted against one another. In the end, individual liberty triumphs; it reins in and severely limits the egalitarian tendencies of the culture.

Property and the Work Ethic

One of Hochschild's young but needy respondents, who earned only $6,000 a year in 1976, echoed the Harrington themes of hard work and acquisition. She thought that people could very well make money if they made up their minds not to be lazy. She saw herself as an ambitious achiever, despite her poverty (p. 29). She also expressed Adam Smith's concept of the "unseen Hand" that converts interest into social utility (p. 30).

Respondents at the other end of Hochschild's economic spectrum also celebrated the virtues of free enterprise. A forty-eight-year-old businessman told her how hard work and luck had brought him from a childhood of poverty to the position of a businessman. He was owner of a business that allowed him the luxuries of suburban life and enabled him to support two children in graduate school (pp. 30–31). He thought welfare payments were bad for the poor, morally corrupting. Welfare taught them to be content with living on a dole rather than to embrace the work ethic (p. 31).

One of Hochschild's needy respondents described the operation of the system of free enterprise as something resembling a Hobbesian war of all against all. "There's always going to be conflict, jealousy. . . . Everybody's out to beat everybody, and it's just human nature to try to get away with everything you can. . . . People are fighting each other—it's a good thing. The more he fights, the more rewards he gets" (p. 38). Like Hobbes's, the conflictual framework of this respondent resembled one of natural physical necessity rather than an institutionalized system of economic order governed by principles of justice.

In the conception of economic freedom under consideration, liberty and equality come together at only one point—in the equal right of all to compete for material well-being. It is significant that in Jefferson's first draft of the Declaration of Independence, the word "property" appeared in place of "the pursuit of happiness." The famous triad of natural rights announced by the Declaration enshrines an equal right of all Americans to personal freedom and security and to compete in the marketplace. That these are introduced in this document as God-given inalienable rights appears to place them in the context of the politics of conscience rather than in the realm of interest politics. But the justification of individual rights with both these languages is characteristic of American political culture. It has also been argued that the religious categories employed by writers like John Locke and his American successors were adopted by the rising middle-class intelligentsia as a useful way to legitimate for all an economic and political system that this new class found personally profitable.[16] Whatever the semantics of the matter, it should be stressed that liberty as free enterprise runs contrary to the norm of equality. It produces social stratification and an elite structure in society.

The overriding importance of liberty as freedom to acquire property is found throughout American history. Despite his political egalitarianism, Jefferson was a free enterpriser, as were his Federalist opponents. Men like James Madison, who helped develop a complicated constitutional system of separated, divided, and balanced authorities, thought that the "first object of government" was to protect "different and unequal faculties of acquiring property." "All men must be free to seek their immediate profit and to associate with others in the process," declared Madison.[17]

And so things have remained, through the creation of the Horatio Alger success myth in the last part of the nineteenth century down to the present. "There is probably no people on earth," wrote a nineteenth-century immigrant to the United States, "with whom business constitutes pleasure, and industry amusement, in an equal degree with the inhabitants of the United States of America."[18]

Survey research has borne out the continued authority of the profit motive for Americans. In a 1979 study, 91 percent of the respondents disagreed with this statement: "The government should limit the amount of money any individual is allowed to earn in a year." And 73 percent supported this proposition: "The profits a company or business can earn should be as large as they can fairly earn." In a 1975–77 study, 54 percent of the public agreed that the profit system teaches the value of hard work and the importance of the drive to succeed, while only 16 percent thought instead that it brings out the worst qualities in people.[19]

The Rejection of Economic Equality

In view of these opinions, it is not surprising that when "equality" is translated from the realm of moral estimate and social compassion to the domain of economic activity, the American public should denigrate it. In his pioneering study of 1962, Robert Lane found that the blue-collar workers he interviewed had a positive fear of economic equality. The existence of a superintending economic elite gave them a sense of security. Lane's respondents did not sympathize with people lower than them on the economic scale. Nor did they wish themselves to be raised, by government policy, to a level they had not achieved by personal effort. Were a demand for leveling to capture the public mind, they thought it would destroy individual incentive. (They had internalized the work ethic very well.) Lane's subjects had also given up hedonic desires in order to achieve something like middle-class respectability.[20]

Fourteen years later, in her 1976 update and revision of Lane's study, Hochschild found that the same kinds of attitudes still existed. One of her needy respondents remarked that the rich must have worked hard for their money and that they deserved it (p. 112). Here, inequality is legitimated by attribution of the work ethic to the successful. Another subject spoke disparagingly of the welfare state for leveling society. This person viewed the system as a "gigantic rip-off" by the lazy. Welfare recipients whose stories he recounted "just want to keep their booze, car, and that's it." The "deserving poor" did not come into his ken (p. 116). In summary, this research indicated that the people who supported equality in what Hochschild called "the socializing domain" supported economic inequality (p. 118). In specific cases, they usually sought a ground for legitimating differentiation. In viewing the system as a whole, however, they tended to accept it as though it were a fact of nature (pp. 122, 125).

Survey research conducted both before and after Lane's and Hochschild's reports of their interviews in a specific New England locale showed that outright rejection of economic equality by rich and poor alike held true for the nation as a whole. In 1937 and 1939, in the midst of the Great Depression, only 30 to 35 percent of respondents to national *Fortune* polls supported redistribution of wealth from rich to poor by taxation. Even more than 46 percent of those in the lowest quarter of the income scale did not favor such a measure. Of the unemployed, a bare majority of 54 percent were ready to seek redistribution in 1939, while only 44 percent supported such a view in 1937. When in March 1939 the poll used the word *confiscation* to describe the measure and pitted the individual's freedom to earn against the requirements of the "public good," support for the measure was only half of that registered in the less radically worded poll.

This was true for the national average and for the poor and unemployed categories as well.[21]

Polls carried out in 1974 and 1976 yielded results similar to those of forty years earlier. In the 1976 poll, 51 percent of blue-collar workers were in favor of the proposition that "the government should tax the rich heavily in order to redistribute the wealth." Interestingly, however, only 47 percent of the unemployed held this view, which was also the percentage of the nation as a whole in favor of this position.[22]

EQUALITY AND PUBLIC POLICY

Despite the rejection of absolute equality of condition by a majority of all social groups, there is no question that the American egalitarian tradition has greatly influenced public policy over the generations. The national faith in the equal worth of all human beings has passed over into public measures designed not to produce economic leveling but to ensure broadly defined equality of opportunity for all persons. From the passage of the Thirteenth, Fourteenth, and Fifteenth Amendments to the Constitution down to the civil rights legislation of the 1960s, blacks gradually achieved a large measure of legal, political, and social equality with whites. Here, the meaning of "equality" has been interchangeable with the concept of "freedom." Equality of opportunity has meant equal freedom.

Lyndon Johnson's War on Poverty, despite its many administrative failures, gave large numbers of blacks, as well as poor whites, greater equality of economic opportunity than they had ever before enjoyed, and it brought millions of blacks and poor whites into the ranks of the middle class. Over roughly the same period, women achieved greater equality with men. Large-scale welfare programs like those of the War on Poverty were not intended by their authors to create a permanently dependent class in American society, like that feared by Lane's and Hochschild's respondents. They were aimed instead at making all Americans self-reliant, independent persons. As Lyndon Johnson himself described his objective, "The War on Poverty is not a struggle simply to support people, to make them dependent on the generosity of others. . . . It is a struggle to give (them) a chance."[23] So, as one moves from the private world of individual economic endeavor to the world of public economic and social policy, the American view of equality changes once again.

A Positive Role for Government

Despite their fear of economic equality, the subjects of Lane's 1962 study, unlike nineteenth-century exponents of free enterprise or today's libertarian or economic conservative, did not view government with suspicion. They saw "big government" as working for them. Hochschild's study of 1976 revealed a similar attitude overall, despite some fears of the corrupting effect of welfare programs. One needy respondent, reflecting on the role of government in society, saw government as the protector of private property, but she also wanted the government to prevent property from inflicting great harm on the poor. Like Lane's subjects, she was aware of the reality of private power as a repressive force, and she viewed government as a democratic countervailing power. Fair prices and salient community needs dominated private rights and community needs for her. She did not expect all of this to emerge from the unseen hand of the market. Rather, she saw a more progressive tax structure as an important device for establishing this balance. With more tax revenue from the rich, the government could "eliminate college tuition, increase social security payments, guarantee job training and jobs with a livable income, and provide national health insurance" (p. 149). When directly confronted with the question of equalizing property, this subject backed off from equality. Yet in considering public policy, she favored redistribution. To bring these divergent lines of thought together, she espoused the concept of a guaranteed minimum income but rejected the idea of putting a ceiling on incomes (p. 151).

Another of Hochschild's needy respondents expressed pessimism about the ability of government to effect redistribution. He saw taxes as high because of graft by politicians. His mind was filled with traditional American stereotypes of government officials as conniving rascals who cannot be trusted, an attitude that served to reinforce his acceptance of economic stratification and to blunt hope for greater equality. He preferred no taxation at all to progressive taxation by a government he could not trust (pp. 152–53). But others among Hochschild's respondents expressed greater optimism about government. The extent of existing equality pleased them, and they were hopeful the egalitarian trend under government auspices would continue (p. 156). Their faith in public redistributive measures was expressed, however, with the qualification that it should extend only to equality of opportunity, not equality of result (p. 158).

Tension between the Politics of Conscience and the Politics of Interest

In measuring the views of her well-to-do subjects on egalitarian policies, Hochschild found tension between principles attached to what we call the politics of conscience and the politics of interest, both of which the subjects had internalized. But, on margin, she found greater support among the rich for more equality than was dictated by their own material self-interest (p. 165). One of the wealthy subjects was in favor of guaranteed jobs and public programs of job training. She thought that Social Security should have a redistributive effect, and she favored tuition subsidies for college students and loans to medical students. In the latter instance, she saw such equalization of opportunity for some as beneficial to the whole society in the long run (p. 166). She also supported national health insurance. But in evaluating the idea of a minimum income, she wondered whether it would be fair to those who had succeeded on their own (p. 167). Another well-to-do subject resolved the tension between freedom and equality by viewing private property as an instrument for achieving freedom, though not as an end in itself. And he was ready to entertain the idea of more egalitarian policies to achieve that goal. Overall, the respondent was "less protective of differentiating property rights than many of the poor, and his egalitarianism sometimes dominated his economic self-interest."[24]

In the late 1980s and early 1990s, tensions between the egalitarian politics of conscience and the libertarian politics of interest increased markedly within the American middle and working classes. In changed electoral behavior, in the resulting activity of the Republican-led 104th Congress, and in the decisions of the U.S. Supreme Court, the tension seems to have been resolved in favor of individualism and self-interest. As early as 1986, James Kluegel and Eliot Smith wrote that "compared to 1969, the public is ever more likely to agree that we are spending too much money on welfare and to deny that people on welfare try to find work to support themselves."[25] Nevertheless, sympathy for those on welfare remained consistently high. By 1995, that sympathy seemed to have disappeared. Democrats and Republicans continued to vie with one another to present bills that extensively cut federal taxes and that radically overhauled the redistributive welfare system. Republicans also attempted to devolve large new welfare responsibilities onto state governments through the device of block grants. In *Adarand Contractors v. Pena* (1995),[26] the Supreme Court, in holding that the Constitution "protects persons, not groups," adopted an individualist principle that could overturn federal programs that give special preference to minorities in the name of greater racial equality in the workplace. In another decision, the Court held unconstitutional the creation of a Georgia congressional district with a black majority, calling it a racial gerrymander. It had been artificially carved out of a mixed community to ensure the election of a black member of Congress.

Governmental direction has also been giving way to individual freedom in another area. As part of their "Contract with America," Republicans attempted to give businesses relief from the high costs of health, safety, and environmental regulation. Democrats, by contrast, have maintained the sovereignty of public goods. They have insisted, however, that proposed rules be cost-effective. Free up individual enterprise and shrink the size and cost of government!—these are the watchwords of the day.

Beginning in the 1930s, the egalitarian politics of conscience was successively embodied in the programs of the New Deal, the Square Deal, the Fair Deal, and the New Frontier. From these programs emerged a centralized welfare state dedicated to establishing job security for the working person, financial relief for the unemployed, financial and medical security for the aged and

dependent, the equalization of civil and social rights, a guarantee of equal educational opportunity, and safeguarding of the environment. Up to the 1960s,
working- and middle-class white voters found their interests congruent with
those of black citizens in supporting the downward redistributive policies of this
liberal welfare state. But after 1964, issues of race and taxes gradually eroded the
coalition. As Thomas and Mary Edsall summarized this trend, "The costs and
burdens of Democratic-endorsed policies seeking to distribute economic and
citizenship rights more equitably to blacks and to other minorities fell primarily
on working and lower-middle class whites who frequently competed with blacks
for jobs and status, who lived in neighborhoods adjoining black ghettos, and
whose children attended schools most likely to fall under bussing orders."[27]

In this way, the reform plans of Lyndon Johnson's Great Society led eventually to the conservative presidencies of Richard Nixon, Ronald Reagan, and
George Bush, and more recently to the overturn of the long-lived Democratic
majority in Congress. This remarkable turnabout in public attitudes was not
engendered by a simple callousness in the hearts of middle-class Americans
about the plight of the poor and underprivileged. Survey data show that a very
large majority of white Americans remain favorable to the principle of equality
in racial policy.[28] Nor can it be said that the public have suddenly become conservative after having subscribed for fifty years to liberal ideals. These labels are
properly applied only to the elites that vie with one another for public attention.
In a 1980 poll conducted by the Center for Political Studies, nearly 40 percent
of the sample could not even give a definition of the terms *liberal* and *conservative.*[29] These data tend to support the view of E.J. Dionne Jr. that "America's
cultural values are a rich and not necessarily contradictory mix of liberal instincts and conservative values."[30]

The new negative view of egalitarian welfare policies was engendered by
three developments: the threat to self-interest noted above, a changed life situation for an increasing number of Americans, and the failure of many Great
Society programs to accomplish the ends for which they were intended.

The threat to low- and lower-middle-income whites living in large urban
areas has been not only financial (the tax burden of the welfare state) but also
physical. Living adjacent to ghetto areas, they have experienced steadily rising
crime rates and an increase in street violence associated with increased drug
use, activities that have accompanied the breakdown of the family structure
among minority groups. Great Society policies came to connote for them a permissive attitude toward drug abuse and higher incidences of illegitimacy, welfare
fraud, and crime in the streets.[31] At the same time, an increasing number of
Americans were experiencing changes in life situation and lifestyle that brought
with them changes in political attitudes. Dionne wrote that "new jobs in the
service industries promote individualism. The decline of the small town and old
urban ethnic enclaves and the rise of new suburbs, exurbs, and condominium

developments further weaken social solidarity. . . . In the new politics, each voter is studied and appealed to as an individual."[32]

Last, the promise of the Great Society embodied in the welfare legislation passed during the years of the Johnson administration was not fulfilled. Some programs, such as Head Start, may indeed have made a positive difference for minority educational achievement. But relief payments to unwed mothers, if they were not a primary cause of an increased incidence of illegitimacy, at least aggravated this social problem. Young girls who simply had a desire for motherhood were able to fulfill their wish with public support. Also, the vast majority of poor families headed by married couples were ineligible to receive support from the Aid to Families with Dependent Children (AFDC) program, and this was a factor in family breakups. For a time, wages for unskilled labor were so low that heads of families (and single people as well) found that they could do better on welfare than by employment in low-paying jobs. Lacking benefit packages in such jobs, they also had no substitute for Medicaid to cover health-care costs, and so they returned to the welfare rolls. In short, America had a permanent underclass of demoralized people who subsisted with public help and could find no way out of their situation. In this context, the family structure of ghetto minorities came apart. Spouseless women head more than 90 percent of welfare families today. Drug use is rampant in the inner cities, and street violence, characterized by an increasing number of gang conflicts and random shootings, is escalating.

Democrats and Republicans, liberals and conservatives, are today agreed on the nature of the unhappy situation in the inner city. What they disagree on is how it can be remedied. In the 1994 congressional elections, the majority of politically conscious Americans evidently decided to give Republicans an opportunity to enact their conception of change, although their programs, as always, would be subject to the institutional and political complications inherent in the policy process.

CLEAVAGE WITHIN THE POLITICS OF CONSCIENCE

We have described the increasing emphasis in American political culture on individualist values and the growth of antitax and antigovernment sentiment in terms of a tension between the politics of conscience (understood as an egalitarian public good) and the politics of interest, with the latter's taking on a new preeminence. We can also understand this change as the result of a cleavage within the politics of conscience. We noted elsewhere in this chapter that the earliest manifestation of our politics of conscience was in colonial Puritanism, which identified the common good (or public interest) with fulfilling God's law. All persons are equal as children of God; they are also equally obligated to obey His moral code. They are free, but free only to do that which is fitting, noble, and good. Preeminent in the catalog of good and noble acts are hard work, living a pure life sexually, dealing fairly with one's fellows, and being model husbands, wives, and children—what we today call "family values." Only later did the politics of conscience come to emphasize political, social, and economic equality as the essence of the common good. To have the view that slavery is contrary to God's law embodied politically in the Thirteenth and Fourteenth Amendments required a civil war. Later came civil rights acts and the welfare state of the Great Society to give reality to the ideal of human equality in the social and economic realms.

Both concepts remain central to our moral culture today. Dionne has described their relationship in the public's mind:

> Polls (and our own intuitions) suggest that Americans believe in helping those who fall on hard times, in fostering equal opportunity and equal rights, in providing broad access to education, housing, health care, and child care. Polls (and our own intuitions) also suggest that Americans believe that intact families do the best job at bringing up children, that hard work should be rewarded, that people who behave destructively toward others should be punished, that small institutions close to home tend to do better than big institutions run from far away, that private moral choices usually have social consequences. Put another way, Americans believe in social concern and self-reliance; they want to match rights and obligations; they think public moral standards should exist but are skeptical of too much meddling in the private affairs of others.[33]

But despite this continued dual centrality, the two ideals do not readily dovetail. They seem to be in fundamental conflict. During the heyday of the welfare state, the liberalism that embodied the egalitarian conscience came, under the influence of Republican rhetoric, to mean to the electorate favoring blacks over whites, a permissive attitude toward drug abuse, increased illegitimacy, welfare fraud, crime in the streets, homosexuality, anti-Americanism, and moral anarchy among the youth.[34] Liberal programs could not develop the work ethic, and the bureaucracies administering these programs were seen as desiring to keep the poor in place, in order to serve their own interest.[35]

Cultural war has broken out between liberals who are critical of the free market in economic life, because it promotes inequality, yet are ready to celebrate laissez-faire in cultural and sexual life, and conservatives who want constraints and controls in the areas of culture and sex but advocate an entirely unconstrained market.[36] Conceived as a surrogate for the dissolving moral ties of civil society, the welfare state as now viewed by conservatives corrodes the social ties that form the foundation of good government.[37] To sort out the problem properly, one writing team has called for a forum "for a tough-minded exploration of issues of individual conduct, family structure, patterns of socialization, and other so-called moral/cultural matters."[38] In the meantime, representatives of the two visions of what conscientious politics demands do rhetorical battle with one another before a bewildered public that agrees with the basic principles of both visions.

CONCLUSION

In the past, Americans have sometimes been able to resolve tensions between conflicting values through the device of pragmatic compromise. One writer has contended that "in philosophy, Americans accepted the ambiguities and contradictions of the Lockeian tradition. The primacy of sensation and the centrality of the moral sense could flourish at once, as long as each of these theories . . . did not push too far."[39] It is a habit Americans have displayed since the earliest days. The Constitution of 1787 is a prime example of its prevalence. It represents a grand compromise, or rather a whole series of them, designed not theoretically but in a practical way to reconcile energy at the center of the political system with liberty in its parts. John Mercer, commenting in 1830 on *The Federalist,* which aimed at justifying this instrument of government to a diverse people, noted that this work "addresses different arguments to different classes of the American public, in the spirit of an able and skillful disputant before a mixed assembly. Thus from different numbers of this work, and sometimes from the same number, may be derived authorities for opposite principles and opinions."[40] On the other hand, some results are not so happy. Political paralysis in the face of urgent issues is perhaps the most dangerous. Evidence that this is so is presented in other parts of this book.

CHAPTER 4

Ethics and Public Policy Analysis

IS THERE A WAY to bring the competing values that constitute American moral culture systematically to bear on policy choices? In addition to being objective technician, client advocate, and issue advocate, can the policy analyst function also as ethicist?

Over the past few decades, ethicists—persons formally trained in the discipline of moral philosophy—have appeared in many areas of American public life. They consult with hospital house staffs and with public decision makers and study commissions, and they draft codes of ethics for legislators, administrators, and business firms. They also teach courses in medical ethics, business ethics, legal ethics, and, most recently, public policy ethics in university graduate programs. The cult of the expert in modern life, combined with the optimism of American culture, sometimes leads us to think of the ethicist as a moral problem solver who can deal with questions of good and evil, right and wrong in the way that a technician might get a malfunctioning computer or copying machine running efficiently. Properly, however, an ethicist is a clarifier of issues in moral choice and a stimulator of precise and systematic thinking about how one ought to behave in a difficult choice situation. The prospective policy analyst or administrator who takes a course in public policy ethics can hope to be trained to perceive moral issues, conscientiously to grasp and appreciate the range of values that are at stake in a policy choice, and to employ a rational method of ethical decision making rather than relying on hunch and intuition. Learning these things does not make a citizen, policy analyst, administrator, or legislator into a professional ethicist. Instead, it helps one to function at work as an ethically sensitive and morally informed person.

DEONTOLOGY AND UTILITARIANISM

It is interesting to observe that two schools of moral philosophy currently popular among ethicists correspond to the two leading value traditions in American culture that we described in the last chapter. Deontological ethics, also called

Kantian ethics, displays in its key assumptions the values of the politics of conscience, while utilitarianism embodies the principles of the politics of interest.

Kantians place special emphasis on the equal rights of all persons, because of every person's moral freedom and rationality. The special worth of every individual is grounded in his or her ability to grasp principles of right and to respond to the idea that right ought to be done, rather than that the demands of passion or desire be served. The Kantian proposes as a paramount moral rule the "categorical imperative"—that one should act only on maxims that can be universalized as principles of law without producing a situation that would frustrate the end at which they aim. Thus, to borrow money with the mental reservation not to repay it would be self-frustrating, since no money would be lent if the maxim were published as a universal rule. It is therefore morally wrong to borrow money with no intention of repaying it.

In its second formulation especially, the categorical imperative displays its affinity to the politics of conscience. Kant stated the principle as a practical imperative: "Act in such a way that you treat humanity, whether in your own person or in the person of another, always at the same time as an end and never simply as a means."[1] One can readily see that a rule of this sort fits perfectly with an egalitarian social policy program. All human beings, because of their dignity as free and rational agents, have equal rights to participate in the political process (which ideally legislates self-consistent general laws), to exercise a wide sphere of freedom in speech and action, to receive equal treatment before the law, to have equal educational and economic opportunity, and so on.

Utilitarians, by contrast, base their ethics on individual self-interest, understood as the maximization of individual preferences. Preferences, of course, must be aggregated to produce public policy. And the utilitarian rule of aggregation requires that the greatest possible sum of benefits to society as a whole be the criterion of judgment. Thus, social efficiency—the idea that as much value as possible be extracted from scarce resources—emerges as a chief value. There is a running debate within the utilitarian school, however, about how to convert purely individual preferences into social preferences, since individuals remain the judge of what is good for them personally (which is the same as the good as such). At issue are such questions as how interpersonal comparisons of utility can be made, if at all, and how to proceed when intransitivities in social choice appear. ("Intransitivity" is the situation that arises when, in a pairwise choice involving three alternatives, A is preferred by a majority to B and B to C, but C is preferred to A. Such a result contains an irrational group choice.) These difficulties can to a considerable degree be circumvented by assuming, as many utilitarians do, that the free market, in which every individual seeks only his or her own self-interest, is the most efficient aggregator of preferences in producing the largest quantity of utility. Utilitarianism thus walks hand-in-hand with the growing authority of individualism in the popular culture. In some versions, utilitarianism is democratic; what the majority wants is assumed to produce the greatest quantity of good. But this is not an egalitarian doctrine; it is simply another efficiency measure.

CASUISTRY

A third school of ethics has been developing increasing authority among ethicists, partially because of their frustration with the one-sidedness of deontology and of utilitarianism. Although both deontologists and utilitarians aim to serve the welfare of individuals, the first school is preeminently egalitarian in thrust, while the second gives special emphasis to efficiency. Moreover, neither school is able to reconcile conflicting values. Casuistry, an ethical system grounded in the principles of Aristotelian ethics, is equipped to mediate systematically between competing sets of values (e.g., liberty and equality) and to effect trade-offs between them.[2] In the academy, casuistry functions analogously to the pragmatism of the popular culture. Like pragmatism, casuistry eschews abstract judgment and rejects deduction from universal principles to "practical imperatives [regarded] as applying invariably and without exception."[3] Casuistry stresses the importance of giving primary weight in moral judgment to the special circumstances of a situation involving moral choice. These circumstances indicate the appropriate value or combination of values to be served. Approaching moral choice in this way, we realize that "rules and principles can never take us more than part of the way." Required instead is "human perceptiveness and discernment . . . 'equity.'"[4] This concern produces a case method of moral judgment, similar in its procedures to the method of common law.

The casuist works with socially agreed-upon values and organizes them within a taxonomy of moral (and immoral) actions. This requires that actions be described in such a way as to show the relationship between a specific kind of action and a general moral principle. It is, for example, agreed that "unjust killing" is a bad action. But what are examples of just and unjust killing? In international law, which expresses important aspects of the universal moral consensus, it is an accepted principle that killing an armed combatant in a civil war, where moral and legal agreement have broken down, is a morally acceptable (though deplorable) action. International law also holds that genocide—the ruthless massacre of unarmed populations to achieve the extinction of a particular ethnic group—is a wanton moral evil. These principles furnish paradigms of morally acceptable and unacceptable actions. Now, when confronted with a particular act of killing in a specific context, the casuist will approve or disapprove it by giving it a name that carries moral judgment. Thus, in judging the killing of Kosovar Muslims by Serbs, the casuist must ask, "Is this a case of civil war, or is it rather genocide that we are witnessing?" When the ethicist has collected as complete a body of relevant data as possible, he or she must give a moral name to what has been found and act accordingly. The underlying assumption of the procedure is that the complete description of an action or set of actions carries with it a moral judgment. In making that judgment, one marries the particulars of circumstance to a universal moral name, a marriage that constitutes a complete moral notion.[5] Moral principles and maxims considered abstractly do not yield moral judgments. For the casuist, they produce such judgments only when they are prudently combined with as comprehensive a canvassing as possible of the particulars of an action.

Sometimes, the casuist may even feel called on to make up a name for an action—for instance, when it constitutes a new paradigm case in a taxonomy of actions. Julius Kovesi suggested that one might call an untruth told to protect a hidden Jew from discovery by the Nazi Gestapo a "saving deceit" rather than a lie.[6] (The word *lie* is a moral name that signifies evil.) The central principle in all this is that the casuist always works from a careful assessment of particulars up to general principles in moral analysis, never deductively from principles to particulars.

In their book on casuistry, Albert R. Jonsen and Stephen Toulmin illustrated casuist ethics with a number of cases involving the dilemmas physicians face in interpreting and applying public policies.[7] Physicians often must decide whether to follow the maxim "act to preserve life" or the maxim "mercifully refrain." The first maxim is associated with the paramount value of human life; the second attaches to the value of preventing suffering, also a primary medical goal. A paradigm case of preserving life—one in which the first value is manifestly overriding, without complicating circumstances—occurs when an otherwise strong and healthy person's life is threatened by something the physician can readily remedy without inflicting unusual or long-drawn-out pain, as when appendicitis is treated by performing an appendectomy. An uncomplicated paradigm case of "mercifully refraining" from prolonging life might be one in which a ninety-year-old person who is suffering from a painful cancer and whose lungs are collapsing can be kept alive for a brief time only by a system of artificial respiration. In the case of a defective newborn, however, the physician's decision is complicated by the fact that the patient is at the beginning of a life that under some circumstances may be relatively long, happy, and productive but under others will be of doubtful length, very poor quality, and attended by constant pain and suffering. In such a difficult case, the physician must weigh and balance the competing values of life and avoidance of suffering by a most careful assessment of the modes of treatment available and of surrounding facts that permit prediction of what kind of future is most probable for the child.

Jonsen and Toulmin pointed out that in the case of a defective newborn, the physician's problem is compounded because "Congress has passed legislation that sets the problem of withholding care from the newborn under the general heading of child abuse and neglect."[8] In other words, by placing the act under the paradigm of abusive treatment, the law biases the issue by implying that withholding care from a defective neonate is ipso facto bad. It seems therefore to exclude the possibility of giving consideration to the suffering that goes with severe birth defects. This points to the need for training legislators, as well as the policy analysts who assist them, in framing legislation so that it encompasses all the values at stake in a policy choice—the need for the comprehensive consideration of issues in casuist fashion.

We can also use the case of the defective newborn to illustrate the conflict between utilitarianism and deontology and the manner in which casuistry can bring their values together. A majoritarian utilitarian would give weight to the vast social resources used in sustaining the life of a defective infant; in essence, the utilitarian would attempt to attach a dollar value to that life. The deontologist would make a judgment by giving attention only to the welfare of the child but might be at a loss as to how to assess the value of painful life. (From his examples in the *Groundwork for the Metaphysics of Morals,* it appears Kant himself discounted pain in favor of life.) The casuist would give moral weight to cost, to the value of human life, and to the value of diminishing suffering and would focus on assessing and manipulating the circumstances in such a way as to optimize all three values.

A casuist approach to ethical questions can also help reveal the ideological content of what appear to be value-free analytical procedures but that on examination contain either welfare-liberal or libertarian-conservative biases. The "scientific" systems analysis of Great Society programs—called "classical policy analysis"—emphasized "social problem solving, the creative design of public programs, social criticism, and incremental reform, an activist state and public administration [echoing] the basic tenets of American Progressivism culminating in the New Deal and the Great Society."[9] The norms of "classical" analysis were egalitarian and autonomist and therefore clearly associated with the "politics of conscience." This analytical technique gave way during the years of the Reagan and Bush administrations to a new canon, one that was individualist and efficiency oriented. It was characterized by "an emphasis on economizing rationality, incentive structures, the virtues of marketlike arrangements and Lockean conceptions of individual rights more attuned to the resurgent classic liberalism of the 1970s and 1980s."[10] The practitioner of the new method was critical of centralized government and large-scale public programs, such as nationalized health care or extensive aid to education. This kind of analyst was grounded in a school of economics that emphasizes "doctrines of rational individual choice, the logic of efficiency in unencumbered markets, and formal utilitarian calculation."[11]

It was possible for two such different analytical systems, which embody such different value systems, to develop in the United States because of the heterodoxy of liberal culture. "It is possible," wrote Charles Anderson, "to order the guiding values of liberalism in a variety of ways, and the meaning of such fundamental concepts as right, freedom, equality, public interest and the like seems always to be contestable."[12] The ethically self-conscious policy analyst or administrator, adopting a casuist stance, will recognize that the values embodied in both analytical systems are authoritative American values, though frequently contradictory in their demands, and need to be reconciled with one another. The ethical stance of casuistry thus enables the analyst who adopts it to inject a needed note of pragmatism into overly rigid ideological policy debate.

SOME CASES

In this section, we review some cases typical of those that come before decision makers and policy analysts in the course of their daily work. We look at what results from applying the ethical approaches we have considered to the moral issues involved.

The Case of AID and the Single Welfare Mother

A case in the area of welfare policy that revolves around issues of distributive justice was published in the February 1983 issue of the *Hastings Center Report*.[13] It involved a single woman, Ms. S., who requested and obtained artificial insemination by donor (AID) from a private obstetrician, Dr. F. The physician examined her for medical and psychological suitability and obtained letters attesting to her emotional stability and responsibility (in the narrow sense). This was in keeping with the traditional individualist concept of the patient-doctor relationship, in which the physician's moral responsibility is first and foremost to his patient on a fee-for-service basis.

A part-time worker, Ms. S. received $161 in monthly pregnancy welfare assistance. After her child's birth, she filed for and obtained $401 monthly from the AFDC program (replaced in 1996 by the more stringent welfare program known as Temporary Assistance for Needy Families, or TANF). According to the report of the case, Ms. S. knew about and planned to obtain welfare benefits before contacting the obstetrician. Indignant members of the community in which she lived thought she should not have been artificially inseminated while harboring the intent to obtain public support for herself and her baby. Some even claimed that Dr. F. should pay the pregnancy costs. Dr. F. himself was concerned that he had contributed to the abuse of the welfare system. Intuitively, these people sensed that something was wrong. Yet there were no legal restrictions on what the obstetrician had done. Were there clear norms in the culture that might have guided this decision? At issue was the conflict between a woman's right to bear children and society's right to be free of the financial burden implicit in her claim.

When students discussed this case in a seminar at the University of Rochester, they quickly agreed that the obstetrician had no moral responsibility to question Ms. S. about her financial status. His role was seen as restricted to medical questions. Did society have such a responsibility, which should have been written into the law?

How would the casuist answer this question? First, one would have to decide whether a paradigm case that fit the circumstances was available. Was this case analogous to an adoption? If so, it is clear that a demonstration of financial responsibility ought to be required of the prospective parent. But it is also clear that such a requirement rests on a traditional concept of morality. Also, one could question the analogy. Adoption is obviously a privilege, since the prospective parent seeks custody of a child not his or her own, for whom a social agency is acting as guardian. But in the case of AID, the child involved is the claimant's own flesh and blood. Also, the situation is quite new, unlike the petition for adoption. Should it be governed by traditional norms of personal responsibility or by the financial need of the mother?

Reasoning by a different analogy, in the absence of a norm clearly applicable to the case, the class concluded that if an unmarried woman is free to become pregnant through casual liaisons, she is free to become pregnant by the use of a scientific process. If society through its scientific expertise provided Ms. S. with the device by which she became pregnant, society through the AFDC law gave unmarried people the opportunity to cohabit without accepting responsibilities that might follow from cohabitation. No law forbids this, and it appears to be more and more acceptable as traditional taboos on unmarried sex decline and the value of individual freedom takes on new authoritative meanings. While unmarried sex is still frowned on as immoral in some sectors of society, would the act of artificial insemination be as much condemned, since it carries no sexual pleasure with it? Surely, motherhood and childbearing are socially valued things. If these analogies hold, then one would have to ask why the unmarried mother who conceived her child through casual liaisons should morally be entitled to AFDC payments while the unmarried mother who conceived via artificial insemination is not. Intentional acts may be involved in both cases. If they are not, is carelessness about the possibility of impregnation (which implies irresponsibility) better than intentionality?

Some students in the seminar, admitting that they could not distinguish between the two kinds of cases, concluded that AFDC payments should be denied to all unmarried women. The welfare law needed to be changed. In the absence of a clear social norm condemning pregnancy out of wedlock, the warrant for this judgment would be a utilitarian decision that the general pain caused by tax expenditures for the support of illegitimate children and their mothers was greater than the pleasure of mothering and living experienced by the women and children who receive public help. The libertarian attachment to norms of individual responsibility of students who held this view reinforced their position. Interestingly, the 1996 welfare law does place more stress on these values, as its title, "The Personal Responsibility and Work Opportunity Reconciliation Act," indicates.

Coming back to a casuist frame of reference, the class then asked whether other values were involved in the case—now broadened to the question of whether there should be any AFDC payments to unwed mothers. Could this be decided on the basis of a simple utilitarian calculus about comparative pleasures and pains? Kantian values were then addressed for comparison with those flowing from the standard of social utility: social efficiency. At this point, the values of the "politics of conscience" and those of the "politics of interest" were weighed and balanced directly against one another. Within a Kantian frame of reference, one would have to assess the rights of the mothers and children involved to a decent minimum support under the general rubric of individual autonomy and social compassion. In particular, the welfare of children, who would probably be born out of wedlock even in the absence of a public subsidy, had to be considered. Reasoning from this basis, it would appear that society would not have a clear moral warrant to deny single mothers public support. Yet there remained among the students who took this position a sense that somehow society was being put upon, taken advantage of by the individual involved. Just what can individuals asserting the right to autonomous decision about the conduct of their lives claim of society?

But there are other relevant considerations. It is clear that the original Kantian idea of individual autonomy and its correlative social obligation of compassionate support rested on the assumption that the claimant of the right to autonomy was herself a morally responsible person. And the test of moral responsibility was willingness to engage only in actions that could be universalized without producing contradictions (the categorical imperative). But there is a question in this case whether the behavior of the AID recipient could be universalized. Universalized, the rule would have to take the form of a proposition that anyone wishing to enjoy a private value at public expense would have a right to claim public support. If everyone acted on this rule, the public treasury would be bankrupted. The AFDC law would therefore have to contain a provision to exclude from its coverage women who do not behave in a socially responsible way in the use of their reproductive capacities. This would have the effect of excluding from public support not only AID recipients but all unwed mothers as well.

It is the case, however, that contemporary definitions of autonomy do not include the Kantian notion of moral responsibility. One criterion of autonomy in the language of today's bioethics is "competency." Tom Beauchamp and James Childress have argued that it is commonly thought that

> a person is competent if and only if that person can make decisions
> based on rational reasons. In biomedical contexts this standard entails

that a person must be able to understand a therapy or research procedure, must be able to weigh its risks and benefits, and must be able
to make a decision in the light of such knowledge and through such
abilities.[14]

Nothing is said about the individual's willingness to submit his or her maxim to
the test of universalizability. (In a later section of their book, Beauchamp and
Childress wrote of "autonomous suicide" and its criteria. That would be moral
nonsense to Kant, who argued in his *Groundwork for the Metaphysics of Morals* that suicide cannot be universalized.) Viewed this way, the problem takes the
form of a conflict between a traditional concept of morality and a modern
understanding of individual freedom. In the recent literature of ethics and public policy, one frequently finds arguments calling for the restoration of such traditional concepts in the name of the common good.

When faced with a conflict between primary social values, such as freedom
of lifestyle or compassion for helpless children, on the one hand, and the utilitarian need to economize public resources, on the other, the casuist's choice is
dilemmatic. The casuist ethicist might feel compelled to engage in imaginative
policy experiments to reconcile the opposed values. Alternatively, one might
make the hard choice and sacrifice one value for the other. Another solution—
though doubtfully a morally sound one—would be to pass the decision along to
another jurisdiction. This was the course chosen by Congress in 1996 when it
substituted block grants to the states for the federal policy of welfare entitle-
ments, thereby leaving many of these decisions to state policymakers.

The case just reviewed would not have been so difficult were it not for inno-
vative technology. Indeed, without the opportunity for impregnation by artificial insemination, there would not have been any case at all. For women
impregnated in a natural way, the provisions of the AFDC law were clear,
regardless of marital status. The novel method of impregnation in this case
posed the essential dilemma over what norms are to be judged applicable. The
question that needed answering was this: To what situation with established
norms was that of the single welfare mother analogous?

It is above all the proliferation of ethical dilemmas occasioned by technological innovation in a wide variety of fields that has caused the increased interest in systematic ethical analysis in recent years. Technology has created moral
problems that simply did not exist and could not have been envisioned previously. Because of its capacity to develop cogent reasoning by analogy of known
to unknown cases, casuistry is especially suited to this kind of rapidly and constantly changing environment.

In particular, new capabilities to manipulate human characteristics through
technological instruments have created an urgent demand for adequate ethical

analysis. These new and emerging forms of power include genetic engineering, cloning, and mind-altering pharmacology.

Technologies of Human Enhancement

To what extent and under what circumstances is it morally acceptable to employ psychopharmacology to change human behavior? Using Prozac to relieve painful stress and to diminish agitation and sudden rage brought on by premenstrual syndrome (PMS) in some women seems to result in pure benefit. But what of the increasing use of the drug Ritalin to quiet fidgety children in the classroom and to improve their academic performance? Ritalin is perhaps more efficient than traditional means of pedagogical improvement, such as reductions in class size. But does its efficiency in achieving a given end legitimate its morality?

To address this question, the casuist asks whether chemically induced docility and concentration will further other classroom goals, such as the encouragement of self-discipline. Americans see the educational experience as multifaceted, and casuistry requires that the achievement of a particular end within the educational system give due recognition to the multiple goals involved. Thus, is a chemical solution to the problem of order in the classroom compatible with the service of these multiple ends? Women suffering from PMS may be helped only by mood-altering drugs. But is this also true of fidgety children?

The answer to this question probably lies in assessing the degree to which classroom order and the other goals of education can be attained through such measures as reduced class size, good teaching, and adequate discipline. As one writer has put it, "Technology, purely because of its power and efficiency, seems to cheat us of the experience of accomplishment, which is something valued in distinction from the achievement of [a particular] end."[15] Applying this view to the educational system, one could reasonably conclude that Ritalin should probably be reserved for those children who are clinically hyperactive and cannot otherwise be brought to good order. This may well entail better definition and measurement of the widely discussed condition of attention deficit disorder.

Questions similar to these arise when we consider the future possibilities of genetic manipulation, a technique that Lee M. Silver has labeled reprogenetics. For example, when it becomes technically feasible, will it be morally appropriate, through germ-line gene therapy, to enhance human cognitive abilities? In Silver's view, "After the desire to have children, the desire to have successful children is the next strongest force driving parental behavior."[16] In other words, should genetics be employed to increase intelligence and academic capacity? Answers to these questions require weighing and balancing the various goals of the entire educational experience in order to determine how the end of scientifically induced intelligence fits with the many other attributes of the good human life. If, for example, we were to provide only those who can afford the treatment the means to improve the intelligence of their progeny, so that they might compete more effectively with others, the casuist would conclude that this is socially inappropriate.[17] One might then suggest that intelligence enhancement across the social spectrum would be desirable. However, before assenting to this proposition, we would have to consider the value of integrating such characteristics as compassion, generosity, and altruism as well. Enhanced intellect alone might become simply a tool of individual self-glorification and arrogant domination. Genetic manipulation in itself makes no judgment as to the desirability of conscious scientific intelligence enhancement; it simply poses the question.

Environmental Ethics: The Problem of Short-Run Utilitarianism

Environmental pollution is an area in which the casuist method is more difficult to employ than in the foregoing cases. This is because casuistry assumes the possibility of achieving compromise on social differences in values and purposes. The politics of environmental pollution, however, are tied to a deep conflict between two utilitarian values in our culture, which are not readily compromised: prosperity and full employment today versus healthy living associated with environmental integrity in the future. An example is the tension between the welfare of the industries in the Ohio valley, which emit smoke that produces acid rain, and the health of the forests and lakes of the northeastern United States and eastern Canada. In these areas, acid rain is gradually destroying timber stands, as well as all life in numerous lakes.

Political pressures from economic interests have been great enough to weaken legislation that would compel a cleanup among the polluting industries. Such a cleanup would substantially increase the costs of production. Because private economic calculation computes efficiency and productivity only for the moment, and with reference to the private profits of particular firms only, it cannot factor in long-run social costs of present-day pollution. And the magic "unseen hand" of the market is not able to produce future social well-being. It is possible, however, for analysts to calculate social costs and benefits and to establish surrogate values for things not traded in a market. There is nevertheless no clear and certain way to give dollar value to social costs that emerge several years down the road. So one may be left with a reduction of the ethical dilemma to purely political terms. Nor have efforts of deontological argument in the literature of environmental ethics, employing rights language with reference to future generations and to nonhuman entities, been more than halting. Is it meaningful to say, for example, that animals and plants have needs and interests and that ethical status derives from these things? But if species have needs, do not buildings also? Is there anything, then, that would not have moral standing under this rubric?[18] Would a new ethic of the common good that moves away from radically individualist premises help to cope with this dilemma? To develop such an ethic would require not only a break with utilitarianism and deontology. It would demand a rethinking of the fundamentally individualist assumptions of American political culture, out of whose matrix the formal systems of ethical theory proceed.

CHAPTER 5

American Democracy and the Fragmentation of Consensus

IN WESTERN DEMOCRACIES, electorate attitudes and party systems have been expected to provide broad frameworks of preferences within which specific policies can be formulated. Traditionally, parties have been seen as representing coalitions of voters and as facilitating the election of policymakers who would respond to the interests of these coalitions. When these coalitions remained stable, they provided a basis for coherence in governmental policy and a predictable policy environment for the analyst. But many analysts contend that in recent years, democratic electorates have become increasingly volatile and divided and have thus been unable to give consistent guidance to public officials. These electorates are in flux, and no one is certain what direction they are headed. But it is clear that current trends pose important challenges to the political skills of elected officials.

Destabilization of electoral coalitions began in the 1970s and continued through the millennium. Changing political currents lead to oscillating policies. The environment of the policy analyst becomes kaleidoscopic. The electorate provides little direction for elected officials, who begin to think increasingly in terms of short-term tactical approaches, which, in turn, provides meager support for policy analysts. In such conditions, short-term political considerations often override policy analysis. Currently, students of the policy process are in the midst of an ongoing political mystery: Has an era of Republican ascendancy arrived, or will oscillation between the two parties continue? Signs of both possibilities coexist uneasily.

The policy analyst must expect to continue to function in an uncertain environment. If electoral stability were again to become the norm, then presumably the analyst would be in a better position to develop and implement rational procedures in decision making. Whatever the future holds, the policy analyst must be aware of electoral realities, since these are important constraints on the behavior of elected officials. This chapter focuses on two questions: What is happening in the electorate? What do these developments bode for the future? The bulk of the material in this chapter is based on studies of the American system. However, some important electoral changes in other Western democracies have been studied in greater detail. To treat these trends fully, we refer also to these non-American polities.

THE "NEW CLASS" AND POSTMATERIAL VALUES

One major trend postulated in recent years is that postindustrial society has given rise to a "New Class." In this view, expertise and education are key resources of postindustrial society, and mind work is the dominant form of activity. Those who operate within this paradigm increasingly set the political agenda and structure the acceptable boundaries of political action.[1] A practical outcome of these developments has been a fracturing of the political party system, which had been based on materialistic economic interests, and a lessening of that system's ability to develop coherent party positions on the issues. The problem is most obvious in the parties of the left, such as the Democrats in the United States, a party described by some as having a "split personality." But even Republicans have similar challenges—as the aftermath of their impeachment actions against President Bill Clinton demonstrates.

New Class Democrats (those who are younger, college educated, and in professional and managerial jobs) take issue positions different from those adopted by "Old Class" Democrats (those older, without college training, and in blue-collar occupations). New Class Democrats are less interested in the "bread-and-butter" issues than are Old Class Democrats. On some questions, they clash with the Old Class Democrats. For example, they favor the pro-choice position in the abortion controversy, strong environmental protection, racial equality, and freer sexual relations. Old Class Democrats are more conservative on these issues. The result is a deep ideological split within the Democratic Party.[2] If the Democrats select someone perceived as liberal on lifestyle issues (such as George McGovern in 1972), the party stands to lose the support of the Old Class Democrats. At the same time, through the various reforms that have opened the party to "democratic" influence, the New Class has considerable power to structure the party's official positions. The result has been that the Democrats have experienced difficulty in holding presidential coalitions together.

It is not only the Democratic Party, though, that faces problems as a result of this new class division. William S. Maddox and Stuart A. Lilie argued that the terms *liberal* and *conservative* are no longer clear guides to the political positions of Americans.[3] They contended that at least two separate issue dimensions are needed to categorize individuals' ideological positions: government intervention

GOVERNMENT INTERVENTION
IN THE ECONOMY

		FAVOR	OPPOSE
EXPANSION OF PERSONAL FREEDOM	FAVOR	Liberal	Libertarian
	OPPOSE	Populist	Conservative

Figure 5.1 Matrix of Ideological Types

Source: Modified from William S. Maddox and Stuart A. Lilie, *Beyond Liberal and Conservative* (Washington, D.C.: Cato Institute, 1984), 5.

in the economy and expansion of personal freedom. As figure 5.1 shows, juxtaposing these dimensions results in four ideological groupings.

Those who favor government intervention in the economy and expansion of personal freedoms are liberals in this scheme; conservatives favor less government intervention in the economy and are not in favor of expanding personal freedoms; populists are for government involvement in the economy but against expanding lifestyle freedoms; libertarians are against government intervention in the economy but favor expansion of personal freedom. The net result is *two* national parties with split personalities.

Self-identified Democrats tend to be largely liberals and populists (the two factions correspond somewhat to the New Class–Old Class distinction already discussed). Republicans, in contrast, are largely conservative and libertarian. Voting behavior is clearly affected by which stance one adopts. Libertarians voted for Nixon, Ford, and Reagan from 1972 to 1980, and conservatives did the same. Populists supported Nixon, then Carter twice. Liberals supported McGovern and Carter twice. Through the 1990s, a libertarian-conservative alliance managed to survive. This relationship is likely to continue if economic issues dominate political campaigns. On the other hand, if lifestyle or social issues become dominant, the Republicans may find their apparently powerful coalition splitting in a manner similar to the fate of the Democrats in 1972. In that year, populists deserted the Democrats because they saw McGovern as too liberal on social issues; at the same time, New Class liberals found his social liberalism to their liking. Although the inherent tension within the ranks of the Republican Party has not as a rule been a particularly great problem, it did surface during the Clinton impeachment hearings and the trial in the U.S. Senate, as more moderate Republican governors criticized the congressional wing of their party for its fixation on impeachment.[4]

Exactly what kinds of people make up the various ideological categories? In 1984, Maddox and Lilie noted that liberals were younger (under forty-one), had some college education, were less religious or were Jewish, came from all income levels, and were from the Northeast and West. Populists were of the New Deal generation or older, had a high school education (or less), made relatively little money, were working class in background, and were 24 percent nonwhite. Conservatives were people who came of political age in the 1950s or earlier; they came from all educational levels, were middle to upper income, and almost completely white. Finally, libertarians were—simply—those once referred to as Yuppies. They were under forty-one, had college degrees, earned middle to high incomes, and were largely white and not religious. The liberals and libertarians were the two fastest-growing segments of the voting electorate. Populists had already begun to decline as a proportion of the electorate. They were, literally, dying out, to be replaced by liberals and libertarians. While conservatives retained their share of the electorate, they were an aging group, too. The electoral division among these four ideological perspectives was rather even and would last into the next decade. In 1992, Kenneth Janda, Jeffrey M. Berry, and Jerry Goldman calculated that 26 percent of Americans were liberal, 25 percent populist, 28 percent libertarian, and 21 percent conservative.[5] The result of this relatively even distribution was that an element of instability had been introduced into partisan politics.

The origins and rise of the New Class are important because much research suggests that this phenomenon is part of the electoral change affecting most of the Western democracies. The most persuasive explanation for the rise of the New Class is Ronald Inglehart's needs theory.[6] He argued that people growing up in a time of scarcity tend to develop "materialist" attitudes. They are so concerned with survival needs—food, shelter, clothing—that they see government's primary responsibility to be the provision of these basic material items. Those who mature in times of abundance, however, such as have existed in the Western world since World War II, take the satisfaction of basic economic and material needs for granted. They instead view government and politics as vehicles for self-expression, for advancing their opportunities for self-development and fulfillment. They are the "postmaterialists."

Inglehart offered two basic propositions to explain these trends:

1. *A scarcity hypothesis.* An individual's priorities reflect the socio-economic environment; one places the greatest subjective value on things that are in relatively short supply.

2. *A socialization hypothesis.* The relationship between socioeconomic environment and value priorities is not one of immediate adjustment; a substantial time lag is involved, for one's basic values to a large extent reflect the conditions that prevailed during one's preadult years.[7]

Findings indicate that younger people and those who grew up in wealthier homes are most likely to be postmaterial in their orientations—in the United

States, Great Britain, France, West Germany, the Scandinavian countries, and even Japan. On political issues, they are more sympathetic to women's rights, efforts to ameliorate poverty, environmentalism, the antinuclear movement, and, in general, lifestyle freedom. Furthermore, postmaterialists are less likely to accept traditional values. Their orientation is secular and agnostic. For them, God has little importance. They accept homosexuality and sexual permissiveness and prefer easy divorce. In contrast, the materialists are *most* likely to accept traditional values. According to Inglehart, it is "precisely those who experience the least economic and physical security in their lives, that have the greatest need for the guidance and reassurance that familiar cultural norms and absolute religious beliefs provide."[8]

Chapter 3 discussed two core value orientations in American thought: a politics of interest and a politics of conscience. At one level, these concepts seem applicable to the conflict between materialists and postmaterialists. Materialists emphasize government's responsibility to focus on economic issues. In this regard, liberals want government to ensure minimum wages, fair treatment of workers, and generous unemployment compensation. Conservatives prefer government to carry out policies to enhance the profitability of market enterprises. Either way, there is a preoccupation with securing and advancing material, economic benefits. Self-interest is the underlying motive.

Postmaterialists are somewhat more difficult to categorize, since there are elements of the politics of both interest and conscience in their belief structures. Clearly, a politics of conscience grounded in a sense of the common good and a commitment to equality is an important component of the postmaterialist orientation. Postmaterialists want government to allow free expression for all (a key part of the politics of conscience). In practical policy terms, they support racial and gender equality and the environment. Their sympathy for these positions reflects their belief that individuals, at one level, should subordinate their narrow self-interest to a greater good. On the other hand, as individuals, this element of the electorate practices and strongly supports a self-centered lifestyle. As long as the economy stays relatively healthy, there appears to be an inexorable movement toward postmaterialism. In Europe, the number of those ranking "high" on a postmaterialist index contained in survey research questionnaires increased 13 percent between 1973 and 1990.[9] By the 1990s, postmaterialists represented a plurality, and they now outnumber materialists in Western Europe and the United States. Nonetheless, they are not yet in the majority (many citizens are neither materialist nor postmaterialist, but somewhere in between).

Because they have grown more active politically, postmaterialists will have considerable ability to shape the political agenda. Paul Abramson and Inglehart noted that "since postmaterialists will remain a minority, they will often be on the losing side of many political conflicts. Thus, the growth of postmaterialism could lead to a growing number of disaffected but articulate and politically active Europeans, increasing the potential for political protest."[10] Postmaterialists will continue to have agenda-setting power but not effective governing power. Therefore, those responsible for governmental policy in the industrialized democracies may expect to face increasing conflict and division in their electorates.

The effects of these changes for the policy analyst will be both direct and tangible. In Germany, postmaterialists are most skeptical of the North Atlantic Treaty Organization (NATO), are most opposed to nuclear weapons in their country, and are more likely to place themselves on the political left. It was this element, for example, that most strongly opposed the commitment of German ground troops in the 1999 confrontation between NATO and Serbia over Kosovo. Jane Y. Junn concluded that "increasingly more educated, active, and politically powerful individuals opposing nuclear weapons deployment will soon be in a position to disagree with, and disrupt current NATO strategic policy."[11] This obviously has powerful relevance for American foreign policy in the future. Those who undertake policy analysis related to foreign policy must monitor the electoral configurations behind the government policies of other nations if their recommendations are to be useful.

The extent of one's materialism or postmaterialism is affected by economic conditions at a particular point in time (referred to as "period effects" by students of public opinion). One important finding, based on studies of Western European countries over three decades, is that the inflation rate has an effect on the degree to which individuals are materialist or postmaterialist. For each "generation," as the inflation rate goes up, postmaterialist values diminish. It is also clear that each successively younger generation has grown more postmaterial than its older cohorts.

Despite the increase in inflationary pressures in the late 1980s and the modest decline in the number of postmaterialists, the ratio of postmaterial to materialist citizens in Western Europe is now in favor of the former. There appears to be a similar trend in the United States, although the data are not as complete as for Western Europe. The United States enjoyed a healthy economy throughout the 1990s. As a result, one would expect that the proportion of postmaterialists in the population has increased.

Findings from a wide variety of studies indicate that the emerging postmaterialist generation has begun to cause political dealignment (a weakening of party ties in the electorate) in many European democracies. Voting and issue views are increasingly shaped by whether one is material or postmaterial in orientation. Nevertheless, European parties continue to be largely based on the more materialist tradition of social class. The result is a poor fit between the perspectives of postmaterialist voters and the socioeconomic class bases of political party support.

This disjunction is one of the reasons for the development of "Green" parties in Western Europe. Postmaterialists are not satisfied with the traditional parties of the left. These parties continue to emphasize material issues relevant to the interests of the working class and their poorer constituents—precisely the issues deemed less important by postmaterialists. As one response, these voters have moved to support newer "Green" parties in a number of countries, such as Germany and the Scandinavian states. But in the United States at this time, there are really no viable alternatives to the Democratic and Republican Parties. H. Ross Perot's Reform Party has done well by historical standards for a third party, but—except for some maverick winners like Jesse "The Body" Ventura, elected as a Reform Party candidate to the governorship of Minnesota—it has not had great success electing officials to office.

The Republicans have been able to do reasonably well among younger, postmaterialist voters (i.e., the "libertarians").[12] But these voters are not likely to stay on board the Republican ship if traditional values are emphasized in the implementation of public policy. In the long run, there can be a sorting out of the ideological strains currently in evidence. In the short run, the tension within the party systems of the Western democracies will continue. In the United States, more specifically, the longer-term future may well be one dominated by liberals versus libertarians, with residual numbers of populists, conservatives, moderates, and those who are nonideological. For the next decade or more, though, there will likely be continuing instability among the factions within the two American political parties.

WHAT HAVE YOU DONE FOR ME LATELY?

Over the past few decades, commentators have spoken of a new and invidious source of individualism in the United States. Christopher Lasch's *Culture of Narcissism* and Robert Bellah et al.'s *Habits of the Heart* have depicted this as cancerous in its rejection of common interests and values. Individuals take advantage of opportunities in order to further their self-interest. The effort to improve themselves and advance their interests obscures the larger social context. Pursuit of economic self-interest or self-fulfillment reduces to a minimum any inherent concern for the larger interests of society. In many respects, this characterizes the basic motivation of contemporary materialist and postmaterialist citizens and their representative interest groups and places them squarely within the politics of interest.

In terms of elections, this new individualism engenders in voters a "What have you done for me lately?" calculus. If people see incumbents as not having done well by them, they will vote against them. Samuel Kernell noted that in the Western democracies, people increasingly do not vote for candidates; they are more likely to vote *against* them.[13] Indeed, there is evidence that negative voting routinely takes place in the United States. People want quick answers to sometimes difficult problems; if such responses are not forthcoming, they oust the incumbent administration and try again. In times of economic difficulty, like the 1970s, the predictable result will be governmental instability. No policy guides for the future are provided by such voting—only approval or disapproval of past performance. The policy analyst working in Jimmy Carter's Environmental Protection Agency would have had to switch gears dramatically to function in the agency in Ronald Reagan's early administration.[14] This hardly provides the conditions for rational, future-oriented policy on the environment.

The increasingly short-term orientation of the electorate has an impact on candidates for office. For members of Congress, this sensitivity to the electorate leads toward increased errand running and constituency service and away from developing a coherent policy orientation. For presidential candidates, it may encourage overselling of inflated promises on which delivery is improbable or impossible.

Kernell quoted Henry Kissinger as saying,

> There is the problem that as the pressures of their electoral process have increased, governments have become more and more tactically oriented. The more tactically oriented they are, the more short-term their policies. The more short-term their policies, the less successful they are. So we have the paradox that governments following public opinion polls begin to look more and more incompetent.[15]

Examining the electoral politics of Western democracies, including Australia, France, Great Britain, the United States, Japan, and Germany, Kernell contended that similar processes exist in all these countries. Assuming that these societies would continue to face chronic economic problems, he argued that candidates for high office would try to outdo one another in promises about their abilities to turn the economy around. Once in office, however, the winner would be unable to carry out those promises. Hence, the leader (and his or her party) would be discredited and ousted at the next election—to be replaced by the leader of the opposition party, who would also have promised too much in the way of results.

As this scenario unwinds, voters become increasingly disenchanted. They no longer vote *for* candidates to leadership positions; they now vote *against* incumbents. If economic conditions remain unstable, governments are forced to endorse austerity measures, which in turn will lead to greater mass discontent. Kernell concluded that "about all the new austerity offers modern capitalist democracies . . . is elite conflict, on occasions ideological stridency, and regime instability."[16]

In the United States, presidential popularity makes a difference in the balance of political power. This is one resource that can assist a president in getting his policy initiatives approved by Congress.[17] But what helps shape the level of popularity? If Kernell was right, judgments about a president's performance that are tied to real-world events ought to predict people's approval of a president better than abstract values would. In an important essay, Charles W. Ostrom and Dennis M. Simon developed a statistical model to explain and predict presidential popularity. They considered the role of unexpected events, legislative success of a president's program, the degree of tension with the former Soviet Union, people's judgments about the state of the economy, existence of war, and a "honeymoon effect" (a boost in presidential standing after elections or some sympathy-evoking event, such as an assassination attempt). Each of these factors does, in fact, affect mass approval of the president. "Thus, . . . public assessments of presidential performance are anchored in the real world."[18]

Nor are these findings contradicted by Ronald Reagan's "Teflon effect," for the data do not support its existence. Ironically, Republican frustration about President Clinton's often high standing in the polls in his turbulent second term echoed Democratic frustration with Reagan's high standing in the eyes of the public. Doubtless, President Clinton's standing followed the same logic as Reagan's—and there is nothing supernatural about it. Providing a month-by-month prediction of Reagan's approval ratings, Ostrom and Simon anticipated his levels of approval quite accurately—based on data derived from other presidents' tenure in the office. For instance, as the economy declined in 1981 and 1982, so did Reagan's job performance rating, as it has done for other chief executives. When the economy improved and foreign policy crises occurred (with the concomitant "rally 'round the flag" effect), Reagan's approval rating rebounded. In short, there is nothing mysterious about mass response to a president. Approval is based largely on public assessments of a president's job performance. Still, Republicans wondered why the public was not outraged with President Clinton as result of revelations from the Starr Report and the subsequent impeachment proceedings. It appears that—despite his obvious personal moral failings—Americans felt that Clinton's performance as president was good, reflecting a dynamic similar to the one that occurred for Reagan.

One issue raised by these events is the extent to which the American people are inclined to hold presidents or any other high officials accountable for their behavior, other than as that behavior affects the citizenry's pocketbooks. If all are equal under the law but voters are not willing to apply that standard to public officials because they are seen as having "brought home the bacon" for the people, serious questions follow. It appears clear that President Reagan at least violated the intent of Congress with some of his foreign policy decisions regarding supporting rebels in Central America; clearly, President Clinton at least skirted outright perjury in testimony about the Monica Lewinsky affair. However, as long as both were perceived as performing well in terms of facilitating economic prosperity, Americans tended not to penalize them in approval ratings for their rather cavalier approach to the rule of law. In the long run, repetition of such behavior and this kind of citizen response to it might undermine the traditional view that the United States is an empire of laws and not of men, to paraphrase the English political philosopher John Harrington.

Analysis of data from 1952 through 1992 suggests a number of points about presidential elections that indicate the growing salience of the "What have you done for me lately?" orientation in the electorate. Over this period, incumbents were increasingly evaluated on the basis of their past performance. Non-incumbents across the board were more likely to be judged on the basis of expected performance. Performance consistently outweighed policy as a predictor of electoral support.[19] The only exception over this period was the 1964 Johnson-Goldwater election, which had a strong policy mandate component. Although the elections of 1972, 1980, and 1992 also had a policy mandate component, it was weak in comparison with the performance factor. This emphasis on performance is significant because policy questions are more likely to deal with long-term considerations, while performance factors tend to be tied to short-term voter satisfaction.

The Carter-Reagan contest of 1980 is normally viewed as a straightforward retrospective judgment—and rejection—of the performance of incumbent Jimmy Carter. Although there is some evidence of a modest policy mandate for Reagan that year,[20] retrospective rejection of Carter was clearly a more significant factor. The 1984 Reagan-Mondale race also featured a retrospective judgment (positive in this case) of the president's performance. Demonstrating the power of "What have you done for me lately?" voters actually preferred Mondale's future and past policy positions to Reagan's, preferred Mondale as a person, and observed that Mondale was probably more capable than Reagan. But they believed the president had done a good job—so they disregarded their distaste for his policies, for him as a person, and for his capabilities.[21] These data provide a remarkable demonstration of the power of retrospective judgments.

In congressional elections, there is a very strong retrospective element: voters reward members of Congress for the services they render. As long as incumbents bring home the pork, serve as ombudsmen, and take credit for government projects, voters will continue to support them. This has been an American tradition of long standing, and legislators are aware of its importance. The policy-oriented congressional election of 1994, in which Republicans united and ran under the banner of the "Contract with America," might have hinted at coming changes in this respect. However, the 1998 election appeared to be more about public weariness of partisan bickering—and a rebuke to the Republicans' zeal to impeach and convict President Clinton—than about policy per se.

Retrospective voting creates pressures to do what it takes to get the public to see that an incumbent has done something for them lately. Short-term (or tactical) decision making that overwhelms long-term considerations may result. There is some evidence, for example, that in presidential and majoritarian parliamentary systems, manipulation of the economy may be timed to coincide with elections. National leaders may tend to "juice up" the economy just before elections and try to "cool" it down afterward. Under such conditions, policy analysts in budget offices will discover pressures to subordinate a long-range budgetary approach to the short-term fiscal maneuvers of their political superiors.[22]

REALIGNMENT, DEALIGNMENT, OR WHAT?

Realignment is the shift to a new, stable alignment in coalitions that have supported the parties. Realignment is associated with the development of a new political agenda and a new set of programs and policies. Has the United States experienced one recently? Is it experiencing one now? If so, is the realignment stable and firm, or is it "hollow"?

How these questions are answered helps sketch the picture of the political future. A solid realignment can provide the policy analyst with a sense that there will be greater stability in the decision-making environment and in institutions than there has been recently. If realignment is not in sight, however, electoral volatility and policy instability will continue, as political figures try to appease a public that provides no direction. Across many Western democracies, to paraphrase Bob Dylan's old song "Ballad of a Thin Man," *something* is happening, but we don't quite know what it means.[23]

One plausible explanation posits 1964 and 1968 as critical U.S. election years in which the racial issue brought about significant change in political coalitions. In this scenario, the culmination of those two elections came in 1994, when Republicans swept control of Congress and solidified gains in statehouses throughout the country. This argument sees the following events as linked to the critical nature of the 1964 election:

1. From the 1940s until 1964, Republicans were more moderate and Democrats were more conservative in votes on civil rights bills in the House of Representatives and Senate. After 1964, Democrats in Congress became more moderate to liberal than Republicans in this area.

2. Voters picked up on this. They correctly perceived that the Democrats had become the more liberal party on civil rights.

3. There seems to have been a resulting differentiation between new party identifiers after 1964; new Republicans were more conservative and new Democrats more liberal on racial issues.[24]

This chain of events could help explain the defection from the Democratic Party of blue-collar workers and southern whites, since both groups are conservative on racial issues.

Apparently, the large-scale movement of southern whites away from the Democratic Party was part of a two-stage process. First, between 1964 and 1968, many southern whites—especially young ones, but some older ones as well—came to see themselves as less Democratic. Their party identification as Democrats weakened, fewer voted for Democratic presidential candidates, and they increasingly supported Republican candidates in subpresidential races. This describes a dealigning process "in which traditional party coalitions dissolve without new party coalitions being formed to take their place."[25]

Second, there was a shift toward Republican identification. In 1980 and 1981, for instance, a dramatic shift toward the Republican Party occurred among whites in Florida.[26] Younger voters were once more the key group, although a smattering of older conservative-segregationist Democrats joined the rush. Additionally, many southern whites seemed to carry a kind of "dual" identification. They saw themselves as Republicans in national elections (for president and Congress) and as Democrats in state and local elections. This dual identification seems to have begun developing in, as one might have guessed, 1964.[27]

Studies of realignment tend to locate the important election period as 1964–68, pointing to race as part of the answer about why the change occurred and to dissatisfaction with Democratic presidential performance as another. The case for realignment, thus laid out, seems fairly persuasive. Indeed, one major work on the American voter concluded as a simple statement of fact that in those years, we experienced realignment.[28]

However, 1992–96 appears also to have been a key period in electoral dynamics. This position is even more persuasive if the 1994 election is taken into account. In that year, Republicans stunned Democrats in elections for the House, the Senate, and many state offices across the nation. And it appeared that Democrats would not fully recoup their losses soon. Many of the new Republicans entering the House of Representatives came from districts that were fairly conservative and Republican in background. There had been a massive move of southern whites from the Democratic Party to the Republican Party over the previous thirty years, producing the final denouement to the drama begun in 1964,[29] with race likely the underlying issue. Democrats would be unlikely to win very many of these seats back with moderate-to-liberal candidates. In addition, the built-in advantage that Democrats had had since the New Deal era in terms of outnumbering Republicans had disappeared, partially because the New Deal generation was dying off. (In 1999, the *New York Times* noted that by one government estimate, "World War II veterans are dying at a rate of more than 1,000 a day.")[30] Currently, about as many Americans call themselves Republicans as Democrats. Also, more Americans now define themselves as conservative, which seems to indicate a measurable move to the right in the electorate.[31]

In 1998, Earl Black contended that the partisan balance nationally was even, the result of Republicans becoming electorally vibrant in the Deep South. He concluded:

> With the decline of southern sectionalism, the Republican Party has become a national party in congressional elections for the first time since Reconstruction. Old-fashioned sectional conflict has dissipated, but sectional considerations continue to pervade national politics through the conservative agenda pursued by Republican congressional leaders from the South. As it has been in presidential politics for some time, the South is now at the epicenter of Republican and Democratic strategies to control Congress. In order to comprehend the dynamics of national politics, it is more important than ever to understand the South.[32]

In a related study, John Petrocik and Scott Desposato found abundant evidence that the rapid decline of the Democratic Party in Congress in the 1990s was not due solely to redistricting of electoral districts in the South. The redistricting plus the changing patterns of party identification together produced the results leading to Republican control of Congress in 1994.[33]

When all these bits and pieces are put together, they suggest that realignment has taken place and that a sea change in American politics has occurred. These developments could provide the basis for a more predictable working environment for the policy analyst for some years to come. On the other hand, however, the realignment does not appear to have led one party to become sufficiently dominant to create a stable policy environment. There are likely to be oscillations between parties if the current realignment proves at all stable, given what appears to be a fairly even partisan division.

Even if one party were to have something like a decided electoral advantage over the other, aspects of electoral change suggest that the stability of voter realignment may not be as great as in the past. Both parties have experienced a weakening of voter loyalties that is part of a general weakening of the partisanship in the electorate. For this reason, Martin Wattenberg referred to the realignment as "hollow." Political parties seem to be less salient and important to voters.[34] Some evidence suggests that much of the gain in Republican identification is performance-based, a function of Ronald Reagan's successes as president. In an increasingly candidate-centered age, party does not have the same value as a cue for the electorate as it used to.

Furthermore, the Republicans are unlikely to make many more gains in the House of Representatives. If Alan I. Abramowitz is right, the districts now controlled by Democrats in the House tend to be more moderate to liberal and thus are unlikely to elect very many conservative Republicans. In his view, "Republicans may find it difficult to add to their currently fairly narrow majority in the House."[35] If this analysis is correct, consolidating and expanding recent gains will not be easy for the Republicans.

Finally, if the electorate's penchant for voting on the basis of performance does not change and the Republicans are perceived as not performing well, the strength of Republican support can be expected to erode. This, for example, might be part of the explanation as to why Republicans were surprised in the 1998 midterm elections, in which a president's party—for the first time since 1934—actually gained seats in the House of Representatives. The public's distaste for the Republican House's performance in the impeachment process certainly contributed to this. Realignment may not be what it used to be. Thus, Walter Dean Burnham's observation that "1994 represents one of those rare elections from which bearings will have to be taken for a long time to come. . . . The shape of American politics will very probably never be the same again"[36] might best be taken as tentative. The electorate's attachment to the "What have you done for me lately?" syndrome suggests that the 1994 election may be less than fundamental in its long-term ramifications. Moreover, the increasing importance of the media must be considered.

In many instances, candidates have come to rely more heavily on the media than on the party in their campaigns. As early as 1978, data gathered during the congressional elections indicated that as media spending increases, the candidate becomes more salient to the voters than his or her party. Candidates today function more as electoral entrepreneurs than as partners on a political team linked by a common party. Moreover, media affect voters' behavior in other ways. People consider television news to be the most trustworthy, dependable source of what is going on. Yet reliance on television as a news source leads to an inability to distinguish candidates' positions and so reduces voting turnout rates, since those who cannot see differences between candidates are less likely to vote. More generally, greater dependence on television for news is associated with lower levels of political knowledge, interest, and participation, and, paradoxically, the effects are greatest for those with the most education. Thus, television news may be reducing Americans' ability to judge parties and candidates and may thereby be rendering the electorate more volatile.

Additionally, there is abundant evidence that the media have an impact on politics and public agenda setting.[37] Those issues that are most focused on by the media tend to become accepted as the vital issues of the day—and government will often begin to focus on these issues rather than on others that may actually be more substantial. For instance, why did the United States become involved in Somalia? Media images led Americans to awareness of the serious human suffering in that country, and they began to believe that this was an important matter about which something needed to be done. Political leaders followed public opinion, and the United States took part in a humanitarian endeavor that ultimately failed. In the process, other African countries with as great a set of problems—but no television cameras to record them—were ignored, and their unique circumstances never penetrated the agenda. Similarly, during elections, emphasis by candidates on specific issues through extensive and sophisticated media advertising can lead the electorate to perceive these as key agenda items.[38]

These trends indicate that election outcomes will probably depend more and more on the short-term effects of candidate evaluation and on specific issues of concern to relatively small numbers of lightly motivated voters rather than on the long-term force of party identification.[39] As Wattenberg noted during the Reagan era,

> Even if the Republican surge is a long-lasting one, it will be of limited importance as long as partisanship in the electorate continues to decline. Given the most ideal conditions for party revitalization in decades, all that occurred [in 1984] was a stabilization of the decline. With an incumbent unable to run again, and with what will most likely be fractious campaigns for the presidential nomination within both parties, it seems likely that the conditions in 1988 will be such as to foster further party decline. The candidate-centered age will be with us for a long time to come, regardless of whether the next political era will be a Democratic or Republican one.[40]

Furthermore, much of the debate over realignment in the United States ignores the value changes that seem ongoing as postmaterialism gains and liberals and libertarians become more numerous at the expense of conservatives and populists. Although Republicans are surely benefiting now from the changes that are occurring, there is no solid evidence of firm electoral stability yet. Identification with party is still weak, and party programs cover potentially uneasy coalitions, as demonstrated, for example, by the expressed concerns of moderate Republican governors that the Clinton impeachment battle had diverted the party from its central message for the voters.

If there is to be a stable mass realignment of the "traditional" kind, it is still in the future. "What have you done for me lately?" will probably remain the key question asked by contemporary individualists. Instability and volatility are likely to remain dominant. Even though it appears clear that there has been realignment, it seems fated to be hollow for the next decade or so. There is unlikely to be the stability needed to maximize the usefulness of policy analysis in areas in which values conflict, although in certain technical areas (e.g., water resources or traffic planning) the analyst may remain unaffected. Short-run, tactical needs of politicians will continue to dominate and remain a part of the landscape within which the policy analyst labors.

THE PARTY ORGANIZATION: RESURRECTION OR REQUIEM?

As voters have become less politicized and less oriented toward party, the conclusion of many students of American parties has been that these organizations have gone into decline. Party decline is a source of anguish to political thinkers, many of whom contend that the parties are the only viable mechanism for organizing political discourse in the United States. The two parties, by competing with one another for votes, present alternatives to the citizenry and thus help to structure debate and, ultimately, policy. The decline of party organization, then, is lamented as making the American system more susceptible to interest-group influence.

Frank J. Sorauf, in fact, claimed that the likeliest future of electoral politics is individual candidate-centered and interest-group-sponsored candidacies, with some residual influence of the political party.[41] Ultimately, this course of events would render the electorate ever more volatile and make still less likely stable electoral majorities. This would introduce further uncertainty into policymaking, with short-term political considerations becoming more important for elected officials as they jockey for position to gain the support of groups. The prospects for rational decision making aided by policy analysis are hardly promising under the gloomier projections.

Nevertheless, some scholars argue that party organizations—at all levels of government—are making a spirited comeback. At the local level, county parties became much stronger as organizations from 1964 through the decade of the 1990s. They became more active in fund raising, in distributing campaign literature, in arranging political events, and in voter registration drives, although there was little budgetary support for the local parties and few had even part-time staff to operate their organizations on a day-to-day basis. At the state level, there has been a striking increase in the strength of party organizations. From the 1960s into the 1990s, more and more state parties developed permanent headquarters, hired professional leadership staff on a full-time basis, implemented more specialized staff operations, increased their budgets, and began to operate party programs either directed at building the organizations further or at assisting party candidates in campaigns. Researchers have noted that the Republicans have progressed much more rapidly than the Democrats in these areas. Thus, although both parties at the state level are much stronger organizationally than in 1960, the Republicans have clearly outpaced the Democrats in this respect.[42]

Changes at the national level have also helped strengthen the parties. In *Democratic Party v. Wisconsin* (1981),[43] the Supreme Court recognized the power of the national party organization to make rules that must be adhered to by state government. Both parties—but especially the Republicans—have become much more ambitious in their fund-raising efforts. The party organizations collect funds and then disburse them to specific candidates for office or to some state party organizations. They even purchase advertising time on television for generic commercial campaigns on behalf of the party. It is worth noting that the Republican Party has evolved further than the Democrats in terms of party organization. This is surely one of the factors contributing to Republican gains at the local, state, and national levels in recent years.

On the face of it, parties seem to be coming back and are increasingly able to play the role that democratic theorists have consistently advocated for them. But some problems remain. A case study of party organizations in the Pittsburgh area found that party activists are not really party loyalists as much as supporters of particular candidates or party leaders. Indeed, many activists are trying to advance their personal ambitions through party involvement.[44] And even though national party organizations are donating money to candidates for office, the party contributions are dwarfed by the influx of political action committee (PAC) money.

Despite the problems just noted, the venerable American parties may well be evolving into important shapers of policy debate. Stronger party organization might help introduce some order into the present electoral uncertainty. First, as noted above, party organizations at all levels of government have become more vital institutions. They are, simply, more *capable* of affecting the structure of policy debate.

Second, party organizations seem to be working toward creating more of a "team" sense and developing greater party unity. In 1978, the Republican Party's various national organizations (Republican National Committee and both the Senate and House Republican Campaign Committees) began targeting aid for candidates at all levels of government who needed help and who had a chance of victory. The national Republicans also paid for television advertisements extolling the Republican Party and its candidates for office ("Vote Republican! For a change!"). The ads seemed to somewhat improve Americans' image of the Republican Party. These effects could lead to increased power of the national party over those candidates beholden to it for assistance, which might translate into more party influence on elected officials' decision-making behavior. Other evidence shows that party voting in Congress has been increasing since 1968; that is, Republican members of Congress increasingly vote against Democrats, with fewer party crossover votes (technically, party cohesion has been increasing on congressional votes). This may be a measure of the parties' increasing potency as an influence on policy debate and decision.[45]

Third, party organizations—by working hard at getting out the vote on election day—can affect election outcomes (and hence render party candidates more beholden to the organizations). Activities by county parties accounted for about 7 percent of the vote in 1984 in selected statewide and national elections. That is a substantial independent impact—one that could easily affect winning and losing.[46] However, despite the effectiveness of mobilizing voters through the party organization, some evidence indicates that mobilization activities declined from the 1960s into the late 1980s. Indeed, one key reason for the decline in voter turnout over those years appears to have been diminished efforts by parties and other political actors to contact people directly. Instead, more emphasis was placed on the media to reach voters. And, as noted, the reliance of voters on television actually may demobilize the electorate.[47]

Fourth, leadership in the House of Representatives has in some respects strengthened over the past few decades. The postreform Congress that emerged from the internal changes of the 1970s has been characterized by greater exercise of influence by the majority party leadership and the devolution of power to subcommittees (see chap. 6 for further discussion of these issues).

It appears that Democratic members of the House, realizing that wider distribution of power could prevent them from mobilizing to create majority coalitions to win on the floor, decided to fashion stronger leadership tools. Thus, the conditions for more effective leadership stemmed from greater decentralization. In the absence of such leadership, though, fragmentation could be enhanced and policy immobility would become the order of the day. To avoid this, Democrats turned over to their leadership more power in selecting committee members, including more control over the influential House Rules Committee. House Democratic leaders used this increased power base to become more equal partners with the president in setting the national agenda. Functionally, they were more successful during the Reagan administration on issues of concern to the leadership than they had been in previous Congresses, indicating a strengthening of party government—at least in the House of Representatives.[48] Under Speaker Newt Gingrich, the Republican leadership in the House was able to maintain especially tight control over the majority during the first session of the 104th Congress,[49] although that began to dissipate in later Congresses, and his successor, Dennis Hastert, found the leadership position considerably more challenging. Taken together, these points paint an overall picture of a somewhat revitalized party structure (especially Republican organizations) influencing voters and elected officials. At this time, there is evidence that party organizations may be serving to bring some order back into the policy process; it is premature to say anything stronger, though, given the apparently deep and pervasive roots of the electoral division and volatility described earlier in this chapter.

THE POLICY PROCESS

An understanding of the trends and relationships within the electorate is important to explaining and predicting the movement of issues in the policy process. Studies indicate that voters' beliefs and the positions of the political parties are in a general sense influential in moving issues onto the government's agenda. For example, in interviews with policymakers in the areas of health and transportation, John W. Kingdon found that 57 percent of this sample believed that public opinion generally had played an important agenda-setting role, 50 percent thought elections had been significant, and 29 percent saw parties as being important.[50] These findings indicate that citizens—through their votes, opinions, and/or parties—can have an effect on the first stage of the formal policy process. This fact makes the existence or threat of electoral disorder that much more significant in terms of its eventual effects on public policy.

The postmaterialist phenomenon in the electorate has weakened the parties. At the same time, the power of interest groups, especially single-issue interest groups, in the agenda-setting stage of the policy process has grown. In Kingdon's study, interest groups were seen as important in getting issues onto the agenda in almost three-fourths of the case studies examined, and over 50 percent of those interviewed saw them as politically influential. These findings indicate that groups have significantly more impact at the agenda-setting stage than do political parties, elections, or public opinion in general. The problem posed for the policymaker and the policy analyst stems from the narrowness of group orientations, which is in turn reinforced by postmaterialist views among the electorate. Parties, in their representation of sizable aggregations of electorate preferences, retain the power to move issues through the policy process. Their weakening has meant that issues are now brought to the agenda by interests capable of gaining public and official notice—but rarely capable of maintaining sustained support throughout the policymaking process. Analysts can provide useful explanations of the plight of the homeless or the effects of acid rain, and interests can make sufficient public outcry to obtain legislative notice of these problems. But movement toward effective remedial action remains at the mercy of the demands and maneuvers of many other interests.

The policy process has become an obstacle course composed of both procedural and substantive pitfalls. In this respect, the disorientation of the electorate is mirrored in the fragmentation of the legislative and executive branches. Difficult decisions in these branches require majority coalitions of some duration, for victory at one point may only increase the intensity of the opposition at the next. Charles O. Jones argued that "the result is a system of layers of numerical majorities in elections, in referenda, in committee action, in roll-call voting, in court decisions. It is true, of course, that pluralities are sometimes accepted, but it is also true that those who rely on pluralities are likely to be limited in their exercise of authority and subject to criticism."[51]

Public opinion is a key influence on the actual policies adopted by national and state decision makers through legislative votes, executive actions, or judicial decisions. Public opinion affects what government does.[52] While there is stability in the broad contours of public opinion,[53] it moves to and fro within those broader channels, as argued throughout this chapter. Although it was conceivable that 1994 might portend the introduction of a new, more conservative stability into the political system, that has not been borne out, and this seems to be in keeping with historical trends. James Stimson's research, for example, suggested oscillation in the "mood" of public opinion from liberal (early 1960s) to conservative (with 1980 as the high point) back to liberal (late 1980s to mid-1990s).[54] Finally, of course, it appears that a realignment has taken place—with the end result being a fairly even partisan split. If this is so, then neither party can expect to have enough of an edge to establish a stable decision-making environment. The nation is most likely to experience political control moving back and forth between the parties, reflecting the effect of short-term forces unique to each election.

At any one time, public opinion is fragmented among liberals, libertarians, populists, and conservatives, with ramifications for policymaking. The divisive effects of the electorate in the decision-making process were demonstrated graphically in the Senate's consideration of President Nixon's program for reforming family assistance. Representative Wilbur Mills, chair of the Ways and Means Committee, was twice able to put together sufficient support in the House of Representatives to obtain passage. Both times, however, the ideological disagreements in the Senate produced a three-way division that stymied the bill's supporters from putting together a majority for passage. These differences closely reflected three of the four electorate divisions described by Maddox and Lilie. One grouping (populist) supported the measure; another (conservative) opposed it as too generous; the third (liberals) saw the plan as too restrictive on the rights of the poor.[55] In what may be a portent for much domestic policy in the future, the Republicans avoided this kind of stalemate in 1996 by packaging the AFDC program into a block grant and giving the states much greater discretion in the details of welfare administration.

Other alternatives designed to circumvent the difficulty of fashioning majorities on policies focus on weakening the wording of legislation so as not to offend anyone deeply or on distributing benefits so broadly that most of the legislators can anticipate advantages for their constituents. The first approach contains the seeds for trouble at the implementation stage, since the ambiguity of the policy package provides little guidance for the supervising agencies. The result tends to be an unraveling of the program by a variety of interests adept at exploiting the legislature's vagueness in their favor. In the second instance, resources can be spread so thinly that the program is bound to be ineffective. For example, during the Johnson administration, purchase of legislative support for the Model Cities program required so many promises of funds from the program that the program's administrators were simply unable to provide the kind of concentrated aid envisioned by the authors of the legislation.

The implementation phase of the policy process has always been fertile ground for interests to exploit the waning of public commitment to programs. In some cases, it may be possible to construct coalitions of sufficient durability to enact reasonably precise policy, but over the long term, public interest will dissipate while the interests directly affected by the policy will remain.

The next stage in the policy process, evaluation, which is often invoked as a primary activity of policy analysts, can likewise be highly politicized. Program evaluation refers to studying government programs to determine if (1) they are meeting their goals, (2) their impacts are being achieved in as cost-effective a manner as possible, and (3) their day-to-day operations are proceeding smoothly and as desired. This appears to be a straightforward task for the policy analyst—to use appropriate social science methods to determine how well a program is functioning. However, some programs—such as Women, Infants, and Children (WIC) and Head Start—are extremely popular, and critical evaluations tend to be downplayed, since they have become "sacred cows" in the public mind.[56] Thus, program evaluation may also, to some extent, be hostage to the vagaries of America's democratic process.

Obviously, if the electorate is moving more markedly toward a self-centered individualism, there will be even less sustained support for administrators who attempt to advance broad public purposes. Jones touched on the kind of environment created by contemporary electoral conditions:

> A weakened presidency, a more pretentious Congress, a steady Court, an expanding bureaucracy, enfeebled political parties, disinterested voters, burgeoning group activity, and a changing governmental policy structure—these developments both reflect and contribute to the social change that has characterized recent decades. Anthony King concludes that "American politics has become, to a high degree, atomized." Majorities must still be gathered, but it is much more difficult to build a lasting coalition.[57]

The lack of consensus on basic values in the electorate has serious consequences for the policy analyst, whose attachment to careful, rational approaches to issues constitutes the core of his or her occupational calling and, perhaps, orientation toward life. The immediacy of the needs expressed by the electorate pushes the policy analyst toward incremental policymaking. He or she must be sensitive to the quickly changing attitudes of a volatile electorate and will find the cautious, small steps of the incremental approach to issues more effective than solutions requiring long-term commitments. Moreover, the fragmented character of the institutions of the policy process in many instances also makes this stance one of necessity rather than preference.

CHAPTER 6

Policy Analysis and the Political Arena

WHEN DEALING WITH governmental institutions, the policy analyst confronts the structural manifestations of basic political values and the power of pluralism. The American people have had an enduring preference for government divided into many separate and largely uncoordinated units. The Founding Fathers' concern for the protection of liberty resulted in a tripartite division of the national government and a federal relationship between that government and the states. These structural arrangements have effectively limited the possibilities for efficient government through centralized direction. The divisive encroachments of social interests have fragmented the policy process further and have led such scholars as Lowi, Olson, and Huntington to voice concern about the direction of American democracy.[1] But experience with recent attempts to bring greater coherence into the policy process demonstrates that Americans continue to have little enthusiasm for coordinating or centralizing governmental institutions.

Coexisting, at times rather uncomfortably, with this distrust of centralized government has been a strong democratic spirit among Americans. Not only have Americans preferred fragmented governmental institutions; they have also insisted that these fragments be highly accessible to the people.[2] Furthermore, the larger the number of units and subunits of government, the greater the number of points at which citizens can "plug into the system," a fact not lost on the proliferating number of organized interests spawned by the nation's pluralistic society. This attachment to direct popular access was significantly reinforced by the Johnson administration's preference for making citizen participation a prerequisite to the implementation of federally funded programs at the local level. These requirements have often made life difficult for local policymakers and have at times raised questions about the viability of grass-roots participation.

The policy analyst intent on bringing to fruition the findings of a carefully designed and executed study may discover too late that the traditional political preferences of Americans often create impassable political roadblocks. At the national level and in many state and local jurisdictions, vested interests are adept at exploiting institutional fragmentation to obfuscate and delay even the most rationally defensible plans. The policy analyst must recognize the obstacles to orderly deliberation that the American political context poses and be prepared to work within the often emotional and chaotic conditions engendered by organized interests. Just as successful administrators within America's governmental bureaucracies have had to develop acute political skills, so, too, must the mature policy analyst move beyond applying analytical techniques to an understanding of the political and normative environments in which findings and recommendations will be considered.

An Incremental Policy Process

Any policy analyst hoping to develop a more comprehensive sense of his or her position will inevitably confront the fact that the dominant theoretical framework for policy interpretation is itself limiting in perspective. To date, the guiding rationale or theory undergirding the policy process has been incrementalism. As perhaps its chief scholarly spokesman, Charles Lindblom has built a persuasive case for the rationality of step-by-step policymaking. His position has been that incrementalism "is in fact a common method of policy formulation, and is, for complex problems, the principal reliance of administrators as well as of other policy analysts. And . . . it will be superior to any other decision-making method available for complex problems in many circumstances."[3] Pressed for time and information, policymakers cannot defer decisions, and it makes good sense for them to focus on specific incremental changes from current policy. Thus, the cautious, politically wise administrator can retain a tentative stance and need not stray far from the known parameters of policy.

The administrator aims, in Lindblom's words, for "satisficing" decisions rather than the (rarely achievable) optimal resolution of a problem. He or she chooses an objective that could be viewed as a step in the right direction over an objective that calls for a definitive resolution of a problem or issue. From this position, an administrator can convey an image of moving toward the solution of a problem and at the same time retain the tactical flexibility to make revisions in response to feedback. There is no question that the incrementalist perspective meshes well with the bureaucratic conservatism and fragmented nature of the policy process and that it creates a comfortable environment for the analytical technician. Careful study and slow, step-by-step development of policy are ideally suited to a process that features many centers of power.

Health-Care Reform

A naive disregard for the advantages of incrementalism accounts in large part for the failure of the Clinton plan for health-care reform to pass Congress in 1994. The plan's principal architect was Ira Magaziner, a liberal health-care guru with a strong penchant for sweeping change rather than incremental adjustment. Hillary Clinton, the second major architect of the plan, was Magaziner's devoted student and powerful political sponsor. The two shared a common approach. According to an administration official, Hillary Clinton "was always of the 'big bang' school." She scathingly dismissed behind their backs those who wanted to go slower—mainly the economic advisers—as "the incrementalists." Gloria Borger described the result: "After endless (secret) health care seminars, they [the Clinton administration] delivered a grand thesis on reform. . . . Trouble was the politicians couldn't stomach either Magaziner's academic fervor or his plan."[4] The *Economist* agreed, accusing Magaziner of acting "like a parody of a consultant, intent on producing a perfect plan and blind to the demands of democratic politics."[5]

The plan suffered in part because it was devised in a politically insulated environment rather than in a politically relevant one. Had President Clinton chosen to have the plan developed by a joint congressional commission that included Republicans and that was headed by a respected legislator—such as Daniel Patrick Moynihan (D-N.Y.), then chair of the Senate Finance Committee—its chances for legislative passage would have been far greater. Democratic congressional leaders compounded the administration's error. According to Moynihan, health-care reform was over "about midday on 6 February 1994," when Democrats controlling the powerful congressional committees decided not to open up the debate to dissenting Republicans.[6]

Finally, an incremental approach to health-care reform would strongly suggest the value of starting from the political center and working outward. Moderates like Moynihan, Senator John Breaux (D-La.), and presidential counselor David Gergen urged the president to take such an approach. But Hillary Clinton's and Magaziner's less incremental approach, one that started at the left and edged toward the center, prevailed with the president. This strategy proved far more vulnerable to opposition attacks and public skepticism.

The Space Program

A major problem with incrementalism, in theory as well as in practice, is that it can provide neither the rationale nor the structure to support areas of public policy that require long-term planning and commitment. This shortsighted, self-interested characteristic of incrementalism seriously undercuts the efforts of policy analysts to provide coherence to the policy process and its goals, just as it has undermined the viability of Social Security and Medicare and efforts to maintain them. America's manned space program has also illustrated the shortcomings of a policy process without either the institutional bases for long-term undertakings or a theoretical model able to provide coherent direction.

Examining the manned space program in 1975, Paul R. Schulman noted that it was one of a species of programs "distinguished by their demand for *comprehensive* rather than incremental decisions; synoptic rather than piecemeal outlooks and vision. These policies are characterized by an *indivisibility* in the political commitment and resources they require for success."[7] He argued that such programs cannot begin in small portions. They require "critical masses" of political and resource commitment at their inception and at crucial points in their implementation.

In response to Sputnik and President John Kennedy's early enthusiasm, the manned space program obtained sufficient support to gain the funding necessary to land a person on the moon. But by the end of the 1960s, the centrifugal forces of policy fragmentation had begun to weaken America's commitment to the space program. Other priorities were crowding onto the public agenda and claiming their share of resources. At the same time, the lessening of support for the space program translated into lowered morale and competence there. The best people left to deal with new challenges, and those who remained did not retain the esprit de corps that had been generated for the lunar landing. Lowered morale made it increasingly difficult to maintain a high level of "hardware reliability and quality control," and insiders began to voice concern about the number of "glitches" occurring in projects.[8]

Programs requiring the level of commitment of the space program are not capable of a "steady-state" existence. They are, Schulman argued, fundamentally unstable. To maintain support at a high level, their administrators must articulate goals that will capture more resources. "The escalation of goals is a major requirement and a major dilemma of non-incremental policy."[9] For a time, the shuttle program instituted by President Nixon provided an important new goal for the space program. But it is clear that before the tragic *Challenger* disaster of January 1986, the space program was again striving for public commitment. That effort included sending civilians into space, which resulted in publicity and—in the cases of Senator Jake Garn of the Senate Appropriations Committee and Congressman Bill Nelson of the House Science and Technology Committee—direct political support.[10]

The public expectation of repeated successes placed pressure on the National Aeronautics and Space Administration (NASA) to continue to produce public events. Some of this was the result of attitudes encouraged by NASA's own public relations. Even the Rogers Commission Report, which was limited to investigating the cause of the *Challenger* accident, noted the "relentless pressure on NASA to increase the flight rate."[11] Situated in a fragmented policy process requiring an immense political effort to sustain continued heavy commitment, NASA was under constant pressure to perform at an exceptionally high level of technological complexity.

Schulman concluded his prescient piece by remarking on the inappropriateness of public policy models based on immediate concerns or self-interest for programs requiring exceptional levels of resources. He suggested that many of America's most serious problems required such programs. Schulman's conclusions indicate that ongoing movement toward important policy goals may require the analyst to assume the role of advocate or at least to become allied with organizations capable of sustained political pressure.

The fate of the superconducting supercollider program reinforced the points Schulman had made. Projected as a 54-mile tunnel in Texas through which atomic particles would be accelerated in the quest for the smallest particle in the universe, the supercollider in 1987 was expected to take several years to complete at a cost of $4.4 billion. By 1993, cost estimates had risen to $11 billion, and despite the completion of 14.7 miles of tunneling and the expenditure of $1.6 billion in federal money, Congress killed the program in that year. Critics of this decision rightly saw it as the triumph of incremental, short-range considerations over "long-term scientific investment."[12]

Despite perceptive critiques of the incrementalist approach, there are no indications that it is about to be replaced or seriously challenged. The simple fact is that it fits exceptionally well with American political culture and institutions. It encourages gradual changes that are minimally threatening to organized interests. It facilitates the maintenance of policy fragmentation and citizen accessibility. And it provides stability and protection for the wary bureaucrat. The continued viability of incrementalist thought and practice ensures that definite limits on the boundaries of policy innovation and levels of programmatic support will remain obstacles to those hoping to wrestle with larger and more lasting goals.

A Fragmented Congress: The More Things Change, the More They Stay the Same

The American preference for weak, accessible government was fairly easy to translate into practice during the lengthy period from Jefferson's election as president in 1800 to Franklin D. Roosevelt's election to that office in 1932. Domestic and foreign policy problems throughout this period (except during the Civil War and World War I) were relatively easy to manage and therefore required little governmental coordination. As a rule, the national government did very little during this period. Numerous state and local governments that afforded a great deal of access to their constituents carried out the bulk of the responsibility of governing.

For its part, the national government replicated to a large extent the highly decentralized pattern set by state and local governments. The dominant branch of the national government was its most fragmented branch, the Congress. The politics of Congress was primarily patronage politics operating on an individual-to-individual or group-to-group basis.[13] Direct dealing with individual congressmen was the hallmark of the system. Coordinated national policymaking was not its purpose.

The Great Depression of the 1930s, and more specifically the election of Franklin D. Roosevelt as president in 1932, brought two fundamental changes to the American political system. First, the balance of power and responsibility shifted decisively from state and local governments to the national government. Second, the focus of leadership *within* the national government shifted from Congress to the president. The president was now expected to provide leadership for the nation as a whole on a continuing basis. This expectation, backed by Congress's massive delegations of power to the executive branch and by a burgeoning bureaucracy with its claims of administrative expertise, clearly placed the president in a preeminent position he had not enjoyed from 1800 to 1932.

Yet even in this new era of vastly expanded national government and presidential preeminence, the American people did not abandon their preference for fragmented government and their desire to have direct access to governmental units. Instead, they made the best adaptation possible under the vastly altered circumstances. The adaptation centered mainly on Congress.

While the president was expected to lead and coordinate, Congress was expected to play a representative role. State interests, district interests, and local interests had representation and access through their congressmen. To perform this function, Congress was expected to remain fragmented. Voters did not elect their senators and representatives to coordinate national policy or to lead the nation. They elected them, as they had in the past, primarily to represent their states and districts.[14]

Congress and the Subgovernment Phenomenon

The subgovernment phenomenon was and is an ingenious adaptation of the public's desire for direct access to the realities of the new era of big government. While not unknown before 1932, subgovernments proliferated and matured after that time. The committees and subcommittees in both houses of Congress are the central points of the subgovernments. They make recommendations to their parent bodies concerning the authorization and funding of government programs.[15] These recommendations are frequently, if not always, adopted by the House or Senate without major changes because rarely is either body in a position to challenge the expertise of the committees and especially the subcommittees.

A congressman typically seeks membership on committees or subcommittees that will give him power over programs of particular importance to his state or district. Many constituents with a strong interest in certain government programs belong to well-organized interest groups seeking direct access to the part of the government that oversees these programs. A link of mutual political advantage is formed between the congressman and the key interest groups in the district or state. The interest groups gain direct access, through the congressman and his committee, to the part of the decision-making process that directly concerns them. The congressman gains the political support of the interest groups, often in the form of campaign contributions for an upcoming election.

The congressman's committee or subcommittee and the concerned interest groups form two parts of a subgovernment. The third part is the agency in the executive branch that administers the programs of direct concern to the congressman's committee and the interest group. The agency is linked to the congressional committee or subcommittee because the authorizations and appropriations it needs usually depend on the committee or subcommittee recommendations. Interest groups that establish links with the pertinent committee or subcommittee of Congress also often serve as the clientele for agency programs and in the implementation of programs can provide a grass-roots political base for the agency. Thus, a three-way linkup of mutual interest, sometimes depicted as a triangle, is formed between the committee or subcommittee, the affected groups, and the appropriate executive agency. Obviously, analysts employed by congressional subcommittees and interest groups have a clear sense of the policy directions in which their work should be pointed. But the subgovernment relationship works its will on agencies as well and encourages the "proper" orientation of analysts there also. It is quite possible, of course, for the participants in a policy issue to accept the general validity of analytical findings but to disagree about their importance. In such cases, the policy analyst has contributed to framing debate, even though the form of the final decision will rest with the policymakers themselves.

The triangular schema is in many ways an accurate description of parts of the American policy process and is often useful in describing day-to-day policy dynamics. As used here, the idea of policy subgovernments also encompasses the broader idea of policy networks, which include the possibility of vertical, "picket fence" relationships among national, state, and local actors in particular policy areas. Within subgovernments, common professional, personal, and ideological associations influence not only policy preferences but also the beliefs that support them. Subgovernments are, then, more than good working relationships. They are the creators, preservers, and promulgators of particular values.

In 1995, with the appearance of a Republican majority in the House and Senate, the number of subcommittees in the House was substantially reduced. This organizational change was accompanied in some instances by legislation creating block-grant program funding. By eliminating funding for individual programs, the block grants weakened the access of interest and clientele groups to agency personnel and to the financial support designed specifically for them. Thus, through organizational change within Congress and legislation that severely weakened claims by special interests on the U.S. Treasury, Congress seriously diluted the force of some subgovernments. Other subgovernments, such as the powerful one protecting the interests of veterans, remained essentially undisturbed.

Students of the policy process have noted that over the past few decades, subgovernments have been increasingly subject to interests external to those involved in the core relationships. With regard to the agricultural subgovernments, for example, environmental interests have at times raised concerns about the use of particular pesticides, and advocates for the poor have insisted on the availability of surplus agricultural products for their clients. In other subgovernments, such as education and housing, civil rights groups have insisted on being heard. Often, these interventions into the cozy triangular relationships originate in advocacy groups or policy study groups. In such contexts, policy analysts can occasionally be exceptionally influential in shaping policy on specific issues.

While these subgovernmental relationships are most salient at the national level, they also exist at state and local levels, for any competent agency director will recognize the need to build a base of political support. Similarly, the student of policy analysis must develop awareness of the networks within which his or her proposals will be considered and formulate strategies that alleviate suspicion, uncertainty, and opposition whenever possible.

Congress and Constituent

The subgovernment phenomenon greatly increases direct access to contemporary "big government" largely on a group-to-group basis. Constituent services, in contrast, increase citizen access largely on an individual-to-individual basis. Like the subgovernments, constituent services have proliferated since 1932. Also like subgovernments, they are sustained as much by public expectations as by congressmen's wishes. Both subgovernments and constituent services are devices by which congressmen bring an impersonal national government "down home" to the voters in the states and localities.

The nature of constituent services is illustrated by a communication sent by former congressman Charles Wiggins to his constituents in the 39th Congressional District of California. "Need Help with a Federal Problem?" asks the headline. The communication goes on to advise the constituent: "If you are experiencing a problem with Social Security, educational assistance, Veterans Administration, Immigration, Internal Revenue Service, Postal Service, Environmental Protection Agency, Federal Energy Office, or any other federal agency, please contact me through this office."[16]

The enormous amount of time a congressman spends on constituent services is a further impediment to coordinated policymaking by Congress. As one congressman observed, "One reason we are not able to formulate better national policy is because we have become the ombudsman and the last hope of individuals who are despairing of dealing with the federal bureaucracy." Yet Congress has consistently refused to act to improve direct administrative access for citizens and thereby relieve its members of their role as political intermediaries.

In fragmenting its operations through subgovernments and constituent services, Congress has retained to a remarkable extent the highly particularized group-to-group and individual-to-individual politics that characterized its operations from 1800 to 1932. Congressmen believe, and the evidence clearly supports them, that they are acting in accord with what the public expects. A 1978 poll, for example, showed that while the public rated Congress *as a collective body* poorly (31 percent approval), they rated *their particular congressman* highly (62 percent approval).[17] Congressmen are well aware that their reelection depends much more on their performance as individual representatives than on the performance of Congress as a collective body.

The 1970s: Fragmentation Prospers in a Decade of Congressional Reform

During the 1970s, Congress instituted the most important procedural reforms since the House of Representatives stripped its Speaker of his far-reaching powers in 1910. The reformers of the 1970s did not set their sights on the fragmented structure of Congress. Instead, they sought primarily to democratize its internal procedures. By concentrating on the latter while deemphasizing the former, they increased the fragmentation that already existed.

Two important results of the reforms were (1) a dramatic decrease in the power of committee chairmen, and (2) an equally dramatic increase in the powers of subcommittees and their chairmen. Before the 1970s, it had been virtually impossible to remove a committee chairman once the seniority rule had placed him on his perch. (The seniority rule mandated that the committee chairman be the majority party member with the longest continuous service on the committee.) During the 1970s, the Democrats, acting as the majority party in both the House and Senate, asserted their right to vote on, and if necessary remove, all committee chairmen. In 1975, House Democrats voted to remove three committee chairmen under the new rules. In 1973, House Democrats had enacted a "Subcommittee Bill of Rights" that sharply curtailed a committee chairman's power over the subcommittees under his jurisdiction.[18] For the most part, the powers lost by committee chairmen were not transferred to party leaders (who might have coordinated Congress) but to subcommittee chairmen and individual members. This further fragmented Congress and strengthened the subgovernment system.

The effect of increased subcommittee power was to narrow even further the policymaking incentives of congressmen and interest groups. When power rested at the committee level, and primarily with the chairman, there was an incentive to coordinate policy, at least at that level. The chairman could pressure the members of different subcommittees to modify and combine their particular preferences into a bill acceptable to him or to the entire committee. Interest groups, working through a particular subcommittee, would likewise have to modify and combine their particular preferences with those of other interest groups in order to get a favorable bill.

The rise of subcommittee power in the 1970s drastically weakened these incentives. Because they could no longer be pressured to modify and combine their policy preferences, subcommittee chairmen and members were more likely to insist on their narrow policy preferences and to align their careers more closely with the small number of interest groups advocating them. Similarly, interest groups were encouraged to insist on their narrow preferences while concentrating exclusively on sympathetic subcommittees.[19] James Sundquist observed that in the postreform environment, "what begins as piecemeal consideration of problems in subcommittees of limited jurisdiction continues as piecemeal action through the legislative process."[20] The effects of this process on efforts to coordinate such areas as environmental policy or health policy are, of course, disastrous. At the same time, the increased fragmentation further encourages the advocacy role of the policy analyst. Whether employed by an interest group or subcommittee, analysts inevitably find themselves moving in narrower political channels. In this environment, concerns about the overall effects of a policy position on health care, for example, may be rather easily replaced by intense support for the narrower interests of hospitals or the medical profession.

The 1970s: What Congress Did Not Do

To say that Congress deemphasized coordination of its fragmented procedures in the 1970s is not to say it gave the matter no attention at all. But with the notable exception of changes in its budgeting procedures, the efforts Congress gave to coordinating its internal procedures came to very little. In these attempts to make the legislative process more coherent and rational, policy analysts supporting change were badly battered by the political power of organized interests that wished to maintain the free rein given to issue advocacy.

Both houses established special committees to make recommendations about how to improve the coordination of internal procedures. The Bolling Committee, established by the House of Representatives for this purpose, recommended reducing the number of committees and subcommittees and altering their jurisdiction. The Bolling proposals encountered determined resistance, much of it in the form of "reverse lobbying."

Normal lobbying occurs when an interest group exerts pressure on congressmen or their staffs. In the case of the Bolling proposals, congressmen and their staffs exerted pressure on the interest groups to lobby against the proposals. Congressmen, their staffs, and affected interest groups all saw a danger to long-standing links of mutual influence within subgovernments. As a result, the Bolling proposals were rejected or greatly weakened.[21] For example, in moves to appease key labor unions and their congressional supporters, the Education and Labor Committee was kept intact, the Post Office and Civil Service Committee was retained, and the Merchant Marine and Fisheries Committee was strengthened rather than weakened. The continued dominance of these centers of power also had unhappy ramifications for the concept of coherent administrative policy in the executive branch. Attempts to rationalize agency structure through reorganization faced the same kinds of pressures as the Bolling proposals from committees and interests that saw their areas of jurisdiction and access threatened by changes in agency structure and personnel. Finally, the *intensity* of the opposition aroused to proposals for greater legislative and administrative coordination has provided an added impediment to comprehensive analysis and planning within the subgovernment network.

A clear contrast emerges between the enthusiasm and determination with which Congress democratized and fragmented its internal procedures and the lack of enthusiasm when efforts to consolidate and coordinate those procedures were under way. Lack of enthusiasm has likewise been the response to proposals, often made by experts outside Congress, to strengthen the party leadership apparatus in Congress while weakening the power of special-interest groups. Such proposals are usually championed as legitimate political devices to centralize and coordinate the internal workings of Congress.

In this regard, Everett Carll Ladd proposed that federal funding be extended to congressional election campaigns. Party committees in each house would administer these federal funds. The funds therefore would go only to central party organs, not directly to candidates. Candidates could raise funds from special-interest groups, but the amounts that such groups could give would be very strictly limited.[22] The purpose of Ladd's proposal was clearly to strengthen the two broad-based national parties as centralizing and coordinating forces in Congress while weakening the power of narrowly based special-interest groups that fragment that body. Congressmen, interest groups, and the public at large all tend to regard strong parties in Congress as an impediment to direct relations between congressmen and their constituents. Therefore, nothing was done in the 1970s to strengthen parties at the expense of interest groups.

On the contrary, in 1973, Congress took action that had the opposite effect. Prompted by business and labor groups, it amended Section 611 of the U.S. Code to allow corporations with government contracts (which included most large corporations) to form political action committees (PACs) that would enable these corporations to contribute money to congressional campaigns. Corporate motives in supporting this change were obvious. The AFL-CIO, however, was motivated by the fear that its political action committee (Committee on Political Education) might soon be included under the Section 611 ban on PACs, because it had a number of manpower training contracts with the federal government.[23]

The amendment of Section 611 was one of several factors that contributed to the explosion in the number of PACs in the 1970s and 1980s. Between 1974 and 1982, the total number of PACs registered with the Federal Election Commission rose from 608 to 3,371.[24] By strengthening PACs, Congress further contributed to its own fragmentation as a legislative body. PACs concentrate on narrow issues and work with congressmen individually, and their advocacy of self-interested or ideologically rigid values has seriously hindered the development of a general normative framework for coherent policy. In contrast to political parties, PACs have little interest in coordinating policy from a national perspective. At the fund-raising and governing stages of politics, PACs are the institutional competitors of political parties.[25] The sizable boost Congress gave to the former therefore served to weaken further the coordinating powers of the latter.

The activities of the "reform decade" of the 1970s did little to change Congress's historical tradition as a highly fragmented body. Indeed, the end of the decade found Congress more divided than ever before. The reasons for this outcome are not difficult to discern. The public expectations of congressmen (that they be first and foremost representatives of their states and districts) did not change during the decade. Therefore, their basic incentives did not change. Reforms that did not conflict with these basic incentives (democratizing congressional procedures) fared very well. Those that did conflict (consolidating and coordinating the committee structures, strengthening the role of parties) had little or no success.

It is, of course, true that Congress has continued to pass major legislation in fairly coherent form over the past three decades. And during the 1980s, the postreform leadership in both houses was occasionally able to draw on sufficient political and parliamentary resources to circumvent the "normal" legislative process and pass significant legislation in a number of areas, including Social Security reform and Gramm-Rudman budgetary controls. Barbara Sinclair traced the ability of the House leadership to use the Rules Committee, persuasion, and coalition building to move legislation through the House. But despite occasional leadership triumphs in that body, Sinclair concluded that House "leaders' resources for directly influencing members' behavior are severely limited."[26] Based on her case studies from the late 1970s and early 1980s, she described leadership control as "tenuous" and heavily dependent on other factors for success in the legislative process.[27] The meteoric rise and decline of Speaker Newt Gingrich in many ways confirms this view.

The 1990s: Congressional Reform Republican-Style

In the landmark 1994 congressional elections, Republicans gained control of both houses of Congress for the first time in forty years. In their much publicized "Contract with America," Republican candidates for the House promised the voters that they would address a wide variety of issues by bringing pertinent legislation to a vote in the House. The very first "contract issues" tackled by the House Republicans in January 1995 dealt with reforms in House procedures. Not since the 1970s had so much attention been given to congressional reform, and in the House, the country witnessed a degree of leadership control unmatched since the early years of the century.

The resulting changes, however, did little to alter the basic pattern of fragmented power in Congress, and, on balance, they increased it somewhat. For example, the new House rules required that committee meetings be open to the public. Only in extreme circumstances, involving such matters as national security or incriminating information, could meetings be closed. Although closed committee meetings have been the exception since the "sunshine laws" of the 1970s, committees had previously been able to close their meetings without stating their justification for doing so. The Republicans simply carried the emphasis on open meetings one step further. Experience indicates that increasing the openness of committee meetings enhances the access and power of organized lobbies and interest groups and that this, in turn, furthers fragmentation in Congress.

House Republicans did make some changes that *reduced* fragmentation within Congress, but only slightly. Three committees (District of Columbia, Merchant Marine and Fisheries, and Post Office) were eliminated in a streamlining move, and the reduction of subcommittees for most committees reduced the number of access points for organized interests. But, on balance, Republican reforms stayed within the historic pattern of congressional reform—a pattern that has fairly consistently honored and enhanced fragmentation.[28]

Discontinuity and Fragmentation

A strong argument can be made that a high level of discontinuity in the leadership and membership of Congress makes the fragmentation of power within that body more prevalent. If this is valid, other Republican proposals regarding Congress could be expected to increase the dispersion of power even more. These included, for example, limiting the terms of committee chairs to six years and the term of the Speaker of the House to eight years. Even more sweeping would be the term limits on all members of Congress proposed in the Republican "Contract with America." By the year 2000, this change depended on the increasingly unlikely passage of a constitutional amendment. But if such an amendment were to be ratified, it would reduce continuity in the leadership and membership of Congress and inevitably increase the volatility of power relationships within the national legislature. Thus, like the liberal Democratic reformers of the 1970s, conservative Republican reformers of the 1990s honored and (for the most part) strengthened conditions that encourage institutional fragmentation.

Republicans and Party Discipline

Although the structural and procedural reforms favored by the congressional Republicans did little to change the fragmentation of power in Congress, party discipline, especially in the House of Representatives, created a more centralized and coordinated power structure than Congress had witnessed for well over half a century. The driving force behind this development was Speaker of the House Newt Gingrich. Most House Republicans in 1995 believed that they owed their newfound majority status to the tireless efforts of their new Speaker. This perception created the loyalty that provided Gingrich with a host of dedicated lieutenants and a working majority of loyal foot soldiers among the Republican rank and file in the House.

In his first months as Speaker, Gingrich defied tradition by ignoring seniority and handpicking committee chairs on the basis of party loyalty. In addition, he established task forces to focus on specific issues and frame them into legislation in a fashion that paralleled the usual functioning of a House committee. Employing the power of party discipline, the Gingrich-led House voted, as promised, on all the items in the "Contract with America" and passed a great many of them in the first hundred days of the 104th Congress. Nevertheless, this remarkable degree of centralization and coordination of power depended to an extraordinary extent on the new Speaker's dynamic personality. This fact alone rendered it fragile. Were anything to blunt the Gingrich mystique among the electorate and/or the House Republicans, the whole system of centralized power that he fashioned might falter. In that case, the traditional fragmentation of congressional structures and procedures would be certain to reassert itself.

This appears to have been what happened. As he tried to balance conservative ideology with leadership of the House, Gingrich found himself in increasing difficulty—a difficulty compounded when he was investigated by the House Ethics Committee. After the 1996 elections, he was forced to fend off an embarrassing challenge from within the party to his position as Speaker. Gingrich met this challenge with a strong assertion of power, but when the Republicans in the House lost seats in an off-year election in 1998, his aura of political invincibility faded perceptibly, and he abruptly announced his resignation from Congress. After Gingrich's authoritarian leadership, J. Dennis Hastert's approach to the speakership represented a marked contrast in style. As Tom DeLay, the majority whip, described this difference for the *New York Times*, "Denny has a completely different style—thank God. . . . Newt had to drive everything and control everything and didn't believe in the committee system at all; Denny's just the opposite."[29] Inevitably, the forces of fragmentation within the House began once again to dominate the policy process.

The impeachment process against President Clinton demonstrated that institutional fragmentation can supersede ideological and partisan agreement. Although the Republicans in the House impeached the president by a narrow margin, they found little help from their colleagues in the Senate. Clearly, Senate Majority Leader Trent Lott knew he did not have sufficient support for conviction of the president, and this undoubtedly contributed to the truncated approach taken to the issue in the Senate. The senators, however, tended to portray themselves as more deliberate, flexible, and less rigidly partisan than the House members, a view growing out of the institutional differences between the two houses and one that surely rankled those in the larger body.[30] On the other hand, comments like the one made by Bob Barr, a House manager of the Senate trial, that "a senator's attention span is probably less than an average juror's, so we'll have to simplify, simplify, simplify" were hardly conducive to building sympathy within the smaller chamber.[31]

THE PRESIDENCY: THE PROBLEM OF FRAGMENTATION IN THE "LEADERSHIP BRANCH"

After 1932, Americans' expectations of the president (unlike their expectations of Congress) underwent a dramatic change. Before 1932, presidents were expected to assert themselves as national leaders only on an intermittent basis. The Great Depression and World War II changed that modest view permanently. The president was now expected to exercise strong national leadership on a continuing basis. The president's job was to chart the nation's course and to coordinate national policies in order to follow that course. Yet even in the "leadership branch," the problem of fragmentation, while not nearly as severe as in Congress, presents serious problems for coordinating public policy.

Presidential Nominations: Reforms Bring Fragmentation

During the late 1960s and 1970s, the Democratic Party enacted historic changes in the way it nominates its presidential candidates. There are interesting parallels between those reforms and the procedural reforms enacted by Congress in roughly the same period. Both sought, with great success, to democratize procedures. In doing this, both radically reduced the powers of established leaders who had helped coordinate operations. Yet neither provided new leadership centers to assume responsibility for coordination. The congressional reforms weakened committee chairmen. The Democratic Party reforms weakened traditional party leaders outside Congress. In both cases, special-interest groups filled a large part of the power vacuum. And in both cases, changes initiated by Democrats led to similar changes by Republicans.

The decline of traditional leaders in the Democratic and Republican Parties led to the decline of an important coordinating function these leaders had performed: coalition building and the construction of minimal normative consensus. Three decades ago, party leaders had the power to pressure special-interest groups to modify their demands as the price of becoming part of a national party coalition that could win the presidency. Using this power, party leaders could act as a buffer between presidential candidates and special-interest groups, especially during the presidential nomination phase. In the postreform era, party leaders are much more limited in their power to modify the demands of special-interest groups on the party or on presidential candidates.

Candidates for the presidential nomination are more than ever dependent on the direct support and approval of special-interest groups.[32] Public postures they must take on behalf of these groups during the quest for party nomination or renomination may render them less able, if nominated and elected, to coordinate public policies for the nation. In 1984, Walter Mondale's highly visible strategy of seeking advance endorsements for the Democratic Party's nomination from labor groups, women's groups, and minority groups led to the damaging public perception that this tactic had compromised him as a national leader.

Ronald Reagan was far more successful for a number of reasons. As the long-time leader of the insurgent conservative movement against established party leaders in the Republican Party, he had probably internalized the programmatic agenda of conservative interest groups more than Mondale had internalized the agendas of corresponding liberal groups. Thus, Reagan projected a stronger image of genuine conviction to the voters. Moreover, in 1980, the general public was moving more in Reagan's conservative direction than in the Democratic Party's liberal direction.

Yet Reagan, like Mondale, was nominated in the postreform environment of strong special-interest groups and weak party leaders. Acting in accord with key items on the agenda of conservative interest groups, President Reagan successfully urged Congress to enact an extremely ambitious military buildup and a package of large tax cuts. In these and other important initiatives, the Reagan people drew heavily on the recommendations of conservative policy analysts from such think tanks as the Heritage Foundation, the Hoover Institution, Claremont Institute, and the American Enterprise Institute. In fact, since the Nixon administration, a fairly extensive network of conservative academic and nonacademic thinkers interested in policy questions had developed. This network meshed easily with the Reagan administration's people and their goals.

Moderate Republican leaders, who were less closely identified with these groups, were concerned from the outset about lack of policy coordination in the Reagan program. How could huge tax cuts finance a huge military buildup? What about the traditional Republican adage that large deficits arise when taxing and spending policies are not coordinated?[33] By 1986, the concerns of the moderates had proved to be prophetic. Even though Reagan was one of the politically strongest and most popular presidents since FDR, his unbalanced fiscal policies raised serious questions about whether any president nominated largely through the influence of interest groups would have the ability to coordinate national public policies. Unlike other postwar Republican presidents, Reagan at least had a majority in the Senate during the first six years of his administration. But the loss of the Senate in 1986 opened the door wider to interest-group politics, and the president's ability to lead dissipated rapidly.

President Clinton also experienced the limitations imposed by a fragmented national government. Although weakened by the fact that Congress was under Republican control for most of his administration, Clinton did achieve significant early policy victories with the North American Free Trade Agreement (NAFTA) and budgetary reform. Nonetheless, much of his administration was characterized by proposals more limited in scope (e.g., reducing teenage smoking, violence in the entertainment media, tinkering with Medicare), and many of these offerings seemed to be in response to the opinion polls that Clinton consulted constantly. They resulted in such a limited form of leadership that Maureen Dowd of the *New York Times* dubbed his administration "the pothole presidency."

The Endless Struggle for Executive Coordination

The executive branch of the national government is composed of thirteen separate departments and 120 special agencies that together employ nearly 3 million civilian employees.[34] Although the president is referred to as the "chief executive" of this vast bureaucracy, his power to coordinate its activities is extremely limited. Of the 3 million civilian bureaucrats, only about 2,700 can be hired or removed at the president's pleasure. The rest are career civil servants, who are hired and fired according to merit principles determined by the Office of Personnel Management.[35]

The primary loyalty of career civil servants is to their agency (which is their permanent working environment and economic support system), rather than to the president (who is to them a temporary political phenomenon). At the top of the career bureaucracy are approximately 4,000 men and women with considerable policymaking powers.[36] Over the years, many of them have established durable relationships with pertinent interest groups and congressmen on key committees and subcommittees. In so doing, they have become one of the links in the subgovernment triangles.

Standing between the president and the career bureaucracy are cabinet and subcabinet officials who serve at the president's pleasure and are supposed to manage their departments and agencies according to the president's priorities. In theory, these officials are "the president's people"; in practice, they are more often "people in the middle." They are subject to pressures from the president and his White House staff and at the same time are expected to respond sympathetically to more narrow agency interests articulated by career administrators who may be supported by key congressmen and clientele interest groups. Although the balancing acts required of cabinet and subcabinet officials at the national level are most salient among the media and general public, the political and administrative cross pressures these officials face are common to politically appointed administrators at any level of the American system. Such conditions can put severe strains on the integrity of the policy analyst, who, caught in the cross pressures of bureaucratic politics, may face subtle and not so subtle pressures to shade and skew findings to fit political needs or expectations. In many instances, however, an analyst may justifiably insist that his or her agency's position requires that a particular emphasis be given the results of a study.

Under these circumstances, it is not surprising that cabinet and subcabinet officials have divided loyalties and often displease the chief executives who appoint them. The phenomenon of divided loyalties helps explain why repeated attempts by presidents to coordinate executive policy through their cabinets (often called "cabinet government") have typically ended in failure. It can also explain why agencies presented with proposals that appear eminently rational in their approach to problems fail to act forthrightly or coherently to implement these ideas.

Strategies for Fighting Bureaucratic Fragmentation

All postwar presidents have expressed frustration at their inability to coordinate policy through the executive branch. Major expansions of the federal bureaucracy in the domestic area have resulted from the initiatives of liberal Democratic presidents who have been primarily interested in establishing substantive programs reaching particular segments of the population. Republican presidents, on the other hand, have often been ideologically unsympathetic to these programs and in any event have been uniformly more interested in achieving administrative efficiency in program implementation. Consequently, recent Republican presidents have found the political power and fragmentation of the bureaucracy particularly frustrating,[37] and they have worked at making it more responsive to their direction. Both Nixon and Reagan provide instructive examples of the possibilities that exist for moving toward a more coherent and presidentially responsive bureaucracy.

What is of particular note with regard to the management efforts of Nixon and Reagan is their recognition of the political forces at work in their administrations and in the intergovernmental implementation of programs. In contrast, President Johnson largely overlooked these political forces by seeking increased control through the Planning, Programming, Budgeting System (PPBS) approach, which he ordered instituted throughout the government in 1965. Johnson no doubt found PPBS attractive because it necessitated the definition of policy goals at the highest levels and then moved resources in line with these goals. In this emphasis on policy outputs, PPBS directly challenged the traditional line-item approach to budgeting, which had become a staple of agency power and incremental policymaking. Furthermore, PPBS was no respecter of organizational boundaries or interests. As B. Guy Peters put it, "In short, PPBS was a dagger pointed toward the central role of the agency in policymaking in the federal government, and as such it could not really have been expected to be successful."[38]

With its emphasis on program outputs, PPBS may in retrospect stand as a turning point in the primary focus of public budgeting theory. As a technique for increased executive control of the bureaucracy, however, it foundered on the opposition of an entire system built around fragmented power. Perhaps somewhat wiser because of President Johnson's experience, Presidents Nixon and Reagan approached the problem of control from routes that did not so blatantly challenge vested power interests. They had concluded that effective program administration required something more politically tangible and persuasive than analytical prowess.

Soon after taking office, Richard Nixon gave up hope of coordinating the executive bureaucracy through his cabinet members. Instead, he used his White House staff as a "counterbureaucracy." Unlike cabinet members, White House staffers have a working environment incontestably dominated by the president, and they must therefore manifest an undivided loyalty to him. Nixon directed his White House staff to oversee an increasing number of bureaucratic activities. Final clearance for bureaucratic initiative was largely transferred from cabinet members to White House staffers.

The "counterbureaucracy" strategy backfired in an ironic way. To exert control over bureaucratic policymaking, Nixon's White House staffers found it necessary to become increasingly involved in administrative details. As they became deeply involved in details, they had less time to oversee important areas of bureaucratic policymaking. Career bureaucrats were increasingly able to make important policy decisions without clearance from a harried White House staff.[39] As a result, policy advocacy moved by default from the White House to the less-coordinated domain of agency turf.

In his second term, Nixon turned to a different strategy of asserting presidential control. He decided to elevate several of his most loyal and effective cabinet members to the status of supersecretaries overseeing clusters of government departments in broad functional areas. The role and size of the White House staff were largely curtailed in Nixon's second term, although three top-level White House staffers were assigned to help the supersecretaries "integrate and unify policies and operations throughout the executive branch."[40] This strategy of presidential control was launched just at the time the Watergate scandals crashed down on the Nixon administration. The scandals weakened and finally destroyed the administration and, along with it, Nixon's second-term effort at presidential control of the bureaucracy.

Ronald Reagan's strategy for asserting presidential control of the bureaucracy was less complex but at the same time more effective than Richard Nixon's. Reagan concentrated mainly on the appointments process. Nixon learned, only after some costly mistakes, that appointing administration loyalists to subcabinet posts was as important as appointing loyalists to cabinet posts. The Reagan administration understood and acted on this axiom from the beginning. Moreover, more than any previous administration, it also emphasized the importance of placing Reagan loyalists in appointive positions *below* the subcabinet level. The Reagan administration thus was able to penetrate more deeply into the executive bureaucracy than any before it and to establish a level of ideological consistency unmatched by any previous administration.

Like Nixon, Reagan recognized the importance of appointees' loyalty to the administration. The Reagan administration, however, was more thorough in the measures it took to ensure that loyalty. In filling some 430 appointive posts, it sought three or four finalists for each post. Interviews conducted by Reagan staffers with eight to ten people who knew each candidate were instrumental in the decision process. Appointees were expected to be loyal to Ronald Reagan and to the conservative movement. Since Reagan had led that movement within the Republican Party since 1968, the two loyalties were mutually reinforcing.

To maintain a high level of loyalty among appointees, the administration utilized, to an unusual degree, an orientation process separate from the bureaucracy. During the transition period, cabinet members learned about their departments from conservative task forces rather than from career personnel in their agencies. Several breakfast meetings with numerous subcabinet appointees were held each year and featured President Reagan, Vice President Bush, and high-level White House or cabinet officials as speakers.[41] If policymakers in uncertain situations tend to act from their political convictions, as the studies examined in chapter 2 suggest, then it seems likely that the Reagan approach to personnel recruitment had the effect of creating a reasonably homogeneous normative framework for the consideration of policy recommendations.

By the end of Reagan's first term in office, his administration had proven more successful than its predecessors in moving the executive bureaucracy in directions desired by the president. Nevertheless, there were severe limits even on Reagan's relatively successful strategy. One of the most important of these was that Congress, as well as the president, has much to say about how the executive bureaucracy functions. Thus, Congress was able to blunt or block many initiatives of Reagan appointees when they were perceived as too zealous in their attempts to redefine or ignore the clear intent of laws specifying the objectives of executive agencies, such as the Environmental Protection Agency. Still, given the broad initiatives undertaken against many bureaucratic interests, the administration was relatively free from internal conflicts. Clearly, the strong ideological stance of the White House encouraged analyses that fit its views and muted analyses that did not.

At the same time, congressmen continued to have an interest in keeping the executive branch as fragmented as possible in order to increase their direct access and that of their interest-group allies to agency personnel. The Reagan administration demonstrated imagination and political effectiveness in attacking sub-government strongholds through the use of block grants. Unlike categorical grants, which are directed at specific programs and administered by bureaucratic specialists who develop close ties with clientele and congressional subcommittees, block grants eliminate many of the specific requirements that necessitate bureaucratic monitoring. They make funds available for general purposes whose details are decided by state and local governments. The block-grant approach generated considerable political support among state and local officials. This backing counteracted the power of the subgovernments, which also found their agency components under heavy budgetary pressures from the Reagan administration's attacks on domestic spending. The results of the Reagan efforts to repackage domestic spending suggest that this approach weakened administrative resistance to presidential directives and that it may have engendered new political networks, perhaps resembling the subgovernment model, at state and local levels.

THE CRISIS OF FRAGMENTED GOVERNMENT: THE LOSS OF FISCAL DISCIPLINE

The American preference for the fragmented forms of the governmental system has made policy coordination in the budgetary process particularly difficult to achieve. The costs of fragmented government were tolerable under the conditions of high prosperity and rapid economic growth that characterized the 1945–65 period. After that time, however, the economy became less prosperous. Slowly but surely, awareness grew that fragmented government could not set spending priorities or control spending in an increasingly difficult economic environment. Efforts to achieve fiscal discipline by coordinating governmental machinery began in the 1970s. Most noticeably at the federal level, these efforts have been under continual strain, partly because they have in many instances threatened the very existence of particular subgovernments. At times, their failure ushered in the danger of a complete breakdown of fiscal discipline.

The Rise and Fall of the Budget Process in Congress

In 1974, Congress established budget committees for each of its two houses. These committees were charged with establishing spending limits for each of the seventeen broad categories in the federal budget.[42] The two committees were expected to bring fiscal coordination and discipline to the numerous other committees and subcommittees that had failed to accomplish either goal in the past.

Although the creation of the budget committees was the most significant step Congress took toward coordinating its procedures in the 1970s, the inherent limits of the process working effectively on its own were severe. A floor vote of either house could overturn the recommendations of its budget committee in favor of the recommendations of its older fragmented and logrolling committees. From the outset, it seemed clear that only with the help of strong presidential leadership would the budget committees win decisive victories for budgetary coordination and fiscal discipline.

In 1981, President Reagan provided such leadership and exercised it largely through the two budget committees. By presenting his proposals for an unprecedented $40 billion in spending cuts to the budget committees and insisting on quick, decisive action on their recommendations, the president forced Congress to vote on broad rather than narrow categories of spending. The older logrolling committees and subcommittees simply did not have time to break these broad categories down into their program-size components and to rally affected interest groups to restore funds for their programs.[43]

Unfortunately, the triumph of the presidentially activated budget committees did not last after 1981. Despite his budget cuts, President Reagan's own budget was badly out of balance and poorly coordinated, partly because of massive defense increases that had to be financed in the face of huge tax cuts. The budget committee leaders were willing to compromise on a number of their own program priorities in order to restore fiscal discipline through the new budget process, but the president was considerably less willing to do so. When the budget committee chairmen and other congressional leaders suggested a bipartisan compromise, which included raising taxes and lowering the growth rate of military spending as a way of reducing federal deficits, the president abandoned the two committee leaders and the new budget process.

By the summer of 1983, the press was reporting that President Reagan "would be perfectly happy to see the budget process fall on its face" rather than alter his priorities on military spending and taxes. Secretary of Defense Caspar Weinberger stated that the president had referred to the new budget process as a "Rube Goldberg machine."[44] Left on their own, the budget committees could win no more decisive victories for fiscal discipline and budgetary coordination. Annual federal deficits ballooned from $60 billion to more than $200 billion in 1986.

The Gramm-Rudman Proposal: An Attempt at Fiscal Coordination by Shotgun

The budget process had been the main hope of congressmen who wished to discipline and coordinate fiscal policy within the Congress. This proved to be impossible without strong presidential leadership that could wrench Congress out of its normal pattern of fragmented decision making and forge a coordinated policy between the two houses of Congress and the president. When President Reagan proved unwilling to lead a sustained bipartisan effort to achieve these objectives, an atmosphere of desperation began to grow in Congress. In this context, the Gramm-Rudman proposal passed both houses of Congress and was signed into law by President Reagan at the end of 1985. The proposal—a kind of self-imposed "shotgun marriage" between the president and Congress—was intended to force the president and Congress to make the compromises necessary to coordinate and discipline fiscal policy. Significantly, Gramm-Rudman became law without going through normal congressional procedures and thus avoided the fragmentation and delay that it would have faced in public hearings, committee debate, and debate on the House floor. Although not formalized, the short-circuiting of congressional procedures became a common approach to dealing with major budget, tax, and Social Security legislation under the Reagan administration.[45]

The Gramm-Rudman bill, passed in December 1985, set a strict timetable for eliminating federal deficits by 1991. The 1986 deficit target was set at $171.9 billion; the 1987 target would drop to $144 billion. In each successive year, deficits would be reduced by $36 billion until they were eliminated in 1991.[46] The "shotgun" feature of the law was straightforward. If the president and Congress could not reach an agreement in any given year about how the deficit should be reduced, deficit reduction would proceed according to an automatic formula that would largely displace both the president and Congress from the process.

The formula designed for the 1987 budget illustrated how the process would work. By 3 February, the president had to recommend deficit reduction legislation, and by 15 June, Congress had to complete it. If the predicted deficit exceeded that year's $144 billion target by more than $10 billion, the General Accounting Office was to formulate across-the-board spending reductions. Approximately one-half of these cuts were to be made in defense spending and one-half in domestic spending. Gramm-Rudman exempted in advance two large spending areas (Social Security and interest on the national debt) and some smaller, less costly social programs aimed at helping mainly the poor. Without question, Gramm-Rudman was an admission by congressmen of their inability to overcome the entrenched fragmentation they had encouraged. Its passage indicated that the inability of the federal government to coordinate fiscal policy (the most basic policy of all) had reached a crisis stage in the minds of the nation's highest elected officials.

In another sense, Gramm-Rudman may have been one of policy analysis's finer moments in the national policy process. The measure was based on a thoughtful judgment of the dangers posed by continued fiscal irresponsibility. Its approach to fiscal discipline combined analytical understanding of the problem, a fine sense of timing, and a knowledgeable anticipation of the realities of the congressional process. Thus, the analytical findings suggesting an effective approach were tempered by reasonable political compromises (e.g., on Social Security) and by providing Congress and the president with an opportunity to reach agreement on their own. But the bottom line on the legislation was that it moved national budget policy in a rational, deliberate manner toward greater control and responsibility. Imposition of the remaining automatic cuts would drastically reduce, or eliminate, many popular domestic programs cherished by Congress and many defense programs cherished by the president. The automatic formula would largely replace both the president's priorities and those of Congress. The supporters of Gramm-Rudman reasoned that the president and Congress would find the prospect of invoking the automatic formula so repugnant that they would be forced to reach their own compromises on deficit reduction.

Gramm-Rudman was launched in a sea of doubt concerning how long the shotgun marriage between the two branches could last, or if it would work at all. The core problem remained one of coordination. As various groups of Americans actually began to experience the effects of automatic slashes in domestic programs, they might successfully lobby Congress to add those programs to the original list of exemptions. Similarly, as slashes in defense spending programs were made, the president might insist on their exemption in the name of national security.

Gramm-Rudman, while very dramatic, was only a law. It neither changed basic political relationships nor modified Americans' normative attachment to divided government. It could therefore be easily weakened or rendered ineffectual. In fact, the law existed under a constitutional cloud from its inception. Twelve House members who had opposed its passage immediately challenged its constitutionality in the federal courts. In July 1986, the Supreme Court declared unconstitutional Gramm-Rudman's automatic spending-cut provisions.[47] Congress had provided that these cuts would be made by the comptroller general, who heads the General Accounting Office, an agency responsible to Congress. The Court concluded that this violated the constitutional clause requiring that the president see that the laws are faithfully executed. It reasoned that placing the comptroller general in charge of automatic budget cuts had the effect of making Congress an executor of the law.

The merits of the decision are less important here than its significance as another ramification of the policy process. In this instance, the courts, yet another part of the fragmented scheme of American government, had been called on to weaken, if not destroy, a crisis-induced agreement reached grudgingly by the deadlocked elected branches of the national government. Gramm-Rudman was not eliminated by the Supreme Court decision, but its effectiveness became very questionable. In particular, who would or could impose automatic budget cuts in the likely event of a presidential-congressional impasse remained undetermined. Congress resolved the question in 1987 by passing Public Law 100-199, which gave this power under strict guidelines to the Office of Management and Budget, an executive agency.

Fiscal Discipline through Political Effort

Even though the Supreme Court had weakened Gramm-Rudman, the law retained sufficient power to prompt political action by the nation's leaders. By 1990, both Republican president George Bush and the leaders of the Democrat-controlled Congress wished to avoid the large automatic spending cuts they saw looming under the provisions of Gramm-Rudman. After extensive maneuvering and one failed attempt at compromise, a bipartisan agreement was finally reached on a five-year, $490 billion deficit-reduction bill. The major points of the compromise were tax rate hikes on wealthier Americans, increased gasoline taxes, and cuts in Medicare.[48]

In addition to specific tax hikes and spending cuts, the compromise included important structural provisions designed to enforce budgetary restraint. Caps were placed on certain kinds of discretionary spending; no spending increases would be allowed on these items before 1996. "Pay as You Go" provisions were applied to entitlement spending programs, including Social Security and Medicare. Congress could increase spending for these programs only if it (1) enacted tax increases to pay for them or (2) cut spending on other programs to offset them.

Independent analysts generally described the compromise as a responsible bipartisan achievement. But the political costs, especially to George Bush, who had promised "no new taxes" in his 1988 presidential campaign, were huge. After this excruciating political battle, President Bush appears to have lost all interest in continuing the battle for further deficit reduction. Further serious efforts in this direction were to be an important part of the policy agenda during the succeeding administration.

By the time Bill Clinton became president in 1993, Congress had set aside the Gramm-Rudman requirements. Nonetheless, President Clinton, fresh from his 1992 victory, was determined to try his fortune against the deficit monster. Whereas Bush (a Republican president facing a Democratic Congress) had by necessity taken the path of bipartisan compromise, Clinton (a Democratic president with a Democratic Congress confronting implacable Republican opposition) was forced to seek a purely partisan majority. The Democrats narrowly prevailed in Congress. Clinton's 1993 budget delivered roughly $500 billion in deficit reduction over five years. This was achieved mainly through new taxes on the wealthy, new taxes on Social Security benefits, and spending cuts in both discretionary and entitlement programs.

Clinton, like Bush before him, paid a heavy political price for his efforts. Many Democratic congressmen who voted for Clinton's budget were successfully attacked on this point by their Republican opponents in the 1994 elections. President Clinton concluded that his 1993 budget, however responsible fiscally, was politically disastrous. He believed it had helped to defeat many Democrats and to produce the resulting Republican majorities in both houses of Congress.

Both Bush and Clinton had put forth substantial "one-time" political efforts to restore fiscal discipline to the national government, and each paid a heavy political price for his endeavor. As a consequence, both retired from the deficit-reduction wars. Although politically difficult, the labors of Bush and Clinton in conjunction with an era of tremendous economic growth removed the specter of expanding budget deficits. The later years of the Clinton administration were marked by controversy over how to deal with budget surpluses, a policy issue rarely encountered in the decades since the 1920s.

With the GOP takeover of the 104th Congress, the initiative on budget control moved to the legislative branch. At this point, constitutionally based institutional fragmentation between the executive and legislative branches was exacerbated by ideological and partisan divisions. The congressional Republicans moved forcefully with a plan to balance the budget within seven years, only to be met by head-on resistance from President Clinton. The result was a political and constitutional stalemate of historical proportions that dragged into 1996 and featured two partial shutdowns of the national government. Incremental movement toward the Republican goals of a mandated balanced budget and rigorously controlled spending seemed inevitable, and by January 1996, President Clinton seemed resigned to slowing the pace of change as best he could through skillful use of the media and his constitutional executive powers. The appearance of budget surpluses in the next few years removed the balanced budget issue from the agenda for the most part; however, the continued divisions between the president and Congress left it highly uncertain that long-term solutions to the financing problems faced by Medicare and Social Security could be achieved.

The source of these budget surpluses, of course, constitutes another policy-related question. Obviously, in view of the fragmentation and partisan rivalries endemic to budgetary policy, they did not emerge from some comprehensive government plan, although spending ceilings established by Congress have had some effect in restraining government expenditures. It is equally apparent that the unexpected and, in many ways, unparalleled economic prosperity experienced during much of the 1990s increased tax revenues far beyond what anyone anticipated. Thus, Americans once again discovered that limited national policy initiatives and economic prosperity can coexist for a considerable period of time, an experience that may well have colored their lack of support for powerful government, a point to which we return in the concluding chapter of this book.

POLICY ANALYSIS AND POLITICAL UNCERTAINTY

The policy process can be unnerving to the uninitiated. The policy analyst is trained in the application of rational methods to problems, and his or her conclusions often possess an aura of certainty. There may not be one best way of dealing with a problem, but usually analysis will suggest two or three clearly preferable alternatives. Unfortunately for the analyst, who may have devoted considerable time and effort to a problem, the policy process can easily proceed to unravel the most tightly reasoned positions or, even worse, may simply ignore them. Constituent interests, agency rivalries, congressional infighting, and external political considerations are but a few of the factors that have priority over rationally based findings and recommendations. The less established the context in which an issue is to be decided, the more unpredictable will be the factors that impinge on the recommendations made.

It should be emphasized that the student of public policy may expect to find political relationships at state and local levels similar to those at the national level. Although political structural configurations will vary, the need of administrators to establish political bases, the power of legislative committees, and the existence of organized interests are common to all levels of American government and to almost all areas of public policy. Where subgovernments have established themselves over time, policy is often reasonably predictable and coherent. In these situations, the advantages of close working relationships, a common sense of mission, and experience can contribute significantly to the effective implementation of routine policy. When this routine is threatened by changes in policy direction or by competing subsystems, established subgovernments have demonstrated time and time again that they can be serious obstacles to the coordinated implementation of public policy and the acceptance of the ideas of policy analysts.

The policy process seems to function most rationally and effectively in the face of crisis. When confronted with impending disaster, or at times just serious difficulties, the actors in the policy process appear able to rouse themselves from the bonds of meandering incrementalism sufficiently to formulate solutions. But their success in taking bold action often depends on their willingness to bypass the fragmented policy process. Often, these situations provide important opportunities for the suggestions of policy analysts. Once the issue is resolved, however, incremental change in diverse directions again becomes dominant, and even the long-term policy commitments obtained can become vulnerable to forces moved by short-term self-interest.

CHAPTER 7

Policy Devolution and Policy Analysis

WITH THE ADVENT of the 1990s, Americans witnessed the interaction of values and politics to an extent rarely seen in the domestic policy process. As discussed in previous chapters, the values of individualism and limited government surged to the fore in 1994 with substantial Republican gains in Congress—gains that in the House of Representatives, at least, derived from heightened opposition to continuance of government programs in their current form. Before the 1994 election, the concept of "reinventing government," which usually meant moving toward more efficient and responsive bureaucracies, had gained considerable attention in the media and in the federal government. Many of the Republicans who swept into office in 1994, however, were not interested in reinventing government; they were intent on eliminating programs and substantially reducing those programs that survived. In the words of William D. Eggers and John O'Leary, "Gore's National Performance Review was touted as revolutionary reinvention of the federal government. But *by its own admission* the NPR did not question *what* the federal government did; the NPR was a halfway measure, looking only at *how* the federal bureaucracy worked."[1] The "how" question was essentially procedural. The "what" question raised primarily by House Republicans was heavily normative and plunged national politics into a rare, but intense, debate over basic values.

A NATIONAL POLICY FOCUS

To this point, our discussion of the policy process has concentrated largely on the activity of governmental institutions at the national level, or politics inside the "Beltway," as the vernacular has it. Since the 1930s, much of the policy initiative in the United States has originated at this level. Numerous centralizing forces played a role in this aggregation of power, which by the 1960s had reached the point that one of the standard textbooks on American government could assert that states were essentially "administrative subdivisions of the national government."[2]

The New Deal began the serious move to greater central power. Its numerous programs for combating the Great Depression necessitated the proliferation of new agencies and the expansion of existing ones. This growth in bureaucracy was further stimulated in 1937 when the Supreme Court removed itself as a constitutional limit on economic and social programs.

The 1960s witnessed the apex of growth in the national government. Lyndon Johnson's Great Society programs occasioned massive governmental outlays that enlarged existing agencies and spawned new ones. Additionally, from the mid-1950s through most of the 1960s, the Supreme Court led by Chief Justice Earl Warren pursued an activist agenda that imposed broad constitutional mandates on the states in the areas of civil liberties and civil rights. Furthermore, the Warren Court was sympathetic to many of the Great Society initiatives.

Foreign affairs also played a role in enhancing federal power. The national government grew significantly during World War II, and the ensuing Cold War required continued attention to national defense. The nation's ongoing struggle with communism greatly strengthened the position of the presidency. In times of foreign crisis, criticisms of presidential power could be portrayed as weakening that office and thus undermining America's defense capability. In the 1960s, the policy issues raised by the war against communism reached their greatest intensity. America's involvement in Vietnam was seen by many people as an excessive response to a minimal threat, a position recently reinforced by Robert McNamara's reevaluation of national policy while he was secretary of defense during this period.[3]

The reaction against virtually unlimited presidential action in the name of national security began immediately after the Vietnam War with the passage of the War Powers Act of 1973, which mandated congressional approval for the commitment of American troops in combat beyond sixty days. The security function of the president and indeed of the national government as a whole became much less salient in the public mind with the collapse of the Soviet Union in the early 1990s. With the Soviet Union removed as a constant threat to the United States, one of the essential underpinnings of citizen support for strong national power evaporated. The United States had become the most powerful military and economic nation in the world, and Americans no longer saw the need to stand solidly behind their government for purposes of security. Even outside the realm of defense, they seemed much less concerned with the need to depend on the central government and became more sensitive to the huge tax-and-spending burdens that the programs from the past thirty years imposed.[4]

INCREASING STATE INFLUENCE

Within the past few decades, the dynamics of American politics have moved the focus for policy change from the national level to the states and, in doing so, have dramatically multiplied opportunities for those engaged in policy analysis. At the same time, the contexts in which analysis occurs have diversified. Not only are there fifty state governments in which to work; a wide variety of think tanks, policy institutes, advocacy groups, and foundations also utilize policy analysts.

Much of the movement of policy initiative to the states can be categorized under the commonly used rubric of devolution. This movement reflects the impact of a number of factors over the past thirty years that have been taking parallel paths toward reducing national power. Historically, President Nixon was the first president to officially recognize the growing demands of state and local officials for greater discretion and policy control. His institution of general revenue sharing, use of block grants in limited areas, and appointment of strict constructionists to the Supreme Court were attempts to limit the expansion of national power in response to the rising unhappiness of state and local leaders.

President Reagan followed up on many of Nixon's beginnings. Early in his administration, he packaged more than fifty categorical grant programs into fewer than a dozen block grants. He continued the practice of appointing conservative justices to the Supreme Court. The input of the nation's governors into the 1988 Family Support Act demonstrated the increasing policy power of the states. An appreciation of this newly acquired status was reflected in the statement that Bill Clinton, then governor of Arkansas, made to the president: "Whether we agree with you or not, we all admit that you've made us more important."[5] Indeed, by the end of the Reagan administration, the office of governor was a highly coveted position in many states, and in the 1990s, forceful and imaginative governors from Massachusetts, New Jersey, Wisconsin, Michigan, California, New York, and Texas were important players on issues involving education, welfare, crime, and fiscal policy. Thus, at the Republican Governors Association meeting in November 1995, the chairman, Governor Michael O. Leavitt of Utah, echoed former governor Clinton's sentiments when he responded to a query as to why none of his colleagues were seeking the presidency with the comment: "Perhaps that would be because it would be trading a very good job for a very bad job."[6]

It is probably fair to say that the actions and events of the Reagan administration fundamentally changed the policy context of American politics. The dialogue over what constituted reasonable and effective public policy shifted perceptibly to the right during this time, although it was not until the Bush and Clinton administrations that pundits and students of public policy began to notice the policy ramifications of this shift.

As early as the Reagan administration, however, political scientists like Hugh Heclo were observing that the subgovernmental relationships that seemed to evolve naturally among congressional committees, agencies, and clientele groups to support programs were no longer the influential force in the policy process that they once were. Heclo suggested that "issue networks" were gaining in influence. He saw these networks as loose configurations of policymakers, media leaders, academics, and advocacy groups who were interested in particular issues and who insisted on being involved in the definition and resolution of these issues. Both John W. Kingdon and David M. Ricci seemed to agree with Heclo on the importance of policy forums, or communities that engage and frame issues.[7]

What we have seen in recent years are trends that continue to weaken the triangular subgovernmental relationships in favor of further diffusion of those who become involved in policy issues. Fiscally, the move to block grants undercuts the strong ties that categorical grants had fostered. Equally important is the increased deference to state policy decisions and the corresponding growth in think tanks across the nation. Many of these changes have been economically driven, in that agencies and groups have been seeking a larger share of the funding pie. However, in Jeffrey M. Berry's view, the postmaterial momentum has also reached into the policy process and is crowding out traditional welfare liberalism. The number of advocacy groups pushing nonmaterial goals (for Berry, the core values of "equality and rights, environmentalism, consumer protection, good government, and family values")[8] has multiplied at a rapid rate, and these groups now impinge significantly on older subgovernments. Additionally, while the more stable subgovernments tend to eschew publicity, these newer interests try to make dramatic use of the media whenever possible. All of these factors have made the policy process even more fragmented and fluid at the same time that they have encouraged greater variety and input into the making of public policy.

Policy analysts have both gained and lost from these changes. The movement away from categorical grants has lessened the need for specialized policy experts attached to narrowly focused programs. Moreover, Republicans at the national and state levels have often found research and analysis units easy targets for budget cuts. The congressional Office of Technology Assessment, for example, was one of the first targets of House Republicans after their triumph in the 1994 elections. On the other hand, the flourishing of private policy institutes has provided other kinds of opportunities for policy analysts.

Although its relationship to the changing federal balance is not often clearly acknowledged, the breakup of the Soviet Union during the Bush administration was also an important factor in undermining the dominant policy position of the national government. The Bush and Clinton administrations clearly felt the aftershocks of America's victory in the Cold War. Both administrations faced restive Congresses and saw the impetus for national policy initiatives wane. Concurrently, the Nixon and Reagan appointees to the Supreme Court, joined by Justice Clarence Thomas, began to grant greater leeway to state legislatures and state courts and to limit the extension of national power.

In *Planned Parenthood* v. *Casey* (1992),[9] the Court, although refusing to overturn the basic right to an abortion established in *Roe* v. *Wade* (1973),[10]

granted states considerable leeway in stipulations surrounding a woman's decision to have an abortion. Here, the majority of the Court discarded *Roe's*
trimester framework in favor of the "undue burden" standard proposed by
Justice Sandra Day O'Connor. This ruling allowed states to prohibit abortion
after the point at which a fetus can survive outside the womb. States were also
permitted to have an interest in promoting childbirth from the point of conception. Thus, waiting periods and consent requirements are permissible as long
as they do not impose an "undue burden" on a woman's decision to have an
abortion. In *Casey,* the Court was clearly unwilling to overrule a major precedent, but at the same time the majority granted considerably more flexibility to
the states than previous courts had been willing to allow. In striking this kind of
balance, the *Casey* decision may provide a kind of paradigm for how more conservative courts will deal with major precedents from the more activist, nation-
alist Warren era, although, of course, the major precedent for *Casey,* that of *Roe
v. Wade,* was a Burger Court decision.

An especially intriguing aspect of the Court's devotion to greater balance in
the federal system has been its resurrection of the need for limitations on
national power, which in the pre-1937 period was often based on the Tenth
Amendment. In *New York v. U.S.* (1991),[11] Justice O'Connor held that Congress
could not require state legislatures to take title to radioactive waste even though
the states had consented to such a mandate. In her words, "State officials thus
cannot consent to the enlargement of the powers of Congress beyond those enumerated in the Constitution." In *U.S. v. Lopez* (1995),[12] Chief Justice William
Rehnquist moved even further with the doctrine of the Tenth Amendment.
Although not directly citing this clause, he held that Congress had exceeded its
commerce powers in its attempt to outlaw the possession of firearms within
1,000 feet of a schoolyard. "We start," he declared, "with first principles. The
Constitution creates a Federal Government of enumerated powers." In the Gun-
Free School Zones Act, Congress had abused its delegated power to regulate
interstate commerce. If the assumptions behind this act were to be accepted by
the Court, Rehnquist found it "difficult to perceive any limitation on federal
power, even in areas such as criminal law enforcement or education *where States
historically have been sovereign*" (emphasis added).

In the closing days of the 1999 term, Chief Justice Rehnquist and four of his
colleagues continued their reinvigoration of federalism. In three cases dealing
with a variety of issues, a five-person majority consistently overruled the position that Congress could make states liable for suit from private individuals or
associations. In the case of *Alden v. Maine* (1999),[13] Justice Anthony Kennedy,
speaking for the Court, asserted, "Although the Constitution grants broad powers to Congress, our federalism requires that Congress treat the states in a manner consistent with their status as residuary sovereigns and joint participants in
the governance of the nation." Kennedy also declared that the "principle of sov-

ereign immunity preserved by constitutional design" entitles the states to be important players in the federal system.

THE 1994 ELECTIONS

The event that seemed destined to move the national government from its preeminent policy position and consciously place much greater policy responsibility on the states was the Republican takeover of Congress in the 1994 midterm election. Compared with previous midterm elections, this was a history-making occurrence. For the first time in forty years, the Republicans controlled both houses of Congress. Norman J. Ornstein and Amy L. Schenkenberg stated, "Using broad electoral history as the predictor, no one would have expected the massive Republican takeover of both houses of Congress in the 1994 election."[14] Walter Dean Burnham characterized the 1994 elections as an "earthquake" and suggested that "the shape of American politics will very probably never be the same again."[15]

Burnham noted that the GOP victories in Congress were accompanied by successes throughout the country, with Republican gubernatorial gains exceeding those in any election since 1867 and with important Republican advances in the state legislatures, especially in the South. Moreover, these election gains were accompanied by a steady succession of switches by incumbent Democrats to the Republican Party. In October 1995, the *New York Times* reported that since the 1992 elections, 137 Democratic elected officials from every level of government had moved into the Republican Party.[16]

For policy analysts hoping to contribute to the policy process, the GOP victories were to have important ramifications with regard to the institutional environment in which they must work. Burnham made this point especially clear with his statement that the "intent of the Republican victors of 1994 is to produce a comprehensive ideological, structural, and policy transformation that goes to the foundations of the American political order."[17] Fred Steeper echoed Burnham's analysis. In his view, the 1994 congressional elections were based on an "ideological polarization" that "brought the New Deal party system to an end."[18] With the decisions of Senators Bill Bradley (D-N.J.) and Sam Nunn (D-Ga.) not to seek reelection in 1996, the prospects for Democratic control of the Senate in the remainder of the twentieth century dimmed considerably, causing Brian Lunde, a former executive director of the Democratic National Committee, to comment that the old Democratic Party, "based on programmatic liberalism, is clearly dying. It's going the way of the Berlin Wall."[19] President Clinton seemed to put the capstone on these sentiments in his State of the Union speech of 23 January 1996, when he declared: "The era of big government is over."

Ornstein and Schenkenberg saw the 1994 Republican victories as the result of the "populist, antigovernment, and antileadership character of the campaign," and they quoted one House freshman as declaring, "My base is more populist than Republican."[20] The Republicans in particular have argued that there is no longer a pressing need for a powerful national government, and in 1994, they were successful in focusing voter resentment against that level of government. It now seems evident that increased latitude to state governments is at least temporarily a rule of the day that many members of both political parties recognize. It should be noted, however, that despite the rather strong rhetoric for sweeping change, no one has seriously suggested the elimination of Social Security (a legacy of the New Deal) or anything beyond careful reform of Medicare (a legacy of the Great Society), two huge national programs.

For the GOP candidates for the House of Representatives, the vehicle for this approach was the now famous "Contract with America," a concise statement of what the Republicans would do if they won a majority in the House.[21] The "Contract" focused on specific proposals to limit national programs, increase state policy discretion, and impose constitutional institutional restraints, such as term limits and a balanced budget requirement. Notably absent from this document were positions on social issues, such as abortion, gun control, and school prayer.

Nonetheless, the programmatic changes proposed by the 104th Congress were of historical importance. While the Supreme Court was resurrecting limits to national power in interstate commerce that had not commanded a majority since the early days of the New Deal, the Republicans in Congress were proposing placing under state authority important national programs that had originated in the New Deal. Aid to Families with Dependent Children, for example, was eliminated as a separate program and packaged in a block grant with a number of other welfare programs. Many of these legislative changes were the outgrowth of experiments tried by state governments or of policy suggestions formulated within think tanks. Some of the changes in welfare approaches can be traced to the 1988 Family Support Act and to experiments in states like Wisconsin that were willing to try new approaches to reducing welfare payments and individual dependency.

STATE POLICY INITIATIVES

In fact, by the 1990s, the states had become the source of most innovation in policy. Oregon had led the way in health-care reform with its attempt to prioritize the kinds of health-care financing it would support. Under Governor John Engler's leadership, Michigan completely revamped its approach to education by removing the property tax base and allowing for the creation of charter schools outside the existing public education bureaucracy. A number of states experimented with privatization of a wide range of functions, including those offered by facilities like hospitals and prisons. New Jersey undertook to deal with sex offenders with "Megan's Law," which allowed neighbors to be informed of the presence of a convicted sex offender in their neighborhood. The "three strikes and you're out" rule, which provides a sentence of life imprisonment for a third felony conviction, began in the state of Washington and eventually found its way into the national 1994 Violent Crime Control and Law Enforcement Act. The term-limits movement gained nationwide impetus with the adoption of term limits in over twenty states, although the Supreme Court refused to allow the states, or Congress, to impose term limits on congressional seats. And in California, under the leadership of Governor Pete Wilson, affirmative action programs were being dismantled.

The list of initiatives at the state level could be greatly extended. The point is that as the executive, legislature, and courts of the national government have begun to withdraw as funding and directing sources, the states have virtually exploded with policy initiatives. In many of these circumstances, policy analysts played important roles that often placed national governmental specialists on the defensive or essentially ignored them.

Changes of this magnitude have not been without their difficulties. States like Oregon and California, which had made early advances in health care and welfare financing, respectively, within the old national programs, saw themselves limited and perhaps penalized by proposed national regulations intended to apply to all states. Additionally, some critics of the devolution of programs questioned whether many states had sufficient expertise and resources to provide for the disadvantaged within their borders. Their argument was that the congressional Republicans were simply devolving national problems to the states. John J. DiIulio Jr. and Donald F. Kettl, for example, contended that much of the "Contract with America" was policy rhetoric that ignored the major administrative problems in implementation that would be occasioned by its passage into law.[22] Finally, those arguing for less government generally seemed to have little tolerance for publicly supported research and analysis. As noted earlier, the congressional Republicans applied their budgetary shears to the Office of Technology Assessment (a congressional agency); they did the same to the Bureau of Economic Analysis and the National Institute of Standards and Technology in the Department of Commerce. At the state level, under the leadership of Governors George Pataki and Christine Whitman, the Port Authority of New York and New Jersey found its Office of Economic and Policy Analysis abolished in September 1995.

PRIVATE-SECTOR POLICY GROUPS

Much of the movement toward the devolution of public policy to the states has been stimulated and guided by private-sector think tanks that have grown in size and number within the past two decades. These relatively recent entrants into the policy equation have been exceptionally important in providing rationales and scenarios for those intent on downsizing the national government, encouraging the growth of private enterprise, and granting more policy discretion to state governments. Not only have think tanks become more numerous; they are also now widely distributed across the country. With their focus on state and local issues and their input into state policy processes, these groups have provided a fund of ideas and initiatives that are independent of the Beltway gurus.[23]

Some policy organizations, such as the Brookings Institution (1916), the Hoover Institution (1919), the Twentieth Century Fund (1919), and the Carnegie Endowment for International Peace (1910), have existed since the early part of the twentieth century. But in the past two decades, the sheer *number* of associations dedicated to providing public analysis of issues and social problems has increased dramatically.[24] Although the rise and influence of these organizations have been the subject of several recent books, Ricci has noted that "no one has yet decided exactly what think tanks are."[25] It seems clear, however, that one guiding principle behind their establishment, from the Brookings Institution to the more ideologically partisan organizations of today, has been the need to link policy ideas more closely to policy action.

Studies of the role and activities of these research organizations naturally tend to focus on those in the nation's capital, but important ones have existed for many years outside the Beltway. Chief among these are the Manhattan Institute for Policy Research in New York City, the RAND Corporation in Santa Monica, California, and the Hoover Institution in Stanford, California. Additionally, research units other than think tanks have existed for many years around the country. Many cities, for example, have municipal government institutes that date back to the Progressive era, and universities as well as many unions have developed research institutes and adjuncts.

Increasingly important today are the numerous private-sector state-level policy institutes that have sprung up nationwide. In 1995, at least forty-eight state policy groups were affiliated with the State Policy Network, headquartered in Fort Wayne, Indiana.[26] Although focusing primarily on state issues, these groups also provided ideas for national programs. They, in conjunction with numerous unaffiliated state and regional think tanks, constituted a formidable conservative-idea network across the country. This network has been reinforced by the American Legislative Exchange Council (founded in 1973). According to David Callahan, 3,000 of the 7,000 state legislators throughout the nation belonged to this organization in 1998, and 22 percent of its model laws that were actually introduced into state legislatures in 1995–96 were enacted.[27] In a tangible sense, the emergence of these conservative groups is another manifestation of a phenomenon that we described in chapter 1—that is, the reaction against using social science analysis to justify government initiatives. But, as might be expected, in response to this conservative movement, by 1998, approximately a dozen liberal state policy groups had appeared and were beginning to have some effect on state policy.[28]

Advocates of new and expanded government programs had no research organizations comparable to the conservative network, and that was one reason why the ideas of the Newt Gingrich Republicans moved so quickly across the nation. In the *New Republic,* for example, Matthew Cooper lamented the inability of the Democratic Leadership Council (DLC) to forge "a popular base." "If the DLC has been a minor player in Congress," he wrote, "it's been AWOL when it comes to building a grassroots movement."[29] Part of the difficulty for liberal supporters of government programs has been the thinning out of sympathetic political leaders throughout the nation. Examining reasons for the "eerie hush" among opponents of the Republican efforts to downsize the national government and devolve its powers, Tamar Lewin of the *New York Times* noted that "the bloc of liberal mayors and governors who could be counted on to protest any attempt to cut back social spending in the years that Republicans held the White House—among them Mario M. Cuomo, David N. Dinkins, Michael S. Dukakis, Henry G. Cisneros, and Ann Richards—have been replaced by more conservative politicians."[30] Thus, analysts supporting existing government programs at the national level found themselves confined largely within the Beltway and defending the status quo against a veritable barrage of arguments for limited government that were presented as being both more imaginative and more efficient.

THINK TANKS AND POLICY ANALYSIS

Think tanks and other private policy groups vary widely in the degree of autonomy from government that they maintain.[31] At one end of the spectrum are privately funded institutes or foundations that operate independently of government while concerning themselves with government policy. These include the Heritage Foundation and the Cato Institute. Other organizations, such as RAND and the Urban Institute, undertake solid analysis but depend heavily on government funding for their survival. This weakens their claims of critical objectivity because it is expecting too much for them to move very far outside the policy paradigms accepted by those who fund them. For example, James A. Smith argued that the Urban Institute's research efforts "embodied the assumptions on which the technocratic reforms [of the Great Society] had been predicated. Although the government had not performed well, more technical knowledge could make it work."[32] In his examination of the limiting effects of policy discourse on poverty policy, Sanford F. Schram made essentially the same point: "From government grants and contracts to a political realism that reinforces the need to impress those in power, the discursive practices of poverty research anticipate the prevailing structures of society writ large. Research gets written in ways that reinforce that structural context."[33] Susan George and Fabrizio Sabelli were more specific programmatically. Commenting on the World Bank's "unquestioned status as the pre-eminent employer of consultants in the development field, a state of affairs coinciding with the much greater dependency of academics, university departments and development institutes on income from consultancy work," they noted the analytical inhibitions that this seems to have fostered: "The direct involvement of so many academics in Bank-funded work is incompatible with a healthy intellectual debate and with pluralism. It would seem that if you can't sell consensus on some issues, you can, arguably, buy it."[34]

Further across the spectrum are the intensely partisan groups devoted to the continuance of particular programs. Often, these groups are quasi-official extensions of agency programs, and many of their studies are heavily funded by the agencies. While creditable studies emanate from these groups, it is not unusual for them to focus on attempting to convince the public of the dire consequences of a termination of funding support for programs to which they have become ideologically and/or financially attached.

Thus, in the summer of 1995, when Congress was considering heavy cutbacks in both the funding and regulatory authority of the Environmental Protection Agency, the National Environmental Law Center released a study of EPA data, which concluded that "millions of Americans live close enough to factories that they are vulnerable to death or illness from accidental toxic releases."[35] That same week, the *New York Times* contained the headline "Weed Killers in Tap Water in Corn Belt." The *Times* reported that the Environmental Working Group, "a private environmental research and advocacy organization in Washington," had found that "tap water in the Corn Belt is dangerously contaminated with agricultural weed killers." The story went on to note that "the study was released as some Republicans in Congress are calling for relaxing regulations on drinking water."[36]

Stephen J. Breyer suggested that this kind of media activity by private policy groups creates "random agendas" for policymakers. By this, he meant that instead of being able to approach environmental risk problems rationally and consistently, administrators are forced by elevated public controversy to make those issues that currently are receiving most publicity important priorities. He concluded that this ultimately undermines public confidence in agency decisions because "the more outside pressures seem to control agency results, the less confidence the public will have in the agency."[37] Thus, in stimulating public concern over perceived risks to health or safety, private policy advocates may over the long haul be weakening the credibility of those very agencies from which they receive support.

Berry has pointed out that "advocacy-oriented think tanks muddy the distinction between "interest group" and "think tank.""[38] Skillful exploitation of the media has contributed tremendously to this "muddiness." Sociologist Barry Glassner has argued that the media have encouraged a "culture of fear" that often exaggerates problems far out of proportion to the threat they pose. Glassner concluded that a "wide array of groups, including businesses, advocacy organizations, religious sects, and political parties, promote and profit from scares."[39] Some in the media have, of course, tried to act responsibly. Michael Fumento, for example, has made a reputation as a correspondent who debunks the current fad among the fearmongers.[40] John Stossel, in an article recanting his days as a "scare" journalist, stated that science is often the real loser in this environment of media frenzy.[41] Glassner also touched on the problems caused for the careful policy analyst by these conditions: "One of the paradoxes of a culture of fear is that serious problems remain widely ignored even though they give rise to precisely the dangers that the populace most abhors."[42] Careful analytical attention to poverty, income inequality, and crime simply cannot compete with the media-induced drama of the exceptional occurrence, even though these may well be sources of the problems that the public most fears.[43]

The role of the policy analyst working in a think tank varies greatly depending on what type of think tank it is. Some excellent policy study organizations, such as the Brookings Institution, utilize scholars from across the ideological horizon. Others, such as the Heritage Foundation and Cato Institute, are conservatively oriented and expect their analysts to be in this mold as well. Moreover, Cato expects its people to be libertarian in outlook. Nonetheless, the credibility of even clearly partisan ideological think tanks depends on the quality of their studies. For this reason, Heritage and Cato insist on high-quality work from their analysts. As Ricci has noted, "Part of winning is to establish a solid reputation, to be regarded around town as knowledgeable, fair, worth listening to, and reasonable enough to qualify for a job somewhere else within the policy community."[44] Berry cited the unusual example of Families USA, a liberal group, and the Heritage Foundation, a conservative group, contracting with the same "highly respected health care consulting firm" for analysis during the 1994 health-care debate. In Berry's view, this "illustrates just how vital lobbyists believe it is to be able to carry highly credible research into battle."[45] The same is true of research groups that contract heavily with government. Here, however, analysts may find themselves inhibited from examining the full range of policy possibilities—alternative weapons systems, for example—and that may limit the usefulness of their work. Government funding is exceptionally important to such analysts, and they make every effort to offer projects and proposals that are responsive to the current thinking within the bureaucracy.[46]

It seems clear that think tanks have had a fairly direct influence on government policies in recent years. The Heritage Foundation, for example, with its 1,093-page *Mandate for Leadership,* provided analysis of a broad range of issues and made suggestions for breaking the grip of triangular subgovernments on national policy. This document served as an important source of ideas for the incoming Reagan administration in 1981. At the state level, the Wisconsin Policy Research Institute worked closely with Wisconsin's governor Tommy Thompson in his efforts to bring his state's welfare programs under control and to reform its educational system. And at the local level, the Manhattan Institute appears to have influenced Mayor Rudolph Giuliani's approach to the problems of New York City.

The example of the Heritage Foundation underlines the attention that has been given to private-sector policy organizations within the Beltway. But the proliferation of think tanks throughout the country has resulted in a broad geographic distribution of important policy ideas. The analyses supported by New York's Manhattan Institute, for example, have had profound national ramifications. The emphasis on reform of tort litigation found in the "Contract with America" owes much to the studies of the excesses of liability litigation emanating from the Manhattan Institute's Peter Huber and Walter Olson, and Elizabeth McCaughey's dissection of the Clinton health-care plan was based on her work at that institute.[47] McCaughey's expertise in the health-care area was established by this work, and it was one of the main factors leading Governor George Pataki to pick her as his running mate in the 1994 New York gubernatorial race. Thus, in a very short time, McCaughey moved from policy analyst to policymaker.

A common characteristic of policy groups outside of Washington is that much of their analysis is concerned with state or local issues. The Claremont Institute in California focuses on statewide issues; its leadership, for example, spearheaded the referendum constitutionally repealing affirmative action programs in that state. Generally, however, these larger and better-financed hinterland research groups are also able to underwrite analysts interested in national issues. Moreover, when state think tanks are examining welfare and education issues, their suggestions may easily have national repercussions, as has been the case with Governor Tommy Thompson's welfare changes in Wisconsin and Governor John Engler's revamping of education in Michigan.

THE POLICY ANALYST IN THE PRIVATE SECTOR

As might be expected, the roles and expectations of policy analysts in think tanks vary, but generally speaking they differ significantly from those of policy analysts in governmental agencies. Analysis within a government agency necessarily occurs within a bureaucratic context that rewards a rather narrow programmatic focus and assumes the importance of the agency's mission. The privately funded think tanks, in contrast, tend to provide more heavily ideological contexts for the analysts.

Each think tank has a particular ideological culture within which a policy analyst must feel comfortable. The Manhattan Institute and the Hoover Institution operate from fairly conservative fundamental positions, and the analysts working within them can be expected to hold similar positions. The Brookings Institution, in contrast, utilizes both conservative and liberal analysts, although its general orientation might be characterized as moderate to liberal. The Economic Policy Institute, the Center on Budget and Policy Priorities, and the Progressive Policy Institute (the research adjunct of the Democratic Leadership Council) can be expected to be fairly consistently sympathetic to the use of government for the solution of economic and social problems. Also affecting the ideological flavor of policy analysis in the private sector is the fact that many of the analysts in the larger research organizations are funded directly by endowments established by philanthropists, and no institute is going to recruit an analyst antithetical to the ideological positions of its major donors. Therefore, while some such organizations may be more independent of external pressures than others, there is no such thing as a completely autonomous think tank.

Winand Gellner has argued that the sophisticated marketing approach of the Heritage Foundation has forced policy research groups that wish to remain influential in Washington to "develop particular market strategies with a considerably stronger ideological stance."[48] Whatever the cause of the move toward a more vigorous public image, today's think tank analysts must expect to help with marketing. Although most are on staff to do lengthy, detailed research, they are also important as public relations vehicles for letting the rest of the world know about their research organization. They work up short position papers, submit opinion pieces to major print media, volunteer for talk shows, and give presentations.[49] At the same time, it is important to emphasize that their work must be of high professional quality. The position taken may be a partisan one, but the analysis supporting it has to be creditable if the sponsoring organization expects to have influence in the policy process and with the public at large.

Think tanks use essentially three kinds of policy functionaries: academic researchers, former government officials, and professional analysts. Academic researchers may be provided residence for a year or more, or they may be contracted for specific research projects while they remain on their campuses. The Ohio Buckeye Institute, for example, has had as many as twenty-eight academics from sixteen college campuses working in cooperation with it, and the James Madison Institute in Florida has worked closely with faculty from Florida State University. Generally, think tank administrators prefer to have academic researchers in residence because this enhances control over research schedules and helps ensure that the scholars will be available for marketing purposes at conferences, on call-in shows, and for op-ed pieces. Typically, the works of academic researchers are in-depth and book length, and usually the sponsoring organization has some arrangements with a publisher to produce and market them or does its own publishing (as do the American Enterprise Institute, Cato, and Brookings). Many of these works are excellent examinations of an issue, but usually they do not contribute directly or immediately to policy decisions, primarily because policymakers do not have the time to read through lengthy analyses. Such works can, however, contribute importantly to the conceptual framework within which issues are interpreted. Thus, Charles Murray's *Losing Ground,* supported by the Manhattan Institute, provided opponents of the Great Society with a basis for criticism and began the long movement toward welfare reform.[50] Some of the better-funded policy research groups also have journals in which their people as well as others report on their research. *Policy Review* of the Heritage Foundation, the *Brookings Review* from the Brookings Institution, *Regulation* published by the Cato Institute, *American Enterprise* representing the American Enterprise Institute, and *City Journal* out of the Manhattan Institute are to be found on the shelves of most reasonably comprehensive magazine stores throughout the nation. And, of course, most think tanks have web sites, many of which provide rapid-fire analyses of breaking events over the Internet. In 1997, Townhall.com, the major web site for conservative organizations, reported 145,000 "hits" a day.

Former government officials have increasingly found refuge in think tanks. Prominent examples are Robert Bork, William Bennett, and Herbert Stein (American Enterprise Institute) and Edwin Meese (Heritage Foundation). As resident scholars, former government officials have provided visibility for those supporting them, have continued to criticize those in power while awaiting a possible return to office, and have occasionally, as in the cases of Bork, Bennett, and Stein, written extended analyses of public issues. Sometimes, of course, such individuals return to power, and when they do, their former think tank colleagues can expect to have preferential access to the official circles of policymaking. According to the *Washington Post,* in his run for the presidency, George W. Bush drew heavily upon fellows from the Hoover Institution who had served in previous Republican administrations, and one assumes that many of those individuals anticipated becoming part of a Bush administration.[51]

The professional analyst works as a resident employee of the think tank. He or she may engage in in-depth studies, as do the analysts at Brookings, but administrators are increasingly interested in immediate impact from their analysts. Those specializing in specific topics, such as the environment, poverty, or nuclear proliferation, are expected to be available to carry their organization's colors wherever these issues are discussed. Specialists on Congress provide short analyses of congressional issues, appear in the media, and serve as panelists at conferences. The Heritage Foundation has in addition used its congressional analysts to provide training workshops for new members of Congress. It should be noted here that the use of resident specialists is a luxury of the larger, well-funded research organizations. Many of the policy groups established at the state level are small operations consisting of perhaps a director and secretary. They depend heavily on less certain, ad hoc funding to undertake individual projects. Some state policy organizations, however, such as the Heartland Institute in Chicago and the Empire Foundation for Policy Research in New York, are substantial think tank operations.

AN EXPANDED POLICY ARENA: PROSPECTS AND CONCERNS

The opportunities for private-sector analysts are in some ways considerably broader than are those for governmental analysts. The policy analyst as policy entrepreneur may find it much easier within a think tank to propose new policy initiatives and to critically evaluate policies already in place. Obviously, the scope of such discretion varies with the proclivities of those directing the organization. Analysts working for organizations dependent on contract financing are more limited in the range of their endeavors. First and foremost, they must attend to whatever projects they have been contracted to complete. Second, although analysts in any organization must be sensitive to the views of those funding them, these analysts may be more reluctant than most to launch a vigorous attack on the vested interests of their funding agencies.

As of this writing, the prospects for continued vigor on the part of think tanks are very promising. The institutional fluidity of the policy process that encouraged the recent growth of policy groups will only be furthered by the devolution of policy initiatives to the states. The outlook for creative policy ideas and for those working in the policy field is thus more auspicious and exciting than has been the case in the past.

Probably the greatest threat to the proliferation of think tanks is posed by budget cuts aimed at parts of the national government. Obviously, think tanks that have depended heavily on government contracts and other forms of funding will be forced to adapt to the tightening of the federal spigot. Some Republican members of Congress have proposed further limits on nonprofit and charitable organizations that receive federal grants in an effort to prevent these groups from influencing public policy at the national, state, and local levels.[52] Such efforts to "defund the left" could strengthen even further the conservative flavor of the think tank world. This orientation was dominant even before federal cutbacks in funding, as Ricci pointed out in 1993. In his words, "In Washington's marketplace for ideas, the conservative story stands almost alone. It is recited confidently, it is packaged impressively, and it appears repeatedly because it is financed faithfully and generously."[53] Certainly, the financial resources of some of these think tanks outstrip those of many colleges and universities. In 1999, the Heritage Foundation was completing an $80 million endowment campaign, and the endowment of the Hoover Institution was estimated at about $250 million. The only cloud on the conservatives' rosy horizon would seem to be the remote possibility that the federal tax code could be changed to undercut the tax deductibility of gifts to not-for-profit educational organizations.

The ideological character of the private-sector research world has occasioned concern among those examining it. Ricci urged liberals to become more effective in promoting policy scenarios within the Beltway "so as to achieve a balanced ordering of whatever facts and theories have accumulated in Washington's various policy communities."[54] James A. Smith expressed dissatisfaction with the ideological partisanship now tied to the extensive marketing efforts undertaken by think tanks. He likened the current situation to one in which "thousands of baskets come down like a flotilla of colorful hot-air balloons and empty their experts upon us."[55] Like Ricci, he was concerned that the linkage of power and carefully crafted knowledge, ostensibly one of the primary functions of research groups, has suffered.

Although the need to achieve a rough ideological balance among think tanks is a valid concern, other aspects of their proliferation hold promise for both the enterprising policy analyst and the commonweal. There is no question that devolution of policy issues to the states in conjunction with the geographical dispersion of think tanks has opened the policy dialogue far beyond what it was two decades ago. This broadened dialogue will complicate many aspects of the policy process, including constitutional law, in which many state decisions will differ from national standards, and term limits on elective office, which will vary from state to state and from state to national levels. Thus, fragmentation and discontinuity in policy seem destined to extend beyond the Beltway. At the same time, the wider scope of policy discussions cannot help but increase the variety of policy proposals and in this respect should broaden the array of ideas from which the policy analyst may draw.

CHAPTER 8

Policy Analysis in the Judicial Process

POLICY DISARRAY AND stalemate in the elected branches of government have encouraged interests seeking assistance and protection to turn to the nation's courts. Relatively insulated from political pressures, courts remain capable of providing reasonably definitive, authoritative responses to the questions brought before them. Thus, there has been a tendency by elected policymakers and the public to defer difficult and controversial issues to what seem to be the impartial, rational processes of judicial procedure. The courts in turn have abetted this movement by easing the requirements for filing suit and by adopting a more activist view of the judicial role. In trying to manage complex social problems, judges have often turned to various forms of social and scientific analysis to complement the formalities of judicial procedure. The courts have never really been comfortable with such approaches, however, and in their grappling with social problems, they have illustrated the policy limitations of the legal process.

THE JUDICIAL PROCESS

Since the days of the early common-law courts of England, Anglo-American judges have served to integrate changing social norms into the law of the land. The framework for this activity has been the common law, and the dynamic has been the adversary process. In the adversary process, the parties to a case present to the court not only interpretations of the facts involved but also their views as to the appropriate rule of law governing the case. In suggesting the proper rule of law, attorneys to a case in which no statute is involved utilize previous judicial decisions, or legal precedents, that support their positions. They in effect ask a judge or a panel of judges to legitimize or penalize a particular form of conduct and thus render it legally acceptable or unacceptable. Judges, in an incremental fashion, draw on earlier judicial positions to determine which view of legitimacy will prevail in the case before them. This decision in turn becomes part of the collection of judicial precedents on which later litigants and judges will rely. As social norms change, new legal arguments are brought before the courts. Judges will act to incorporate some of these into legal rules over a period of time and a succession of cases.

Although the proliferation of statute law has rendered common law, or judge-made law, less influential in many areas, the courts have retained their roles as arbiters of competing social norms. No statute can encompass every circumstance to which it might be applied, and statutory language, no matter how carefully chosen, will require some elaboration by the courts. But precision in statutory language is today the rare exception. It is far more common practice for state and national legislators to skirt controversial social issues through vaguely worded laws intended to leave the definition of their meaning to administrators and judges. In these instances, the primary effect of the legislation is not to solve a particular problem but to provide a structure within which agencies and ultimately the courts can fashion remedial approaches.

Entanglement in the thickets of social controversy has forced the courts to move beyond their power of judicial review, which enables them to declare legislative or executive acts unconstitutional and thus void. In extreme cases, judges have gone so far as to engage in quasi-administrative day-to-day monitoring of explosive and complex situations in order to ensure compliance with court orders. The ultimate sanction behind judicial orders has been the power of the courts to hold individuals and institutions in contempt. Generally, however, judges have tried to avoid such direct confrontations and have attempted to achieve community support through political negotiations and the use of analytical studies of problems. In this approach, activist judges have utilized the ideas of reformist thinkers who have stressed the value of judicial sensitivity to community interests and the findings of social analysis. Nevertheless, judicial activity has not provided policy analysts the degree of support that might be expected. Instead, the courts' use of policy analysis in their attempts to resolve social problems has often illustrated the uncertainties that can arise from the interplay of analysis and values even in a relatively rational and formal institutional context.

The adversary process has been both a boon and a danger to policy analysis. It has had the advantage of increasing the demand for analysts, as neither side in litigation wishes to be found using flawed analysis and at the same time each hopes to be able to point out problems in its opponent's position. As Serge Taylor has noted, the "residual uncertainty" about what courts might do has increased the analyst's status and leverage within agencies.[1] Thus, the technically oriented analyst who wishes to avoid the partisan aspects of policy formulation can still have considerable influence simply by insisting that certain issues have to be examined in order to protect the agency's position should it become involved in litigation. Similarly, an analyst's best strategy within an agency is to provide his or her superiors with thorough and complete analysis so that agency spokesmen do not find themselves caught unprepared by their adversaries.

On the other side of the coin, the adversary nature of the judicial process seems to encourage the role of analyst as advocate and in this respect to strain the integrity of policy analysis as a profession. The freewheeling, emotional nature of many American trials poses one of the more obvious challenges to the policy analyst. For attorneys dedicated to winning for their clients, the rules of the game are extremely flexible, and policy analysts can easily be drawn into this orientation. Taylor suggested that "the mere anticipation that the other side will act to maximize its chances of prevailing on the policy issue, rather than to ascertain the evidence, may maintain a vicious circle in which both sides play fast and loose with the evidence."[2] Even the most reputable analysts can be moved to make arguments and statements that, in the heat of the courtroom drama and the opportunities provided by the media, deviate from their carefully considered conclusions.

APPROACHES TO LEGAL REASONING

From the turn of the twentieth century until 1937, the nation's courts were dominated by a concept of legal reasoning based on formal, abstract constitutional doctrines that tended to favor the interests of corporate property over those of social reformers. Drawing heavily on John Dewey's pragmatic ideas, the reformers argued that judges should move from reliance on abstract constitutional principles to concern for the concrete effects of their decisions on human lives. Probably chief among the academic critics was Roscoe Pound, dean of Harvard Law School from 1916 to 1936.

Pound adapted Dewey's philosophical ideas into what he termed "sociological jurisprudence" and urged judges to recognize that rather than objectively "finding" the law, they were engaged in making it. Sociological jurisprudence was a movement "for the adjustment of principles and doctrines to the human conditions they are to govern rather than to assumed first principles; for putting the human factor into the central place and relegating logic to its true position as an instrument."[3] Instead of shielding themselves behind legal abstractions, judges should consciously undertake an equitable balancing of the needs of social interests through "continually more efficacious social engineering."[4] In this effort, they would replace the artificial logic of the legal syllogism with the findings of social science analysis. Pound urged courts to establish laboratories and reference sources for social science research that would provide judges with accurate information on the social contexts of their cases and the effects of their decisions.

Although Pound stressed the need for empirical data to inform judicial decisions and criticized abstract natural-law doctrines, he remained convinced of the importance of general social norms in judging. The Legal Realist school, however, discounted the importance of tradition and normative standards in deciding cases. As G. Edward White has asserted, "A case, for Realists, was an autonomous entity whose doctrinal significance might well be confined to its own factual context."[5] Legal Realists, such as Jerome Frank, rejected the influence of judicial precedent and guiding legal principles in court decisions, arguing instead that judges should act on a case-by-case basis that left each case governed by the facts and issues specific to it. Because the Realists ignored precedent and the essential normative elements of the law, Pound separated himself from them in the 1930s. Nonetheless, by 1940, Legal Realism had become the dominant form of jurisprudence in American law schools.[6] This development, coupled with the Supreme Court's 1937 retreat from constitutional formalism in the face of FDR's Court-packing threat, marked a level of achievement for reformist legal thinkers that set the stage for greater judicial activism. Realism provided a conceptual basis for reformist courts to attack social evils, but its focus on particular facts and issues evaded larger questions not only about normative standards but about the essential character of institutional processes as well.[7]

SOURCES OF JUDICIAL ACTIVISM

During the 1950s, America's courts, under the guidance of a Supreme Court headed by Chief Justice Earl Warren, began to implement the activist beliefs of reformist jurisprudence. Social analysis became an important input into judicial decisions. Through the opinions of the Warren Court, the nation's courtrooms became refuges for a wide variety of interests that could not obtain satisfactory relief in the political arenas of the policy process.

Racial Desegregation

Among the grievances brought before the nation's courts, racial discrimination came to be seen as the most blatant constitutional failing of America's elected officials. The Warren Court's decisions in this area constructed constitutional bases for increased judicial activism and served as examples of the judicial application of sociological jurisprudence. In the famous 1954 *Brown v. Board of Education* decision,[8] Chief Justice Warren drew on both legal precedent and social science research to support his ruling that racial segregation in public education was unconstitutional. In particular, he argued that regardless of the tangible equality of the racially segregated schools, social analysis had established that racial segregation in and of itself had damaging effects on black children, and his famous footnote 11 invoked psychological and sociological studies for documentation.[9] Whether the Court was persuaded by the social science data or inserted it merely for additional support, its appearance in the decision demonstrated the emergent influence of a jurisprudence and reformist philosophy first articulated in the early decades of the twentieth century. Moreover, concern for the social consequences of the decision at hand was to be characteristic of Warren Court opinions not only in the area of racial discrimination but also in the areas of religion, reapportionment, criminal rights, and poverty. The task of defining problems in these areas and articulating the routes to their amelioration was to fall heavily on the shoulders of students of social analysis.

The Supreme Court's decision in *Brown v. Board of Education* was a momentous event in American history, and it was plainly radical rather than incremental in nature. Nevertheless, the impact of the constitutional doctrine propounded by the Warren Court was markedly tempered by its follow-up decision a year later in *Brown v. Board of Education II*.[10] Here, the Court in effect returned desegregation policy to the realm of incrementalism. In this decision, Chief Justice Warren emphasized the differences in local conditions and the proximity of the district courts to these conditions. Thus, the Court ordered the district courts that had originally heard the cases grouped under the *Brown* decision to monitor implementation of that decision. In this effort, Warren instructed the district courts to utilize their "equity" jurisdiction, an attribute of judicial power that allowed these courts broad flexibility in effectuating the Supreme Court's ruling. Finally, Warren urged that enforced compliance with the *Brown* decision proceed "with all deliberate speed," a phrase interpreted by many as a signal that desegregation should move slowly.

The Supreme Court's early desegregation decisions facilitated and encouraged vastly increased judicial intervention in social issues in at least three major ways. In a purely legal sense, they provided strong precedents from which federal courts could claim authority to invoke remedial powers where constitutional rights appeared to have been violated. Second, the decisions gave greater legitimacy to the analyses of social scientists. This development had less obvious but perhaps more far-reaching ramifications than the legal standards of the *Brown* decision, for it opened the possibility that the basis for legal standing to pursue social issues could be broadened considerably. Essentially, if social problems were to become a concern of the judicial system, then courts could be expected to be much more sensitive to the existence of these problems as defined by social scientists, who, on the whole, have never been hesitant in locating instances of social injustice. Finally, the activities of the National Association for the Advancement of Colored People (NAACP) and other groups confirmed the effectiveness of organization as a means of favorably influencing the judicial process and, ultimately, the supreme law of the land as enunciated by the nation's highest court.

Procedural Changes

The activist ramifications of the early desegregation decisions were reinforced in succeeding decades by the Supreme Court's liberalization of the requirements of "standing to sue," the basis on which litigants may claim an injury that allows them to bring a case before a court. The Court's receptivity to new kinds of cases has given it a much greater role in establishing rules and values for society. Interest groups have also gained in influence as the Court has shown a greater willingness to consider their analyses of social problems.

Ironically, the growth of interventionist government, largely at the urging of one generation of social reformers, created serious concern among a later generation of reformers. This later generation looked to an activist judiciary to correct injustices that they argued were created by the welfare state. These views were articulated forcefully in Charles A. Reich's article "The New Property," which appeared in the *Yale Law Journal* in 1964. Reich contended that government largesse had created a new form of property that was almost wholly dependent on bureaucratic discretion. In their efforts to invoke governmental aid in the cause of social change, previous reformers had "summoned up a doctrine monstrous and oppressive" that in effect made much of society dependent on administrative discretion for economic profit, or, more seriously, for bare subsistence.[11] The administrative process was "characterized by uncertainty, delay, and inordinate expense; to operate within it requires considerable knowhow."[12] Those with sufficient resources could eventually manipulate the system to their benefit; the individual indigent, dependent on welfare and other forms of assistance, remained at the mercy of the bureaucracy.

Reich argued that it was time that government assistance be treated as a form of property protected by adequate legal procedures: "There is no justification for the survival of arbitrary methods where valuable rights are at stake."[13] The inequities of the administrative process should be replaced with judicially enforced due process protections that ensured the application of fair procedures before governmental benefits were terminated. In essence, Reich was saying that the courts should allow standing to individuals and organizations to enable them to obtain protection from administrative bias and arbitrariness, and his article has been credited with influencing the Supreme Court's move in this direction. In particular, his views seem to have found support in *Goldberg v. Kelly* (1970).[14] Here, the Court explicitly rejected the view of governmental aid as a privilege that could be withheld in favor of the view that an indigent's welfare assistance was a legal right that could not be terminated without affording that person proper due process protections.

Although the Court drew back from granting carte blanche procedural protections to those receiving governmental assistance, it continued to widen the basis for gaining access to the federal courts. By 1976, Karen Orren could announce the existence of a markedly more flexible standing test that appeared to stem from a "pronounced disenchantment" with administrative processes among Supreme Court justices.[15] Standing to sue under the restrictive "aggrieved party" standard of the Administrative Procedure Act of 1946 had required a demonstration that a specific statutory or constitutional right had been infringed by governmental action. Thirty years later, this standard had been widened into a judicially protected "zone of interests" that allowed a range of postmaterialist organized interests—including environmentalists, consumer groups, and historical preservationists—to claim the infliction of noneconomic, intangible injuries by agency decisions as the basis for standing to sue.

Orren was especially concerned about the courts' willingness to accept broad definitions of what constituted legally redressable injury. Often, these definitions were formulated by organizations posing as representatives for whole segments of the population, such as consumers or nature lovers. The justices' generosity toward the pleas of organized interests raised the distinct possibility that the particularistic definitions of social problems formulated by these interests would lead to the legal imposition of their narrow normative standards on society at large.

Organized Interests

In the judicial arena, organized interests have not been able to establish the kind of direct access and pervasive influence that they have in other areas of the policy process, but they have become an essential ingredient in the formulation of policy by the courts. Simply in terms of the financial resources necessary to pursue a case, particularly when social issues are concerned, group organization is necessary. Groups have also developed strategies that help ensure favorable court decisions. Chief among these is the use of test cases that are carefully selected to present the facts and issues in a light favorable to the group's position. Often, these cases are filed as class action suits, making them, in essence, suits on behalf of all individuals similarly affected by the governmental action or inaction at issue and positioning the interest-group litigant as the spokesperson for these people. When a class action suit is allowed, the court's decision automatically applies to all persons disadvantaged by the governmental policy, not just to the particular litigants to the case. These strategies, in conjunction with the greater powers exercised by courts and their willingness to consider social science data, have provided organized interests with important power over society.[16]

With the careful use of policy analysis, interests can locate and define social problems of concern to them. They are then able to use organizational resources and legal skills to introduce these data into the courtroom in an effort to obtain a ruling defining and expanding their rights. An excellent example of this approach was provided by the Supreme Court's consideration of a challenge to capital punishment based primarily on statistical analyses of the racial application of the death sentence.[17] The plaintiff's contention was that because proportionately more blacks than whites received the death sentence, its use must be seen as racially motivated. The Court, however, declined to base its consideration of the constitutionality of capital punishment on these statistical data or their general social extrapolation. The Court has also responded to the introduction of "junk science"—scientifically questionable conclusions about health and environmental hazard—into court proceedings by granting judges increased discretion in excluding such evidence, which is often intended primarily to appeal to the emotions of the jury.[18]

EXAMPLES OF JUDICIAL ACTIVISM: SOCIAL AND TECHNOLOGICAL CHANGE

Other examples of judicial activism can be drawn from the fields of public education and institutionalized care. In these areas, it became evident that group efforts to expand rights entailed a significant expansion of the power of the federal courts in society. As the courts exercised this power, they became embroiled in political battles with elected officials and state bureaucracies that quickly overshadowed the input of policy analysts.

After having used the judicial process successfully to obtain the *Brown* decision, civil rights groups maintained continued litigious pressure on local school boards to ensure movement toward integration. The resulting court decisions led to step-by-step increases in the power of lower federal courts. The key decision in this respect was *Green v. County School Board* (1968).[19] Here, declaring its impatience with the pace of school desegregation, the Supreme Court specified that school boards had an affirmative duty to act to remedy conditions of segregation and that district court judges should be more aggressive in seeing that school boards acted constructively. In Bernard Schwartz's opinion,

> Under *Green,* the district courts were now expressly vested with the affirmative duty to supervise the operation of desegregation plans. The clear implication was that they should do whatever they deemed necessary to ensure that those plans proved effective in practice. Discharge of the judicial duty here might well involve the courts in the intimate details of school administration.[20]

The Court further decreed that lower-court judges had the authority to retain jurisdiction of a desegregation case until they were certain that segregation stemming from deliberate state policy had been eliminated.

Racial Integration

The *Green* decision precipitated a flurry of renewed activity among civil rights groups. In Charlotte, North Carolina, District Court Judge James B. McMillan received a petition asking that the local school board be ordered to undertake an effective effort to desegregate the Charlotte-Mecklenburg School District.[21] Although as a prominent member of the North Carolina bar McMillan had publicly stated his skepticism of forced integration, the plaintiffs' analyses and use of precedent convinced him of the illegality of the existing situation and of his responsibility to act. Despite repeated orders from Judge McMillan, however, the Charlotte-Mecklenburg School Board refused to come forward with a desegregation plan that met constitutional standards. Finally, Judge McMillan designated Dr. John A. Finger Jr., an expert on school desegregation policy, to formulate an acceptable plan. In February 1970, Judge McMillan ordered the school board to implement the Finger Plan by the end of the school year; the plan called for the daily busing of 10,000 students to achieve racially balanced schools. Although the public outcry against Judge McMillan's order was tremendous, the Supreme Court unanimously affirmed it in *Swann* v. *Charlotte-Mecklenburg* (1971),[22] thereby imposing a judicial solution on a heated public policy debate being waged throughout the nation.

Despite the volatility of the busing issue, within a reasonably short time after the *Swann* decision, Judge McMillan obtained compliance from the school board. In this, he was aided considerably by the good offices of the Citizens Advisory Group, which acted as liaison between the school board and the court and served to soften for the school board members the impact of judicial directives. In 1974, Judge McMillan approved a revised integration plan from the school board, and in 1975, he withdrew from supervision of the school board, ending seven years of litigation.

Meanwhile, in Boston, District Court Judge Wendell Arthur Garrity continued to have difficulty bringing the school board into constitutional compliance on the issue of racial balance in the schools.[23] In the spring of 1972, Judge Garrity had begun hearings in *Morgan* v. *Hennigan*,[24] a case with which he was to be closely involved for the next decade. During this period, continued opposition by the school board to judicially mandated integration led Judge Garrity to assume administrative control of the Boston schools, an action that involved him in the day-to-day management of the public schools to a degree unprecedented in the federal judiciary. As school superintendent, Judge Garrity set school hours and supervised the hiring and firing of personnel. At a more mundane level of detail, he found himself ordering twelve MacGregor basketballs and six Acme Tornado whistles for South Boston. Concerned also with students' creature comforts, Judge Garrity cautioned those converting elementary schools into middle-level schools to take care to see that the urinals were elevated.[25] But despite prodigious efforts and extraordinary attention to detail, Judge Garrity was never able to obtain the community support necessary to make racial balance a constructive educational experience in Boston.

In June 1974, after hearing testimony on the question of racial discrimination in the Boston schools, Judge Garrity issued a 152-page opinion finding that deliberate discrimination by the school board existed. Then, as an interim implementation measure, he adopted a state Department of Education plan. Like Judge McMillan's plan, this one drew on the input of policy specialist Dr. Finger. It mandated widespread busing, but most serious was its attempt to combine students from white working-class South Boston with students from the black Roxbury area. The intense opposition in these areas to the integration plan led to rioting that in October forced Governor Francis W. Sargent to call out the National Guard to restore order.

During this time, Judge Garrity established a masters' committee to recommend to the court a long-term plan for integration of the schools. J. Anthony Lukas saw this group of six Bostonians as being guided primarily by Edward McCormack, a prominent Boston attorney and politician. After holding extensive public hearings, the masters' committee presented Judge Garrity with a plan that they believed was constitutionally adequate and had broad community acceptance. Judge Garrity, however, rejected important parts of the plan by increasing the number of children to be bused and retaining the combination of the Roxbury and South Boston areas. The result was continued community bitterness and opposition and white flight from the public schools, with the trend line pointing dismally toward a public school system that would soon be predominantly black and poor in its student composition.[26]

Although the contexts and results differed markedly, the desegregation actions of Judges McMillan and Garrity contained parallels that spoke to the policy future of the federal courts. Both drew heavily on analyses of education specialists, both utilized interim groups of community leaders, and both, with varying degrees of success, sought community support. Most important, however, the racial desegregation decisions allowed these judges and others throughout the federal system to develop an arsenal of tools and techniques for enhancing their effectiveness as policy implementers. Essentially, federal judges were creating an image of judicial power that was to carry over into other areas of judicial concern. The opportunities for such intervention increased as courts responded sympathetically to analytical social findings that supported legal efforts to expand the already broadened criteria for standing to sue.

Other Areas of Social Distress

The impetus that the racial desegregation cases provided for judicial intervention in other social areas was illustrated exceptionally well by the record of District Court Judge Frank Johnson of the Middle District of Alabama, whose career has been ably chronicled by Tinsley Yarbrough.[27] In important ways, Judge Johnson's early initiatives in school desegregation were to foreshadow his attempts to reform the state's prisons and mental institutions. What is particularly fascinating about Judge Johnson's approach to social change is that he was not eager to invoke the extensive powers of his position. He acted at an early date to remedy segregated schools in central Alabama, but he never advocated the idea of forced busing of students. And although he fought bitter battles with the authorities of Alabama, he remained throughout reluctant to use the court's contempt power to gain compliance. Judge Johnson was effective as a force for social change because he was intelligent, patient, politically astute, and sensitive to the positions of administrators and the community at large.

In March 1967, Judge Johnson authored the decree of a three-judge federal court requiring the end of segregated schools in Alabama. The objective was clear, but the means adopted by the judges were gradual. The judges met weekly with school district officials from around the state, monitoring their progress toward integration and moving them toward greater compliance. In the meantime, the judges were gradually tightening the standards to be met. In this manner, Judge Johnson and his brethren moved the schools of Alabama toward integration with a minimum of violence. Equally important in the light of his later actions, Judge Johnson's firmness and good judgment won him the respect of the federal appellate courts, which were subsequently willing to grant him a great deal of flexibility in his approaches to other problems.

Judge Johnson's movement into Alabama's mental health institutions began in earnest in October 1970, with the case of *Wyatt* v. *Stickney*.[28] His exercise of judicial power during the litigation of this case was nothing short of sweeping. Although the case was originally filed on behalf of employees who were being cut from the payroll in mental institutions, Judge Johnson informed the attorneys at an early date that he was more interested in the rights of the patients. As a result, the attorneys quickly transformed the case into a class action suit on behalf of the patients in the state's three mental institutions. In March 1971, Judge Johnson issued a preliminary finding holding that the state's mental patients had a constitutional right to "adequate treatment," a position for which he had almost no supporting precedents.[29] Thus, Judge Johnson refocused the case away from the claims of the original plaintiffs and then almost by simple assertion created constitutional rights for the new plaintiffs. After a series of hearings featuring testimony by many experts in the field, the judge issued a comprehensive order with detailed standards to be met by the three mental institutions. To monitor implementation of his order, he established a human rights committee for each institution. The Fifth Circuit Court of Appeals upheld Judge Johnson's decision, and the Supreme Court denied review of the case, making *Wyatt* v. *Stickney* a major constitutional precedent for standards in mental institutions.

Judge Johnson's forays into the Alabama prison system had a firmer constitutional basis than his ruling on treatment of the state's mental patients, as there were numerous precedents in which federal judges had intervened on behalf of state prisoners. After extensive hearings, conditions in the prisons were found to be so bad that the state conceded they violated the constitutional prohibition against cruel and unusual punishment and agreed to work with the plaintiffs in formulating a plan that would pass constitutional muster. In January 1976, Judge Johnson issued a comprehensive order detailing the standards to be met in the Alabama prisons. Following his *Wyatt* approach, he established a human rights committee to monitor state compliance with his order. Governor George Wallace, apparently taken aback by the scope of Judge Johnson's ruling, denied that he had given the state's attorneys the authority to enter into a consent agreement. Although he apologized for his public statements that federal judges should be given barbed-wire enemas, the governor proceeded to appeal Judge Johnson's order. Ultimately, the circuit court of appeals upheld much of the judge's opinion. It did not, however, support his specification of space requirements for prisoners or his order that prisoners be provided with educational or vocational training opportunities. It also disagreed with his use of a human rights committee, arguing that a single master, who could monitor but not intervene in prison affairs, would be more appropriate.

Judge Johnson recognized early in his reform efforts the importance of maintaining continuing communication with the parties to a case and with the political system. He made extensive use of his ties with the "old boy network" in Alabama politics, which went back to his law school days with Governor Wallace and other leading politicians. Nonetheless, he constantly encountered opposition from the state's bureaucrats, who were often backed by Governors George or Lurleen Wallace. His human rights committees met particular difficulties in attempting to work with the Alabama prison authorities; at one point, he had to threaten to reclassify each prisoner personally before cooperation was achieved. Only when George Wallace stepped down from the governor's office did Judge Johnson face a more amenable political climate. At that point, Wallace's successor, Governor Forrest F. James, asked Judge Johnson to appoint him receiver for both the mental health system and the prison system, a request that the judge quickly granted. This development reflected Governor James's desire to remove the federal courts from a supervisory capacity. But, more significantly, it suggested that the state finally had a chief executive prepared to accept responsibility for providing adequate care for the less fortunate.[30]

As judges have moved from dealing with clear constitutional wrongs involving race to social problems that are often vaguely defined and poorly understood, they have faced increasingly effective opposition from other policy bodies, as Judge Johnson's record attests. Such struggles have at times called into question the capabilities of the courts as policymakers. In essence, federal district courts have found it far more difficult to direct large state bureaucracies and state legislatures than to command the compliance of local school boards. Robert A. Burt has argued that "no matter what judges do, they have only limited capacity to command obedience from these mammoth bureaucratic enterprises charged with complex social welfare functions."[31] Not only are the state bureaucracies large and complex; they are also peopled by experts in their fields who have survived and prospered as much through their political skills as through their knowledge. Thus, at the state level, the courts have encountered political alliances and relationships similar to those that have grown so powerful at the national level. When federal judges in New York and Pennsylvania moved into the mental-health area, they found such coalitions particularly resistant to their efforts and effective implementation of their decisions exceedingly elusive.

In New York, in response to petitions filed in 1972 asking the courts to intervene to reform the horrible conditions at the Willowbrook Developmental Center, a state school for the retarded, U.S. District Court Judge Orrin Judd issued a preliminary injunction that attempted to provide an interim remedy until formal judicial proceedings had run their course.[32] A lengthy trial ensued. Before Judge Judd could issue a final decision, the state of New York and Governor Hugh Carey entered into a consent decree, agreeing to meet court-imposed standards. Of these, the most substantive was that the number of Willowbrook's inmates was to be reduced from over 5,000 to 250 within six years. To monitor the changes at Willowbrook and to make recommendations for improvement, Judge Judd appointed a review panel. Almost immediately, the review panel met opposition from the New York State Department of Mental Hygiene. This conflict continued until April 1980, when the state legis-lature eliminated the funding for the review panel and Governor Carey refused to act to provide other monies. Judge John Bartels, who had assumed responsi-bility for the litigation on the death of Judge Judd in 1976, held Governor Carey in contempt for his inaction. The Second Circuit Court of Appeals overruled Judge Bartels's contempt citation, however, holding that a federal court could not force the governor to act contrary to state law.

Subsequently, Judge Bartels appointed a special master to monitor the Willowbrook situation. The transition from Willowbrook as a substandard insti-tutional facility to one that met professionally acceptable housing standards was finally completed in September 1987, and the facility was renamed the Staten Island Developmental Center. In March 1993, Judge Bartels, now ninety-five years old and peering closely at the relevant legal papers to be able to read them, signed off on eighteen years of federal court supervision of the Willowbrook case. The buildings of the former Willowbrook Developmental Center had by that time become part of Staten Island Community College.[33] By 1999, only 2,000 individuals remained in state mental institutions in New York, and that number was expected to dwindle to approximately 800.

In Pennsylvania, District Court Judge Raymond Broderick was also facing sustained obstruction from state officials in his efforts to deal with the problems at Pennhurst State School and Hospital. In December 1977, after a trial of thirty-two days in which he heard testimony from numerous witnesses, Judge Broderick concluded that the only effective remedy for the conditions at Pennhurst was its closure.[34] He ordered the institution closed and its residents transferred largely to community residences. The state, however, maintained that he did not have the authority to order closure or to specify the criteria for Pennhurst's termination as a mental institution. The result was a series of challenges to Judge Broderick's orders that several times reached the Supreme Court. Of particular note here is that the High Court tended to support the state's position, but the Third Circuit Court of Appeals and Judge Broderick were able to interpret its decisions narrowly and thus maintain pressure on the state.

Following his original decision, Judge Broderick had appointed a special master to monitor the closing of Pennhurst. At one point emboldened by New York State's action, the Pennsylvania legislature, with the public support of the head of the state welfare department, halted funding for the special master's office. This action brought a quick contempt citation from Judge Broderick against the state department head. The citation was affirmed by the court of appeals, and the state legislature renewed the funding. Apparently the legislature empathized with Georgia's governor Marvin Griffin, who, when asked how he felt about contempt citations, is reputed to have responded, "Being in jail sorta crimps a governor's style."[35] Although no one went to jail in the Pennhurst case, the state, for a variety of actions and inactions, eventually was assessed over $1 million in fines for contempt of court.

Finally, in August 1982, Judge Broderick dismissed the special master's office and assumed direct control of the case himself. Numerous hearings and orders followed, with the judge continually pointing to the state's recalcitrance. In July 1983, the state and the private plaintiffs to the case reached an agreement to close Pennhurst by July 1986; although this deadline was not met, by the fall of 1986, Pennhurst was close to being emptied of inmates.

Judicial Social Activism in Perspective

As the courts have moved from the protection of racial rights into other categories of social policy, questions have arisen as to the institutional capability of the judiciary to deal effectively with controversial policy questions.[36] Some of the difficulties the courts have faced have stemmed from the essentially political nature of the problems with which they have found themselves dealing, as was the case for Judge Johnson in Alabama. In contrast to the frequent inaction or ambiguous decisions of the electorally responsible parts of the policy process, courts can issue concrete decisions. But they then encounter the problems of institutional and procedural fragmentation in the *implementation* of their decisions. Furthermore, as administrative and legislative policymakers become more adept at dragging their collective feet in response to judicial edicts, it will become even more difficult for the courts to achieve constructive compliance. In this kind of context, judges are almost forced to move from behind the bench into the policy melee to monitor the implementation of their decisions.

In addition to political obstacles to judicial policymaking, the forms and procedures of the judicial process itself limit the effectiveness of the courts. A lawsuit is a formal, often excruciatingly detailed process that limits a court to the initiative of the parties and to the facts and arguments presented by them. A court may, of course, allow other interested parties to participate in argument as amicus curiae (friend of the court) and may request additional information, but a judge's sources of usable information remain severely limited in comparison with those available to other policymaking bodies. As a consequence, in most cases, the vision of the court is bounded by the parameters of an issue as presented by the adversary parties, and the broader social and political aspects of a question receive little or no formal consideration. Philip J. Cooper has noted a tendency for defendants in cases calling for remedial decrees to narrow a judge's perspective by stipulating to the facts or refusing to present a defense. Not only do these tactics deny the judge the "validity check of a balanced adversary process" but they also weaken or dilute the record on which the judge's decision will be based.[37] This narrow focus is reinforced by the natural tendency of judges, as the products of a particular kind of educational and socialization process, to think of issues in terms of rights rather than in terms of alternative ways of resolving complex problems and reconciling conflicting interests. The backgrounds of judges and the institutionalized focus of the judicial process encourage courts to think in terms of the apportionment of blame and the application of proper constitutional remedies at a time when they are being drawn into policy issues more appropriately dealt with in a broader, more flexible fashion.[38]

Efforts by Judge Johnson and the courts in New York and Pennsylvania to reform state institutions were, like the attacks on racial segregation, guided initially by moral outrage. In these cases, the conditions challenged were so bad that the parties to the litigation agreed to their lack of constitutional validity. Consequently, the findings and suggestions of policy analysts that became part of the judicial record did not receive the scrutiny they might otherwise have. Opposition by state bureaucracies to judicial remedies grew only when the extent and costs of these remedies, based heavily on the recommendations of specialists in the areas, emerged.

In these cases, the problematic role of the analyst in the judicial process became apparent. Judge Johnson relied extensively on expert opinions in his detailed implementation orders and in fact attempted to have academic specialists participate in the actual reform of the Alabama prison system.[39] These opinions and efforts were not well received by those shouldering the tasks of day-to-day administration. The confrontation was not simply one of uncaring vested interests versus humane reformers. Judge Johnson's original order detailing cell size, for example, specified a standard nowhere met in the Alabama prison system. Judge Broderick's order closing Pennhurst was based on testimony by those favoring community placement, a position that was soon challenged by other specialists in the field. These professionals argued persuasively that for some mentally disabled, institutionalization was both more effective and more humane.[40]

Although the orders rendered by the judges in these cases had legitimate roots in the professional literature, the original court cases themselves and the ensuing hearings encouraged the full play of the analyst as advocate. A variety of professional associations and reform-oriented advocacy groups quickly joined the various legal efforts. Believing they were engaged in an adversary process, these groups naturally presented their arguments and data in as strong a fashion as possible. When the defendants agreed to many of their challenges, the plaintiffs' views survived in the judicial forum without the tempering, or moderating, effects that active opposition might have had. The courts in turn were denied the wider consideration of approaches that more confrontational interaction could have provided.

The restricted focus of the judiciary makes it vulnerable to exploitation by organized interests. Because they have the ability to initiate and monitor cases throughout the country, organized interests can select for sustained litigation those cases that appear to present the most blatant violations of constitutional rights. To further enhance their chances of judicial success, organizations can employ the services of policy analysts to locate and define judicially cognizable problems that will widen the range of issues on which they can litigate. Thus, in the 1970s, the Sierra Club undertook to challenge every environmental impact statement of the Forest Service's Unit Plan in that agency's California region.[41] The combination of greater use of policy analysis, increased organizational activity, and wider reliance on the test-case strategy has often left the courts responding to "worst possible case" types of behavior. The courts may then impose on everyone living or working in similar conditions constitutional remedies fashioned to deal with such situations. As Taylor has noted, the effects can be unsettling to agencies:

> A court aroused by a particularly egregious case which it regards as "typical," or at least as unacceptably frequent, may therefore operate with an incorrect theory of what caused the problem, and in all likelihood also with an incorrect theory of how to remedy it. In its zeal to fashion a remedy, a court may disrupt agency policy and procedures in ways that the agency regards as much worse than reversing a particular decision, or sometimes even the general policy at issue.[42]

Effective implementation of judicial policy has also become a more serious problem as the courts have intervened in a greater range of social issues. Part of the difficulty appears to be conceptual, and part is clearly institutional. On the former point, Bruce Ackerman argued that within the context of a welfare, interventionist state, activist lawyers operating from a Realist conceptual framework are engaged in an unending quest for reform. In his view, "the activist lawsuit is but a chapter in a never-ending story of the polity's struggle with an ongoing problem. . . . A final judgment no longer suggests that everything worth saying has been said, only that it is best, all things considered, to say no more for a time."[43] In institutional terms, judges are limited in their ability to ensure effective implementation of their decisions because in most instances they must proceed on a case-by-case approach that depends on litigation brought by those adversely affected. Conceptually and institutionally, courts are oriented toward piecemeal adjudication of issues that may never reach areas of policy difficulty in which interest or resources for litigation are lacking.

The conclusions suggested here are not altered by the fact that some judges have undertaken continual, comprehensive monitoring of the implementation of their decisions. Any extensive imitation of these efforts would put an unbearable strain on the resources of the nation's courts, which are already backlogged in many areas. Even when comprehensive orders have been issued, the presiding judges have often found themselves continuously modifying them in response to petitions brought by the litigants.

Under Chief Justices Warren Burger and William Rehnquist, the Supreme Court has been reluctant to act to redress social ills, although it has initiated and expanded constitutional rights for women. Most striking about the Supreme Court under Chief Justice Rehnquist has been the Court's careful scaling back of its activist role in social policy while insisting on the observance of what it sees as the institutional integrity of the constitutional system. Thus, in the 1990s, the Rehnquist Court overturned the item veto,[44] insisted on a census by capitation,[45] voided term limits on members of Congress,[46] and acted vigorously to protect the states from what it saw as congressional threats to federalism.[47] In these decisions, the Court often declared congressional or state statutes unconstitutional. At the same time, the Court reduced its docket markedly, leaving for final decision by the lower courts cases that previous, more activist High Courts would likely have accepted for final review.

The Rehnquist Court's refusal to undertake more active social reform, its deference to the states, and its reduced dockets have relegated important policymaking to the lower federal courts and to the state judiciaries. This has led to a patchwork of law across the states in such areas as individual rights. In the lower federal courts, it has opened opportunities for agencies and advocacy groups to pursue long-term strategies that seek statutory interpretations favorable to their causes.

In a study of the evolution of AFDC, food stamp programs, and programs to educate the handicapped, R. Shep Melnick discovered that statutory interpretation by the lower federal courts was an essential ingredient in the strategy of interests striving for reform. As a result of the civil rights struggles of the 1960s and 1970s, U.S. district courts and courts of appeal gained substantial policymaking powers, and clientele and advocacy groups moved to exploit these venues. Melnick found that these groups, many of which were funded by foundations and by the government itself, had become "sophisticated repeat players with long-range litigational strategies. . . . These groups were well aware of the risks of Supreme Court review, especially on constitutional issues. They adapted their arguments to the new judicial terrain, stressing statutory rather than constitutional arguments and putting more emphasis on winning a string of cases in the lower courts."[48] In Melnick's view, the Supreme Court is no longer where the action is when the detailed implementation of public policy is at issue.[49]

Given the Court's limited view of its role, it now seems to be actively encouraging policymaking in other judicial jurisdictions. This has not only fostered doctrinal variety among state jurisdictions; it seems to be extending heterogeneity across the lower federal courts as well. For example, differences in statutory interpretation among courts of appeal no longer automatically draw the Supreme Court into the fray.[50] Adding to the confusion is that there are discernible ideological variations among the various circuits, with the Fourth Circuit establishing itself as consistently conservative and the Ninth Circuit, the largest in the nation, as consistently liberal. In what must stand as some sort of record, the Supreme Court in its 1996–97 term overruled twenty-eight of the twenty-nine Ninth Circuit decisions appealed to it. It is still too early to determine the overall configuration of the policy process that the Supreme Court is sculpting. However, the current direction seems likely to encourage greater fragmentation in the implementation of national policy by allowing interpretational differences by region and by encouraging interests that lose in one jurisdiction to continue to litigate in others until they find favorable treatment.

Judicial Response to Technological Change

When the courts have moved into policy areas involving the problems caused by technological change, they have faced difficulties as serious as those encountered in their efforts to effect social change. Where science and technology are concerned, judges carry the additional burden of lacking expertise in these areas.[51] Somewhat surprisingly, the courts' attempts to resolve problems wrought by science and technology have made the need for values in rendering final decisions most obvious. In these contests, both sides have drawn heavily on analytical claims, and it has rapidly become apparent that policy analysis does not play ideological favorites. After examining the extensive use of cost-benefit analysis by the Army Corps of Engineers and the environmental groups in their court battles, Taylor concluded that everyone "now realizes that the issue is a value choice."[52] Faced with a lack of fundamental normative consensus and the rapid pace of scientific change, judges have been sorely pressed in their efforts to draw on their generalist backgrounds and a legal tradition based on gradual movement toward legal change to fashion workable accommodations to the demands of social interests. Their approaches to environmental issues provide examples of some of the problems raised by scientific and technological change.

In February 1972, the U.S. Environmental Protection Agency filed suit in the District Court of Minnesota against the Reserve Mining Company of Silver Bay, Minnesota.[53] Reserve Mining extracted iron ore north of Silver Bay, and at its Silver Bay plant on the shore of Lake Superior, it processed the ore into small pellets for shipment to Ohio steel plants. In this process, the taconite waste from which the iron ore was separated was dumped into Lake Superior at the rate of 67,000 tons per day, creating a turbid layer estimated to be 37 miles wide, 3 miles long, and 100 to 300 feet deep. Before the trial began, the case received impetus from the discovery that the asbestos-like fibers from the taconite waste were in the drinking water of communities along Lake Superior, including that of Duluth, approximately 50 miles to the south. These fibers also were present in the air around Silver Bay. After a trial lasting 134 days over a nine-month period, in which experts from both sides as well as court-appointed experts gave testimony, Judge Miles W. Lord found that Reserve Mining was creating a serious health hazard and issued an injunction ordering the plant to stop dumping waste into Lake Superior. This injunction was almost immediately stayed by the Eighth Circuit Court of Appeals.

In November, after lengthy negotiations at the appellate and district court levels, petitions to the court of appeals, and remands by the appellate court back to Judge Lord for resolution of various issues, Judge Lord, without giving Reserve Mining opportunity to be heard, ordered the company to pay the city of Duluth $100,000 in damages. In his order, Judge Lord noted that "I have dispensed with the usual adversary proceedings here, because I simply do not have time to spend, as I did, nine months in hearing, six months of which was wasted by what I find now, and did find in my opinions, to be misrepresentations by Reserve Mining Company."[54] In January 1976, the Eighth Circuit Court of Appeals dissolved Judge Lord's order, returned the funds to the company, and took the unusual step of ordering Judge Lord removed from the case entirely. Finally, in May 1976, after more than seven years of litigation and negotiations, Judge Lord's successor, Judge Edward J. Devitt, in a decision later affirmed at the appellate level, ordered Reserve Mining to pay over $1 million in fines and costs and to halt dumping in Lake Superior by 7 July 1977.[55]

The Reserve Mining case in many ways is a classic example of a clash of values, technology, and judicial procedure. Judge Lord, convinced of the danger of taconite dumping to human health, found himself frustrated by the tactics of the company and the lack of support from his court of appeals. At the same time, the evidence of the imminent danger posed to communities by the fibers in their water was not strong. Although no one disputed the need for action, the real issue for the company was how soon it had to act to find an alternative means of disposing of its waste products. In this respect, Judge Lord, a man of strong convictions, appears to have been frustrated as much by the requirements of the legal process as by the tactics of the Reserve Mining Company.

Congress has also been slow to recognize the difficulties that scientific and technological change pose for judicial policymaking. The National Environmental Policy Act (NEPA) of 1969, which required that government projects be preceded by an acceptable environmental impact statement, was an attempt by Congress to enlist policy analysts in informing and legitimizing governmental decisions. The act is one instance among many in which Congress fairly directly deferred the details of policy questions to the courts and administrators.

Congress's imposition of the environmental impact requirement reflected that body's belief that proper analysis of a project's effects would contribute to protection of the environment and to agreement as to an action's merit. In practice, however, its most important immediate consequence was that organizations intent on preventing environmental damage perceived it as another basis for litigation against governmental agencies, such as the Forest Service and the Army Corps of Engineers. The ensuing lawsuits increased the demand for policy analysts both within and outside government. As the opposing interests clashed in the judicial arena, it soon became apparent that the courts were ill prepared and reluctant to engage in difficult scientific questions. The adversarial employment of analytical findings did not necessarily contribute to greater clarification of issues or certainty about appropriate approaches to their resolution.

Unfortunately for policy analysts and the courts, environmental groups have raised the ante in the policy process significantly with their campaigns against many of the federal dams across the nation. Often, these dams have been in place for decades, and industries have come to depend on them for transportation and power. Nonetheless, environmental groups, including the Sierra Club, argue that the return of rivers to their natural state may justify the uprooting of established communities and economies. In the words of Adam Werbach, president of the Sierra Club, "If we want to actually look forward to the next step of the environmental movement, we're going to have to talk about proactively restoring parts of nature that have been destroyed."[56] Along the lower Snake River, the four dams challenged by environmentalists contribute at least $34 million annually to the port of Lewiston, Idaho. The Glen Canyon Dam forming Lake Powell from the Colorado River has an even greater economic impact. This dam has engendered a local economy of $400 million a year; 20 million people depend on it for water, and approximately 400,000 households use its hydroelectric power.[57] The more activist environmentalists point out that these dams have had adverse effects on the water quality and aquatic life of their rivers and argue that for these reasons they must be "busted." Suggesting that a less obvious agenda may be operative in these confrontations, some commentators have contended that federal dams provide a rallying point for environmental groups that have lost their dynamism. Not surprisingly, these controversies have generated tremendous political activity, and policy analysts for the National Marine Fisheries Service and the Army Corps of Engineers are diligently studying the impact of the dams on the Snake River. It seems clear, however, that in at least some cases, judges will ultimately have to decide whether targeted dams will continue and that they will not have many procedural refuges to which to turn.[58]

The governmental agencies often lost the early challenges to their environmental impact statements because the issues raised were largely procedural. As agencies became more careful about following the proper steps in preparing impact statements, environmentalists turned to questioning the accuracy of the statements. The agencies responded to this tack by preparing detailed analyses and extensive justifications of their proposals. During this phase of the struggle, the agencies were usually successful in court, primarily for two reasons. First, they were able to use their superior resources to "outmuscle" the private-interest groups by providing elaborately documented and detailed analyses and by continuing cases through the various levels of judicial appeal. Second, the courts' unwillingness to delve into complex scientific areas prompted them to give credence to agency positions once they were satisfied that the appropriate procedural standards had been met.[59]

In their attempts to supervise adherence to the requirements of NEPA, the courts found themselves in a highly technical area without a tradition of judicial precedents for guidance and acting under the authority of legislation lacking in precision. As laypersons in the scientific field, judges may have justifiably felt themselves on tenuous grounds deciding substantive environmental questions. But as students of the law, they were specialists in the demands of proper procedure. Thus, in aggressively holding agencies accountable to their own regulations and the requirements of NEPA, the courts were drawing on their particular form of expertise to enhance the legitimacy of their decisions. Although the agencies have been largely successful on substantive issues, the willingness of the courts to act against them in the procedural area created considerable uncertainty as to how comprehensive their impact statements had to be. This, in turn, gave increased influence to the agencies' policy analysts, who were looked to not only for their methodological skills but also for their sense of what facets of an issue might have to be defended in court.

Fundamentally, the experiences of Judge Lord and those judges dealing with implementation of NEPA point out once again the importance of normative consensus to effective policy. Scientific analysis, whether of the physical or social variety, cannot substitute for basic social agreement on a question, nor can it by itself induce such agreement. The effectiveness of the courts in the area of racial discrimination rested not on the findings cited by Chief Justice Warren in footnote 11, but on the widespread belief in American society that it is wrong to treat people differently because of skin color. Despite historical and regional aberrations, the idea of equality of opportunity has constituted a basic normative position for Americans. But in the environmental field and in other areas featuring rapid technological advances, such generally held norms do not yet exist, and, as William Lowrance has suggested, "Special contention arises where somewhat uncertain science intersects with somewhat uncertain values."[60] Where the postulates of science have found agreement over time, there is little room for controversy, although changes will eventually occur even in these firmly held opinions. Alternatively, even without scientific certainty in an area, if a society has an accepted normative interpretation of the world that encompasses that area, there exists a basis for reaching acceptable solutions to problems. Unfortunately, the thrust in today's political culture has been toward greater normative divisiveness and the politicization of scientific findings.

With regard to the latter point, Hugh Heclo has argued that the attempt to paper over ideological divisions by relying more heavily on what appears to be administrative expertise can have serious consequences for public policy and policy analysis.[61] In the current policy context, analysis can quickly become another weapon in the political arsenals of competing camps, resulting in a cacophony of analytical findings and perspectives that deepens cynicism and apathy among the citizenry. Overanalysis of issues, then, may serve primarily to avoid basic normative divisions that are the real sources of difficulty in achieving workable policy. Lowrance has noted that it is much easier to use analytic techniques to identify problems and to demarcate inequities than it is to fashion fair solutions.[62] A culture fragmented by deep value differences renders the question of fairness even more difficult to resolve.

THE LIMITS OF JUDICIAL POWER

Although the Realist movement in American jurisprudence provided an important service by moving the judiciary toward an accommodation with the activist state, it failed to recognize the importance of the broader cultural and political contexts of judicial opinions. The procedures of the legal process and the reasoning of judges have not carried sufficient rational force to inculcate widespread obedience to judicial decrees when the courts have moved into judicially uncharted areas. Judge Johnson experienced the painful consequences of limited judicial power in such circumstances when mental institutions in Alabama met his ceilings on patient populations simply by releasing inmates. Subsequently, some were injured, and others were left wandering around the community. The judge's population ceilings also meant that those who could not get into state institutions were sent to community residences, where conditions were often much worse than in the state institutions. In contrast to Judge Johnson who had to contend with state bureaucracies, Judge Lord had to contend with the corporate power of the Reserve Mining Company, which he found beyond his judicial means of control. Whether rightly or wrongly, many judicial contests between environmental groups and federal agencies appear to have been decided ultimately in favor of those who could muster superior resources. Ackerman argued that judges trained in the Realist perspective are oriented toward "thinking small, instead of placing their particular conflict within a larger framework of structural description."[63] Some of the judges discussed in this chapter moved beyond the facts of a specific case, but in doing so, they had to engage in long, arduous struggles with more powerful political forces without clear conceptual guidance. Others have avoided the larger context of a case by retreating into procedural issues, a stance encouraged by the complex requirements often imposed by Congress on agency decisions.

No matter what theoretical justification is used to support judicial power in an activist state, courts are likely to continue to find their intervention into recently identified social problems hazardous to their status in society. Taylor's view is that courts inevitably possess serious limitations as policymakers in American politics: "Though courts certainly do make policy, they do so without the kind of legitimacy that clothes the policy choices of a legislature or elected executive. Nor, in confronting the agencies, do the courts possess a substitute legitimacy in the form of technical expertise."[64] Not surprisingly, courts have been uniformly reluctant to invoke the draconian power of contempt against recalcitrant public officials who have questioned their ventures into new areas of social policy.

After surveying a range of reform movements in the areas of civil rights, women's rights, criminal rights, the environment, and voting rights, Gerald N. Rosenberg concluded that "U.S. courts can *almost never* be effective producers of significant social reform. . . . Turning to courts to produce significant social reform substitutes the myth of America for its reality. It credits courts and judicial decisions with a power that they do not have." Rosenberg argued that reformers' reliance on the judiciary for help has substantially hindered their various causes in two ways. First, the judiciary can give them only limited assistance. Second, the courts have functioned as a kind of "flypaper" in the policy process by diverting substantial resources away from political activities that could produce important reforms.[65]

Rosenberg's conclusions may be a bit strong, and certainly Melnick specifically disagrees with him.[66] However, there is no question that the judges most successful at policy innovation have displayed shrewdness in balancing their powers against powerful political forces. Cooper argued that for judges, "the truly hard choices come from the effort to meet the elements of remedial adequacy while balancing those demands against the need for limits to discretion, both the more formal doctrinal constraints and the less formal judgmental factors associated with a prudent sense of the court's relationship to the community and its administrative and elected officials."[67] This approach meshes closely with the indirection, or subterfuge, that Guido Calabresi has identified as a common judicial maneuver in volatile cases in which candor and directness would be too socially divisive to allow for effective public policy.[68] If violations of judicially defined rights were to be met on every front with swift and direct judicial action, political and social repercussions would take an even greater toll on judicial authority and status.

Policy analysts have contributed greatly to an understanding of social problems through both definition and clarification. Their suggestions, however, are no more final in the judicial process than they are in other arenas of decision making, and it would be unwise for judges to treat them as definitive. Not only do the conclusions of scholars change; the capability for dealing with problems also changes. And courts often have a difficult time adjusting to rapidly changing technology. Robert V. Bartlett, for example, noted that the methods for counting mineral fibers in drinking water at the outset of the Reserve Mining controversy were crude and not very accurate. The courts accepted this fact, and even though the ability to find such fibers improved dramatically within a few years, their earlier judicial determination continued to carry weight.[69]

The Supreme Court's *Roe* v. *Wade* decision in 1973 provides a more controversial example of the linkage of judicial policy to technology.[70] This decision, which has become the focus of vehement ideological controversy, incorporated Justice Harry Blackmun's proposal of a trimester framework to demarcate the points at which state regulation and prohibition of abortion could begin. At the time of the decision, the third trimester of pregnancy coincided fairly closely with the point in pregnancy at which medical science could keep a fetus alive. Since then, medical technology has been able to keep the fetus viable outside the womb at earlier stages. For a time, this left the Court with the difficult choice of remaining with the rule as originally formulated, even though improvements in science had undermined an important part of its basis, or of revising the law to conform with changing technology. In her dissent in *Akron* v. *Akron Center for Reproductive Health* in 1983, Justice Sandra Day O'Connor explained the problems with basing judicial rules concerning abortion on rapidly changing medical technology:

> [N]either sound constitutional theory nor our need to decide cases based on the application of neutral principles can accommodate an analytical framework that varies according to the "stages" of pregnancy, where those stages, and their concomitant standards of review, differ according to the level of medical technology available. . . . The *Roe* framework, then, is clearly on a collision course with itself. As the medical risks of various abortion procedures decrease, the point at which the State may regulate for reasons of maternal health is moved further forward to actual childbirth. As medical science becomes better

able to provide for the separate existence of the fetus, the point of viability is moved further back toward conception.[71]

Justice O'Connor's opinion was widely cited by those opposing legalized abortions, but it served also as a perceptive statement of the difficulties that policy analysis generally can pose for judicial rule making. In 1992, in *Planned Parenthood of Southeastern Pennsylvania* v. *Casey*,[72] the Supreme Court remedied the difficulties posed by the rigidity of the trimester framework by discarding it entirely and allowing states to prohibit abortions at the point of fetal viability as determined by medical professionals.

The inadequacies of the Realist position, the increased activism of judges, and the heightened debate among students of the courts about the proper role of judicial power indicate that the time is ripe for the emergence of a more sophisticated notion of the political and normative facets of judging. Policy analysis will remain an important input into judicial policy, but it alone cannot and has not provided a firm foundation for judicial decisions. Analytical studies are subject to various interpretations and never-ending methodological critiques. Even when a considerable degree of expert agreement has been achieved on a social issue, it rarely has any staying power. Busing as a means to achieve integrated schools came under severe criticism; some community residences for the mentally disabled were found to have serious drawbacks and spillover effects.[73] Definitions of normality among psychologists and sociologists are in continual flux.

In the environmental area, the ramifications of governmental actions could be extended throughout the ecological chain and, if one wished to assume an expansive perspective, throughout the universe. In terms of threats to the permanence of policy, developments in the area of information technology provide a tremendous challenge, as the boundaries of free speech and privacy are in constant turmoil. The question here is when to stop. What are the cost and other limits acceptable to society? Those attempting to integrate social and scientific analysis into judicial decisions must obtain a clearer conception of what these limits are. At this point, policy analysts have proven much better at diagnosing social problems than at outlining the consequences of remedies. This, of course, may always be the case, but a better understanding of their judicial role should contribute toward narrowing the gap between the two levels of analysis.

The really useful contribution of policy analysis occurs when some degree of normative agreement has first been reached. Robert A. Burt has argued that the normative role of judging should be recognized as paramount in importance. In his view, judges should be seen as something like the high priests of the national conscience whose function is to force the holders of power to assume moral accountability for their actions. Judicial effectiveness from this perspective would be evaluated on the basis of a judge's "capacity to raise issues into high public visibility and force many different people . . . to admit that they are morally responsible for an existing state of affairs."[74] This "moral catalyst" view of judging has the merit of relieving judges of the heavier responsibilities of policymaking and of drawing attention to fundamental issues, but it seems to run counter to the current trend of expecting courts to make definitive policy in a wide variety of areas.[75]

In many respects, courts are now seen as essential components of the policy process. Interest groups regularly regard them as the next arena for contesting policies after the legislative and administrative processes have been exhausted. By loosening requirements for standing to sue and giving greater credence to the legal claims of groups, the Supreme Court has encouraged increased use of the courts for policy purposes. In too many instances, this stance has been reinforced by the irresponsibility of elected officials. The willingness of elected officials to allow Judge Johnson to deal with serious abuses of individual rights came to be known as the Alabama "punt syndrome." Similarly, in New York and Pennsylvania, public officials backed away from commitments or dragged their feet in making them when faced with tradeoffs between the demands of voting constituents and the needs of those too disabled to care for themselves. And school boards throughout the nation found it preferable to be prodded by court action rather than to take responsible, and probably electorally devastating, action on their own to implement constitutional requirements. The judges who have been most successful in implementing their decisions have been those who have candidly recognized the political nature of their position. Perhaps the most serious drawback to establishing the courts as merely an extension of the policy process is that this view opens the judiciary to the forces of relativism and fragmentation that have hampered the other branches of government.

Conclusion

AS THE PRECEDING chapters indicate, policy analysis can be neither optimally performed nor optimally utilized in the highly decentralized and fragmented American polity of today. Institutional reform in the political system could considerably enhance the effectiveness of policy analysis. In this regard, a relatively small number of political scientists, elected officials, and journalists have called for fundamental reforms that aim at coordinating the American governmental system. Most of these ideas are inspired by institutions and procedures found in parliamentary democracies. Parliamentary systems typically give more emphasis to the coordination of governmental powers than does the American system. In addition to suggesting the need for basic institutional changes, we have suggested the importance of a broad perspective on the part of policy analysts themselves. A better anticipation of how the policy process affects analysis and a greater awareness of the cultural values at stake are changes that can be made independently of the more cumbersome process of structural reform.

STRUCTURAL REFORM

Even though parliamentary-type reforms have little political support in America at present, a consideration of them is useful because most Americans are only dimly aware that there are other ways to organize free, democratic societies. Parliamentary proposals give a contrasting picture of how a more coordinated system might operate. We make no attempt here to present an encompassing review of such proposals; instead, we focus on two proposals that affect the election process, which lies at the heart of a working democracy.

Congressional Nomination of Presidential Candidates

Robert DiClerico and Eric Uslaner have proposed that the parties in Congress nominate presidential candidates.[1] In other words, the Democrats in the House and Senate would hold joint meetings and nominate their candidate for president. The Republicans would do the same. Such candidates, if elected, would begin office with a sizable base in Congress. The congressmen of the president's party, having nominated him, would have a larger personal stake in his success. To increase his chances of success, they would gravitate toward a nominee who not only appealed to the general public but also had the skills to work with Congress.

For all these reasons, it can be argued that congressional nomination of presidential candidates would contribute to better coordination between the president and the two houses of Congress. Nevertheless, the idea goes against the grain of American political practice and preference. As noted earlier, American voters show high support for their individual congressmen, but low approval for Congress as a collective body. The latter suggests that they would be ill disposed to grant parties in Congress the collective responsibility of nominating presidential candidates.

Additionally, in most areas of politics and government, American voters have preferred greater direct access (which requires greater fragmentation) to better coordination of political institutions. The existing nomination system, consisting of numerous party primaries and party caucuses, is extremely fragmented, but it affords much greater public access to the presidential nomination process than would nominations confined to Congress.

Electing the President and Congress: The Team-Ticket Proposal

Separate elections of House members, senators, and the president lie at the heart of fragmentation among major power centers of the national government. The team-ticket proposal would have two stipulations and would, of course, require a constitutional amendment.

The first stipulation would be the simultaneous election of House members, senators, and the president every four years.[2] To achieve this, the two-year terms of House members would have to be lengthened and the six-year terms of senators shortened. Also, "off year" Senate and House elections, which occur midway between presidential elections, would be eliminated.

Although coordinated in time, simultaneous elections are nonetheless separate elections. Voters would still be able to "split their tickets." For example, they could vote simultaneously for the Republican presidential candidate and the Democratic candidates for House and Senate. The second stipulation of the team-ticket proposal would prevent this. Voters would be required to vote for a four-candidate party team consisting of the Republican candidates for president, vice-president, House, and Senate, or a team slate of the four Democratic candidates. Voters could not split their tickets.[3]

Perhaps the best place to begin coordinating a fragmented national government is in the minds of the voters. If adopted, the team-ticket proposal would oblige voters first to think about and then to choose their national government as a coordinated unit. Team-ticket elections would virtually end the typical phenomenon of the 1970s, 1980s, and 1990s: a president of one party facing a Congress in which one or both houses are dominated by the other party.

The team-ticket proposal, however, would reduce popular access to congressmen, and for that reason would have little appeal to voters. "Off year" congressional elections, for example, give voters an opportunity to focus more attention on how responsive their representative has been to state and local interests. The two-year terms for the House of Representatives serve much the same purpose.

Voters cherish their right to "split their tickets" in presidential election years for similar reasons. They may strongly prefer the presidential candidate of one party as a national leader, but they also want to be able to vote for the House or Senate candidate of the other party if he or she has been particularly good for the state or the district. The public expectation continues to be that the president will lead the nation, congressmen will represent their state and local districts, and coordination across the branches of the national government will somehow take care of itself.

These expectations have not been unrealistic from a historical perspective. Throughout most of American history, political fragmentation has existed side by side with economic growth and prosperity. Americans can hardly be reproached for perceiving a positive correlation between the two. Only during fiscal and other crises do the American people seem to develop a more critical understanding of the impact of an extremely fragmented political system on the making of public policy, both domestic and foreign. Most important, the merit of reform proposals focusing on the electoral process, in contrast to those attempting to straitjacket Congress, is that they move toward fundamental change in political relationships and attitudes.

ANTICIPATING THE POLICY PROCESS

Without major structural reforms, the policy process will continue to pose important challenges to the policy analyst. Many of these challenges can, however, be anticipated and strategies developed to lessen their impact. The primary prerequisite for the policy analyst is to have an understanding of the complexity of the policy process and an appreciation of the different perspectives and concerns that may be triggered by the recommendations under discussion.

One approach to decision making that has particular merit from the vantage point of the analyst is the PRINCE analysis developed by William D. Coplin and Michael K. O'Leary.[4] Their technique has the advantage of looking toward the point of decision and providing an estimate of how decision makers will respond to an issue. Essentially, the analyst assigns scores to each decision participant, weighting that participant in terms of four factors: salience of the issue, power within the group, issue position, and expected interaction with the other participants. Obviously, the analyst who uses this approach must treat the quantitative results carefully and tentatively. Moreover, to invoke this procedure at each decision point in the policy process would be exceptionally cumbersome and ultimately misleading. Nonetheless, the perspective promoted by the technique at least points the analyst in the right direction.

In an article that touches on the major problem addressed by this book, Peter J. May has noted the difficulty of integrating what he terms "pure" policy analysis with politics. Despite the increase in analytical capacities, a salient feasibility gap remains between the proposals of analysts and their political acceptance and administrative implementation. May suggested that the analyst think in terms of "perceptual maps" and "position maps" that chart the passage of an issue through the policy process.[5] These techniques can help the analyst anticipate the ways in which his or her recommendations will be seen by different policy actors and the political concerns that the recommendations may arouse. With attention to these possibilities beforehand, analysts may be able to avoid the use of unnecessarily antagonistic language and to package proposals as attractively or as innocuously as possible.

One tactic that has been effective in moving proposals through the policy process while retaining analytical integrity has been partisan analysis. Charles Lindblom described this approach as a method for achieving agreement even though value positions differ.[6] The analyst must identify the values of the policymaker that will be served by the recommendations being made. Thus, a proposal to lower taxes might be presented to business as a means of encouraging private enterprise and to unions as a means of increasing employment opportunities. The integrity of the analysis and proposal remains unsullied, but policy actors from different ideological viewpoints still find the policy worthy of support. Again, this approach requires the analyst to have the ability to project realistically beyond his or her study to the forums in which the study will be considered. Partisan analysis will, of course, not be possible under all circumstances, but it does open important possibilities for the more effective use of analysis.

For the most part, the suggestions we have made in this section deal with questions of technique. They do not reach fundamental normative issues. They provide no guidelines for the analyst facing difficult questions in examining a problem and striving to take rationally and ethically justifiable positions.

MOVING TOWARD THE PUBLIC GOOD

In American culture, two concepts of individualism appear to work at cross-purposes in a wide spectrum of policy questions. We have referred to these concepts as a "politics of interest" and a "politics of conscience." Abstract in their thrust, both streams of thought and attitude militate against the adequate conceptualization and treatment of problems of policy. Utilitarian policies, oriented to economic growth, sometimes threaten to destroy ecological integrity. At the same time, an exaggerated concern for individuals embodied in welfare spending may obscure necessities of the common good. As Charles Anderson has asked hypothetically, "Would one uphold the ideal of a free market choice in the face of irreversible environmental destruction? Or pursue equality to the point that no one had the incentive to lift a plow again?"[7] The deep-rooted habits of a political culture are not readily changed. But if there are in a culture secondary ideas and attitudes that run counter to the problematic ones, something of a cure might be wrought by heightening their influence.

Fortunately, American culture has an antibody to the dilemmas posed by a politics of conscience and a politics of interest. It is pragmatism, a habit of the American mind that brings a public into being and organizes its energies for political action. In John Dewey's words:

> The characteristic of the public as a state springs from the fact that all modes of associated behavior may have extensive and enduring consequences which involve others beyond those directly engaged in them. When those consequences are in turn realized in thought and sentiment, recognition of them reacts to remake the conditions out of which they arose. Consequences have to be taken care of, looked out for.[8]

Thus, while an individual eagerness to make money creates Love Canals, the alerted public legislates into existence an Environmental Protection Agency to clean them up. The case-by-case method of the American common-law tradition reinforces this atheoretical attitude.

In chapter 4, we described a method of systematic ethical analysis that embraces the pragmatist attitude: casuistry. The responses of the pragmatic spirit operate without benefit of an overarching theory of the good. They meet the public need in terms of the specific elements of a particular situation. Pragmatism and casuistry are particularistic and situation-oriented in their ethics.[9] Unlike utilitarianism and deontology, they do not start with an ideal theory and attempt to derive proposals for policy from it. As Charles Anderson has put it, the pragmatist approach is to "begin from practice and apply theory to it. Philosophic pragmatists have frequently suggested that principles 'emerge' out of the consideration of a particular problem of judgment."[10]

The cultivation of pragmatism as philosophy and of casuistry as analytical method may help move policymakers toward a flexibility in policy assessment that will overcome the rigidities created by the other, less flexible attitudes that tend to dominate the American mind. It may help to establish an ongoing discourse among these other ideas, a conversation among utilitarians and deontologists that will allow the frameworks for policy analysis and policy decisions to be tailored to the requirements of the particular situation. This way of applying theory to practice requires a conclusion as to

> whether there is a public interest in a specific form of association or collective project. Given the presumption in favor of autonomous collective action, the burden of the argument falls to those who would give good reasons for the suppression or control of practices, or alternatively, their protection and promotion through state action.[11]

This is one way of freeing students of public policy from the value prejudices implicit in the systematic frameworks that have come with the business of policy analysis. Standing back from habitual predispositions, whether the utilitarianism of cost-benefit analysis or the egalitarian stance of Kantianism and welfare liberalism, forces one to look at the policy situation in its multifaceted complexity and pragmatically decide what must be done for the public good.

Not all the suggestions in these concluding remarks are within the control of the analyst, but some of them are. In this latter regard, the analyst can greatly improve the effect of his or her efforts by basing them on a thorough understanding of the policy process and the cultural contradictions on which it rests. If policy analysts can combine this perspective with a casuist approach to specific issues, they can reasonably expect that in most circumstances, they will be able to enhance the utilization of rational analysis in policy decisions.

Notes

INTRODUCTION

1. Theodore J. Lowi, *The End of Liberalism*, 2d ed. (New York: Norton, 1979).
2. Mancur Olson, *The Rise and Decline of Nations* (New Haven, Conn.: Yale University Press, 1982), 70.
3. Alasdair MacIntyre, *After Virtue* (Notre Dame, Ind.: University of Notre Dame Press, 1981), 11.
4. Ibid., 229.
5. Ibid., 102.
6. Samuel P. Huntington, *American Politics* (Cambridge, Mass.: Harvard University Press, 1981), 75.
7. Hugh Heclo, "Hyperdemocracy," *Wilson Quarterly* 23 (Winter 1999): 69.
8. Olson, *Rise and Decline of Nations,* 237.
9. Huntington, *American Politics,* 262.
10. Heclo, "Hyperdemocracy," 69.
11. Eugene Bardach, *The Implementation Game* (Cambridge, Mass.: MIT Press, 1978), 6.
12. Jeffrey T. Pressman and Aaron Wildavsky, *Implementation,* 2d ed. (Berkeley: University of California Press, 1979), 109.
13. Thomas R. Dye, *Understanding Public Policy,* 6th ed. (Englewood Cliffs, N.J.: Prentice Hall, 1987), 350.
14. G. Calvin Mackenzie, *The Irony of Reform: Roots of American Political Disenchantment* (Boulder, Colo.: Westview Press, 1996), 165.
15. Quoted in W. Lance Bennett, *The Governing Crisis: Media, Money, and Marketing in American Elections,* 2d ed. (New York: St. Martin's, 1996), 159.
16. Robert D. Putnam, "Bowling Alone: America's Declining Social Capital," *Journal of Democracy* 6 (1995): 65–78. See also Robert D. Putnam, "Tuning In, Tuning Out: The Strange Disappearance of Social Capital in America," *PS: Political Science and Politics* 28 (December 1995): 664–83.
17. See, for example, Carll Everett Ladd, *The Ladd Report* (New York: Free Press, 1999).
18. Francis Fukuyama, *Trust* (New York: Free Press, 1995).
19. Rosemarie Tong, *Ethics in Public Policy* (Englewood Cliffs, N.J.: Prentice Hall, 1986), xi; Ira Katznelson, "Rethinking the Silences of Social and Economic Policy," *Political Science Quarterly* 101 (1986): 310–13; Bruce L. Payne, "Contexts and Epiphanies: Policy Analysis and the Humanities," *Journal of Policy Analysis and Management* 4 (Fall 1984): 96; Douglas J. Amy, "Why Policy Analysis and Ethics Are Incompatible," *Journal of Policy Analysis and Management* 3 (Summer 1984): 573–91.
20. Judith Jarvis Thomson, *Rights, Restitution, and Risk*, ed. William Parent (Cambridge, Mass.: Harvard University Press, 1986), 94–116.

21. Rosemarie Tong, *Ethics*, 41, notes, "To the degree that the roles of the policy analyst and the subject-area specialist are increasingly indiscernible, so too is it more and more difficult to articulate how a policy advisor differs from a policy analyst or a policy specialist."

22. James C. Scott, *Seeing like a State* (New Haven, Conn.: Yale University Press, 1998), 82.

23. Duncan MacRae Jr., *The Social Function of Social Science* (New Haven: Yale University Press, 1976), 305–6; Duncan MacRae Jr., "Introducing Undergraduates to Public Policy Analysis by the Case Method," in *Teaching Policy Studies*, ed. William D. Coplin (Lexington, Mass.: Heath, 1978), 129–30.

24. William D. Coplin, ed., *Teaching Policy Studies* (Lexington, Mass.: Heath, 1978), xv.

25. Dye, *Understanding Public Policy*, 7–8.

26. Yehezkel Dror, "Policy Analysts: A New Professional Role in Government Service," *Public Administration Review* 27 (September 1967): 200–203.

CHAPTER 1 THE EMERGENCE OF A FIELD

1. Russell L. Hanson, *The Democratic Imagination in America* (Princeton, N.J.: Princeton University Press, 1985), 224.

2. William Graham Sumner, *Essays of William Graham Sumner*, ed. Albert Galloway Keller and Maurice R. Davie (New Haven, Conn.: Yale University Press, 1934), 1:6.

3. Robert A. Scott and Arnold R. Shore, *Why Sociology Does Not Apply* (New York: Elsevier, 1979), 9, 108.

4. Richard J. Bernstein, *John Dewey* (New York: Washington Square Press, 1966), 1.

5. John Dewey, *The Public and Its Problems* (Chicago: Gateway Books, 1946 [1927]).

6. Arthur F. Bentley, *The Process of Government* (Evanston, Ill.: Principia Press of Illinois, 1949 [1908]), 172.

7. Ibid., 177.

8. Ibid., 208.

9. Quoted in Fred H. Cahill, *Judicial Legislation* (New York: Ronald Press, 1952), 73, from Roscoe Pound's *Interpretations of Legal History* (1923), 1.

10. Scott and Shore, *Why Sociology*, 121.

11. Mary O. Furner, *Advocacy and Objectivity* (Lexington: University Press of Kentucky, 1975).

12. Kenneth P. Davis, *FDR: The New Deal Years, 1933–1937* (New York: Random House, 1986), 236–37.

13. Ibid., 234–36, 675.

14. Jurgen Schmandt and James Everett Katz, "The Scientific State: A Theory with Hypotheses," *Science, Technology, and Human Values* (Winter 1986): 40–52.

15. Ibid., 49.

16. Ibid., 48.

17. Ibid., 45.

18. 347 U.S. 483.

19. Michel Crozier, *The Trouble with America* (Berkeley: University of California Press, 1984), 48–49.

20. Aaron Wildavsky, "Rescuing Policy Analysis from PPBS," in *Public Expenditures and Policy Analysis*, ed. Robert H. Haveman and Julius Margolis (Chicago: Rand McNally, 1970), 461–81.

21. For a good summary of the introduction of systems analysis and operations research into government and the criticisms that this engendered, see Thomas P. Hughes, *Rescuing Prometheus* (New York: Pantheon Books, 1998), 141–95.

22. See Paul F. Lazarsfeld, Jeffrey G. Reitz, and Ann K. Pasanella, *An Introduction to Applied Sociology* (New York: Elsevier, 1975).

23. David Easton, "The New Revolution in Political Science," *American Political Science Review* 63 (December 1969): 1051–61.

24. Harold D. Lasswell, "The Policy Orientation," in *The Policy Sciences,* ed. Daniel Lerner and Harold D. Lasswell (Stanford, Calif.: Stanford University Press, 1951), 3–15.

25. Yehezkel Dror, "Policy Analysts: A New Professional Role in Government Service," *Public Administration Review* 27 (September 1967): 197–203.

26. John P. Crecine, ed., *The New Educational Programs in Public Policy* (Greenwich, Conn.: JAI Press, 1982), 21, n. 1; Joel L. Fleishman, "The Creation of a Profession," in *What Role for Government?* ed. Richard J. Zeckhauser and Derek Leebaert (Durham: Duke University Press, 1983), 324–26.

27. Frank Fischer, "Policy Expertise and the 'New Class': A Critique of the Neoconservative Thesis," in *Confronting Values in Policy Analysis,* ed. Frank Fischer and John Forester (Newbury Park, Calif.: Sage, 1987), 103.

28. Crozier, *Trouble with America,* 51.

29. Daniel P. Moynihan, *Maximum Feasible Misunderstanding* (New York: Free Press, 1970), 35–36.

30. Frances Fox Piven and Richard A. Cloward, *Regulating the Poor* (New York: Vintage, 1972), 248–49, n. 1.

31. Carol Hirschon Weiss, "Evaluating Social Programs: What Have We Learned?" *Society* 25 (November/December 1987): 41.

32. Edward Banfield, *The Unheavenly City* (Boston: Little, Brown, 1970).

33. Fischer, "Policy Expertise," 104–5.

34. Henry J. Aaron, *Politics and the Professors* (Washington, D.C.: Brookings Institution, 1978), 158–59; Weiss, "Evaluating Social Programs," 41–42.

35. David B. Truman, *The Governmental Process* (New York: Knopf, 1951).

36. Charles E. Lindblom, "The Science of 'Muddling Through,'"*Public Administration Review* 19 (Spring 1959): 79–88.

37. Ibid., 85.

38. Ibid., 86.

39. Robert Heilbroner and William Milberg, *The Crisis of Vision in Modern Economic Thought* (New York: Cambridge University Press, 1995), 72.

40. Karen Orren and Stephen Skowronek, "Regimes and Regime Building in American Government," *Political Science Quarterly* 113 (Winter 1998–99): 701.

41. Heilbroner and Milberg, *Crisis of Vision,* 93.

42. Ibid., 92.

43. Thomas S. Kuhn, *The Structure of Scientific Revolutions,* 2d ed. (Chicago: University of Chicago Press, 1970). See also Yehezkel Dror, "On Becoming More of a Policy Scientist," *Policy Studies Review* 4 (August 1984): 210–11.

44. Douglas J. Amy, "Toward a Post-Positivist Policy Analysis," *Policy Studies Journal* 13 (September 1984): 210–11.

45. Rosemarie Tong, *Ethics in Public Policy* (Englewood Cliffs, N.J.: Prentice Hall, 1986), 124–25.

46. Douglas Yates Jr., *The Politics of Management* (San Francisco: Jossey-Bass, 1985), 110.

47. Scott and Shore, *Why Sociology,* 142, 144.

48. Ibid., 138–43; Charles E. Lindblom, *The Policy-Making Process,* 2d ed. (Englewood Cliffs, N.J.: Prentice Hall, 1980), 22–25.

49. Laurence Tribe, "Policy Science: Analysis or Ideology?" *Philosophy and Public Affairs* 2 (Fall 1972): 66–110.

50. Martha S. Feldman, *Order without Design* (Stanford, Calif.: Stanford University Press, 1989), 92.

51. Arnold J. Meltsner, *Policy Analysts in the Bureaucracy* (Berkeley: University of California Press, 1976), 282.

52. Tong, *Ethics*, 92.

53. Robert D. Behn, "Policy Analysts, Clients, and Social Scientists," *Journal of Policy Analysis and Management* 4 (Spring 1985): 430.

54. Hank C. Jenkins-Smith, "Professional Roles for Policy Analysts: A Critical Assessment," *Journal of Policy Analysis and Management* 2 (Fall 1982): 88–100.

55. Scott and Shore, *Why Sociology*, 188–89.

56. Meltsner, *Policy Analysts*, 23.

57. Jenkins-Smith, "Professional Roles," 93.

58. Meltsner, *Policy Analysts*, 43.

59. On this point generally, see Peter W. House and Roger D. Shull, *Rush to Policy* (New Brunswick, N.J.: Transaction, 1988), 131.

60. J.M.B. Fraatz, "Policy Analysts as Advocates," *Journal of Policy Analysis and Management* 1 (Winter 1982): 273–76.

61. See David Shenk, "Money + Science = Ethics Problems on Campus," *Nation* 268 (22 March 1999): 11–18.

62. Meltsner, *Policy Analysts*, 274.

CHAPTER 2 RATIONALITY AND DECISION MAKING

1. Karl Popper, *Unended Quest* (La Salle, Ill.: Open Court, 1976), 141–51.

2. Frank Fischer, *Evaluating Public Policy* (Chicago: Nelson Hall, 1995), 17.

3. Ibid., 18.

4. Ibid., 243.

5. Peter deLeon, "Models of Policy Discourse," *Policy Studies Journal* 26 (1998): 147–61; Frank Fischer, "Beyond Empiricism," *Policy Studies Journal* 26 (1998): 129–46; Ann Chih Lin, "Bridging Positivist and Interpretivist Approaches to Qualitative Methods," *Policy Studies Journal* 26 (1998): 162–84.

6. Davis B. Bobrow and John S. Dryzek, *Policy Analysis by Design* (Pittsburgh: University of Pittsburgh Press, 1987).

7. Peter deLeon, *Democracy and the Policy Sciences* (Albany: SUNY Press, 1997); John S. Dryzek, *Discursive Democracy* (New York: Cambridge University Press, 1990); Anne Schneider and Helen Ingram, *Policy Design for Democracy* (Lawrence: University of Kansas Press, 1997).

8. John Dewey, *Liberalism and Social Action* (New York: Capricorn Books, 1935), 27.

9. John Dewey, *The Public and Its Problems* (Chicago: Swallow Press, 1946), 208–9.

10. Harold D. Lasswell, *A Pre-View of Policy Sciences* (New York: American Elsevier, 1971), xiii–xiv.

11. Laurence H. Tribe, "Policy Science: Analysis or Ideology?" *Philosophy and Public Affairs* 2 (Fall 1972): 85.

12. Jeremy Bentham, *An Introduction to the Principles of Morals and Legislation* (New York: Hafner, 1948 [1789]), 2.

13. On the tension between democratic values and policy analysis, see Peter deLeon, "Democratic Values and the Policy Sciences," *American Journal of Political Science* 39 (November 1995): 886–905.

14. Charles Murray, *Losing Ground* (New York: Basic Books, 1984).

15. Anthony Downs, *Inside Bureaucracy* (Boston: Little, Brown, 1967).

16. Arnold D. Meltsner, *Policy Analysts in the Bureaucracy* (Berkeley: University of California Press, 1976), 168.

17. Lawrence M. Mead, "Science versus Analysis: A False Dichotomy," *Journal of Policy Analysis and Management* 4 (Spring 1985): 421.

18. Charles W. Anderson, "The Place of Principles in Policy Analysis," *American Political Science Review* 73 (September 1979): 717.

19. Ibid.

20. Ibid., 719.

21. Grover Starling, *The Politics and Economics of Public Policy* (Homewood, Ill.: Dorsey Press, 1979).

22. Michael Quinn Patton, *Utilization-Focused Evaluation* (Beverly Hills, Calif.: Sage, 1973), 34.

23. Martha S. Feldman, *Order without Design* (Stanford, Calif.: Stanford University Press, 1989), 1–2, 10–11, 93.

24. David Whiteman, "The Fate of Policy Analysis in Congressional Decision-Making," *Western Political Quarterly* 38 (June 1985): 293–311.

25. Peter W. House and Roger D. Shull, *Rush to Policy* (New Brunswick, N.J.: Transaction, 1988), 181.

26. Robert F. Rich, "Uses of Social Science Information by Federal Bureaucracies," in *Using Social Research in Public Policy Making*, ed. Carol H. Weiss (Lexington, Mass.: Lexington Books, 1977), 199–212.

27. Carol H. Weiss, "Policy Research in the Context of Diffuse Decision-Making," in *Social Science Research and Public Policy-Making*, ed. D.B.P. Kallen et al. (Windsor, England: NFER-Nelson, 1982), 534.

28. Feldman, *Order*, 95.

29. Carol H. Weiss and Michael Bucuvalas, "Truth Tests and Utility Tests," *American Sociological Review* 45 (April 1980): 302–13.

30. Meltsner, *Policy Analysts*, 14–15.

31. Emil J. Posavac and Raymond G. Carey, *Program Evaluation* (Englewood Cliffs, N.J.: Prentice Hall, 1985), 263–64.

32. House and Shull comment on these difficulties from the view of practicing policy analysts in *Rush to Policy*, 21–48.

33. John D. Graham and James W. Vaupel, "The Value of a Life," in *What Role for Government?* ed. Richard J. Zeckhauser and Derek Leebaert (Durham, N.C.: Duke University Press, 1983), 176–86.

34. Aaron Wildavsky, "The Political Economy of Efficiency," *Public Administration Review* 4 (December 1966): 296.

35. Edith Stokey and Richard Zeckhauser, *A Primer for Policy Analysis* (New York: Norton, 1978), 86.

36. Edmund Burke, *Reflections on the Revolution in France,* ed. Thomas H.D. Mahoney (Indianapolis: Bobbs-Merrill, 1955 [1790]), 110.

37. Tribe, "Policy Science," 82.

38. Stokey and Zeckhauser, *A Primer*, 201.

39. Susan Welch and John C. Comer, *Quantitative Methods for Public Administration* (Homewood, Ill.: Dorsey Press, 1983), 66.

40. William W. Lowrance, *Modern Science and Human Values* (New York: Oxford University Press, 1985), 142–49.

41. Kenneth L. Kraemer and William H. Dutton, "The Automation of Bias," in *Computers and Politics,* ed. James N. Danziger et al. (New York: Columbia University Press, 1982), 190.

42. James Hansen et al., "A Common-Sense Climate Index: Is Climate Changing Noticeably?" *Proceedings of the National Academy of Sciences* 95 (14 April 1998): 4120.

43. Stokey and Zeckhauser, *A Primer*, 135.

44. Jean Heller, "Syphilis Victims in U.S. Study Went Untreated for Forty Years," *New York Times*, 26 July 1972, 1, 8.

45. Steven A. Peterson with the assistance of Jessica Sicherman, "Schizophrenia and Reification: Who's (Really) Crazy?" *Journal of Social and Evolutionary Systems* 18 (January 1995): 33–53. The basic point here is that our own values and beliefs may become so strong they begin to act as delusions, skewing our understanding and decision making.

46. James E. Anderson, *Public Policy-Making*, 3d ed. (New York: Holt, Rinehart and Winston, 1984), 163.

47. Horst W.J. Rittel and Melvin M. Webber, "Dilemmas in a General Theory of Planning," *Policy Sciences* 4 (1973): 155–69.

48. Ulric Neisser, ed., *The Rising Curve* (Washington, D.C.: American Psychological Association, 1998).

49. Feldman, *Order*, 4–10.

50. William Niskanen, *Bureaucracy and Representative Government* (Chicago: Aldine-Atherton, 1971).

51. Richard J. Richardson and Kenneth N. Vines, *The Politics of the Federal Courts* (Boston: Little, Brown, 1970).

52. See John W. Kingdon, *Agendas, Alternatives, and Public Policy,* 2d ed. (Boston: HarperCollins, 1995).

53. Ibid., 116–17.

54. For example, Daniel Kahneman, Paul Slovic, and Amos Tversky, eds., *Judgment under Uncertainty* (Cambridge: Cambridge University Press, 1982).

55. Stephen G. Walker and Timothy G. Murphy, "The Utility of the Operational Code in Political Forecasting," *Political Psychology* 3 (Spring/Summer 1981–82): 24–60.

56. Thomas E. Cronin, "Small Programs, Big Troubles: Policy Making for a Small Great Society Program," in *American Politics and Public Policy,* ed. Walter Dean Burnham and Martha Wagner Weinberg (Cambridge, Mass.: MIT Press, 1978), 77–108.

57. Patton, *Utilization-Focused Evaluation.*

58. Whiteman, "Fate of Policy Analysis."

59. Meltsner, *Policy Analysts*, 157.

60. Feldman, *Order,* 63.

61. Meltsner, *Policy Analysts*, 269.

62. Fischer, *Evaluating Public Policy*, 19.

CHAPTER 3 THE CULTURAL SETTING OF POLICY ANALYSIS

1. Samuel Huntington, *American Politics: The Promise of Disharmony* (Cambridge, Mass.: Harvard University Press, 1981), 15; David B. Hill, "Rebuilding a Liberal Constituency," in *The Liberal Future in America,* ed. Philip Abbott and Michael B. Levy (Westport, Conn.: Greenwood Press, 1985), 178. Huntington writes that "people sometimes speak of an 'American ideology.' But in the American mind, these ideas do not take the form of a carefully articulated, systematic ideology They constitute a complex or amorphous amalgam of goals and values, rather than a scheme for establishing priorities among values and for elaborating ways to realize values." Citing the work of Philip P. Converse, David Apter, George F. Bishop, and others, Hill points out that "studies of the constraint, or interconnectedness, of American belief systems conclude that only a small percentage of the public possesses an ideology which is reasonably stable over time and which is not beset by apparent internal contradictions."

2. John Winthrop, in his speech to the General Court of Massachusetts Bay Colony, in Vernon L. Parrington, *Main Currents in American Thought* (New York: Harcourt, Brace, 1930), 1:49.

3. Ralph Barton Perry, *Puritanism and Democracy* (New York: Vanguard, 1944), 354, quoted in Herbert McClosky and John Zaller, *The American Ethos* (Cambridge, Mass.: Harvard University Press, 1984), 65.

4. See John G.A. Pocock, *The Machiavellian Moment* (Princeton, N.J.: Princeton University Press, 1975).

5. C.B. Macpherson, *The Theory of Possessive Individualism* (London: Oxford University Press, 1962), 175.

6. Ibid., 176, 177.

7. *Time*, 25 May 1987, 14, 27.

8. Ibid., 27.

9. See Jennifer Hochschild, *What's Fair? American Beliefs about Distributive Justice* (Cambridge, Mass.: Harvard University Press, 1981). It is possible that this study is only regionally valid; however, the national survey findings cited in this chapter appear to show national applicability. Quotations from this book are parenthetically cited. The work serves as a frame for the argument presented in this chapter.

10. McClosky and Zaller, *American Ethos*, 70, 71–72.

11. Cited in ibid., 74. See discussion of this study in William T. Bluhm, *Ideologies and Attitudes: Modern Political Culture* (Englewood Cliffs, N.J.: Prentice Hall, 1974), 91–95.

12. Cited in McClosky and Zaller, *American Ethos*, 75, table 3-6 (Political Affiliation and Beliefs Study, 1958; Civil Liberties Study, 1978–79).

13. Alexis de Tocqueville, *Democracy in America*, trans. M. Reeve et al. (New York: Knopf, 1951), 1:58.

14. Quoted in Parrington, *Main Currents*, 2:76.

15. Ibid., 77.

16. See, for example, Richard Cox, *Locke on War and Peace* (Oxford: Clarendon Press, 1960); William T. Bluhm et al., "Locke's Idea of God: Rational Truth or Political Myth?" *Journal of Politics* 42 (May 1980): 414–38.

17. *The Federalist*, No. 10.

18. Quoted in McClosky and Zaller, *American Ethos*, 101.

19. Ibid., 120, table 4-5.

20. See the summary and evaluation of Lane's findings in Bluhm, *Ideologies and Attitudes*, 85–87.

21. The question read: "Do you think our government should or should not confiscate all wealth over and above what people actually need to live on decently, and use it for the public good?" The results of these polls are analyzed in Hochschild, *What's Fair?* 16–19.

22. Ibid., 18. See also Kluegel and Smith, *Beliefs about Inequality*, 76–81; Sidney Verba and Gary R. Orren, *Equality in America* (Cambridge, Mass.: Harvard University Press, 1985), 253. The latter is a study of views toward equality held by a variety of leadership or elite groups in America. Regarding economic equality, these researchers found that "some (leadership) groups want more income equality, but almost none wants complete equality."

23. Quoted in McClosky and Zaller, *American Ethos*, 89. For a capsulized review of public policies directed toward redistribution of income to the poor, see Kluegel and Smith, *Beliefs about Inequality*, 153–54.

24. Hochschild, *What's Fair?* 169. Samuel Huntington, in writing of tension in American political culture, describes the phenomenon of "creedal passion," which brings on efforts to move ideas into line with practice. See his *American Politics*.

25. Kluegel and Smith, *Beliefs about Inequality*, 154–55.

26. 515 U.S. 200.
27. Thomas B. Edsall and Mary D. Edsall, *Chain Reaction: The Impact of Race, Rights, and Taxes on American Politics* (New York: Norton, 1995), 12.
28. Ibid., 13.
29. Cited by David B. Hill, "Rebuilding a Liberal Constituency," 177–78.
30. E.J. Dionne Jr., *Why Americans Hate Politics* (New York: Simon and Schuster, 1991), 14.
31. Edsall and Edsall, *Chain Reaction*, 10.
32. Dionne, *Why Americans Hate Politics*, 17.
33. Ibid., 14.
34. Edsall and Edsall, *Chain Reaction*, 10.
35. Jean B. Elshtain, *Democracy on Trial* (New York: Basic Books, 1995), 3–4.
36. Ibid., 2–3, citing Dionne.
37. Ibid., citing Robert Bellah et al., *Habits of the Heart* (Berkeley: University of California Press, 1985), 30.
38. Edsall and Edsall, *Chain Reaction*, 16.
39. Henry May, quoted in Michael Kammen, *People of Paradox: An Inquiry into the Origins of American Civilization* (New York: Knopf, 1972), 218.
40. Quoted in ibid., 219.

CHAPTER 4 ETHICS AND PUBLIC POLICY ANALYSIS

1. Immanuel Kant, *Groundwork for the Metaphysics of Morals*, trans. J.W. Ellington (Indianapolis: Hackett, 1981), 36.
2. See Arthur M. Okun, *Equality and Efficiency: The Big Tradeoff* (Washington, D.C.: Brookings Institution, 1975); Albert R. Jonsen and Stephen Toulmin, *The Abuse of Casuistry: A History of Moral Reasoning* (Berkeley: University of California Press, 1988). A portion of the argument of this chapter appeared in William T. Bluhm, "Ethics in Policy Analysis and Public Decision," in *Research in Public Policy Analysis and Management*, ed. Stuart S. Nagel (Greenwich, Conn.: JAI Press, 1995), 195–202.
3. Jonsen and Toulmin, *Abuse of Casuistry*, 2.
4. Ibid., 8.
5. Julius Kovesi, *Moral Notions* (London: Routledge & Kegan Paul, 1967).
6. Ibid., 107.
7. Jonsen and Toulmin, *Abuse of Casuistry*, 308–9.
8. Ibid., 309.
9. Charles Anderson, "Political Philosophy, Practical Reason, and Policy Analysis," in *Confronting Values in Policy Analysis*, ed. F. Fischer and J. Forester (Newbury Park, Calif.: Sage, 1987), 15.
10. Ibid.
11. Ibid.
12. Ibid., 27.
13. *Hastings Center Report* 13, no. 1 (February 1983): 11.
14. Tom L. Beauchamp and James F. Childress, *Principles of Biomedical Ethics* (New York: Oxford University Press, 1979), 69.
15. Ronald Cole-Turner, "Do Means Matter? Evaluating Technologies of Human Enhancement," *Report from the Institute for Philosophy and Public Policy* 18 (Fall 1998): 9.
16. Quoted in Freeman J. Dyson, *The Sun, the Genome, and the Internet* (New York: Oxford University Press, 1999), 109. Dyson is drawing on Lee M. Silver, *Remaking Eden* (New York: Avon Books, 1977).

17. Dyson agrees with the casuists. He offers the hope and belief "that our descendants will decide, in the fullness of time, that the free market should not extend to human genes." Ibid., 111.
18. See Claudia Mills, "Preserving Endangered Species: Why Should We Care?" *Report from the Institute for Philosophy and Public Policy* 5 (Fall 1985).

CHAPTER 5 AMERICAN DEMOCRACY AND THE FRAGMENTATION OF CONSENSUS

1. Everett Carll Ladd, *Where Have All the Voters Gone?* 2d ed. (New York: Norton, 1982).
2. James Q. Wilson, *American Government* (Lexington, Mass.: Heath, 1980), 116–21.
3. William S. Maddox and Stuart A. Lilie, *Beyond Liberal and Conservative* (Washington, D.C.: Cato Press, 1984).
4. It is worth noting the at least short-term negative public reaction to the Republican Party for its role in the impeachment process. For example, see results of "CNN/USA Today/Gallup Poll," www.cnn.com/ALLPOLITICS/stories/1992/02/15/poll.
5. Kenneth Janda, Jeffrey M. Berry, and Jerry Goldman, *The Challenge of Democracy* (Boston: Houghton Mifflin, 1997), 163. For another take on the conflict among ideologies that can produce fragmentation within the parties, see Byron E. Shafer and William J.M. Claggett, *The Two Majorities* (Baltimore: Johns Hopkins University Press, 1995).
6. Ronald Inglehart, "The Persistence of Materialist and Post-Materialist Value Orientations," *European Journal of Political Research* 11 (March 1983): 81–91.
7. Ronald Inglehart, "Intergenerational Change in Politics and Culture," paper presented at the annual meeting of the American Political Science Association, New Orleans, 1985, 2.
8. Ibid., 11.
9. Ronald Inglehart and Paul R. Abramson, "Economic Security and Value Change," *American Political Science Review* 88 (June 1994): 338–39.
10. Paul Abramson and Ronald Inglehart, "Generational Replacement and Value Change among the Western European Public," paper presented at the annual meeting of the Midwest Political Science Association, Chicago, 1985, 21. For a detailed report on this line of research, see Paul R. Abramson and Ronald Inglehart, *Value Change in Global Perspective* (Ann Arbor: University of Michigan Press, 1995).
11. Jane Y. Junn, "German Post-Materialism," paper presented at the annual meeting of the International Society of Political Psychology, Toronto, 1984.
12. Russell J. Dalton, Scott C. Flanagan, and Paul Allen Beck, eds., *Electoral Change in Advanced Industrial Democracies* (Princeton, N.J.: Princeton University Press, 1984).
13. Samuel Kernell, "Strategy and Ideology," paper presented at the annual meeting of the American Political Science Association, Washington, D.C., 1980.
14. See B. Dan Wood, "Principals, Bureaucrats, and Responsiveness in Clean Air Enforcements," *American Political Science Review* 82 (March 1988): 213–34.
15. Kernell, "Strategy and Ideology," i.
16. Ibid., 38.
17. Charles W. Ostrom and Dennis M. Simon, "Promise and Performance," *American Political Science Review* 79 (June 1985): 350; Jon R. Bond and Richard Fleisher, "The Limits of Presidential Popularity as a Source of Influence in the U.S. House," *Legislative Studies Quarterly* 5 (February 1980): 69–78.
18. Ostrom and Simon, "Promise and Performance," 354.
19. Arthur H. Miller and Stephen A. Borrelli, "Explaining Policy and Performance Orientations in the Electorate," paper presented at the annual meeting of the American Polit-

ical Science Association, Chicago, 1987; Merrill Shanks and Warren E. Miller, "Policy Directions and Performance Evaluation," paper presented at the annual meeting of the American Political Science Association, New Orleans, 1985; J. Merrill Shanks and Warren E. Miller, "Alternative Explanations of the 1988 Elections," paper presented at the annual meeting of the American Political Science Association, Atlanta, 1989. For 1992, see Kathleen A. Frankovic, "Public Opinion in the 1992 Election," in *The Election of 1992*, ed. Gerald Pomper (Chatham, N.J.: Chatham House, 1993).

20. For instance, see James Stimson, *Public Opinion in America* (Boulder, Colo.: Westview Press, 1991).

21. Miller and Borrelli, "Explaining Policy and Performance Orientations."

22. See G. Bingham Powell, *Contemporary Democracies* (Cambridge, Mass.: Harvard University Press, 1982), 208–12.

23. For an analysis from the early 1980s that still appears to have some relevance, see Dalton et al., *Electoral Change*.

24. Edward G. Carmines and James A. Stimson, "The Two Faces of Issue Voting," *American Political Science Review* 74 (March 1980): 78–91; Edward G. Carmines, Steven H. Renton, and James A. Stimson, "Events and Alignments," in *Controversies in Voting Behavior,* ed. Richard G. Niemi and Herbert F. Weisberg (Washington, D.C.: Congressional Quarterly Press, 1984), 545–60.

25. Paul Allen Beck, "Partisan Dealignment in the Postwar South," *American Political Science Review* 73 (June 1977): 480.

26. Paul Allen Beck, "Realignment Begins?" *American Politics Quarterly* 10 (October 1982): 421–38.

27. Charles D. Hadley, "Dual Partisan Identification in the South," *Journal of Politics* 47 (February 1985): 254–68.

28. Warren E. Miller and J. Merrill Shanks, *The New American Voter* (Cambridge, Mass.: Harvard University Press, 1996).

29. Alan I. Abramowitz, "The End of the Democratic Era? 1994 and the Future of Congressional Election Research," *Political Research Quarterly* 48 (December 1995): 873–89.

30. Robin Toner, "Shift by Older Voters to G.O.P. Is Democrats' Challenge in 2000," *New York Times,* 31 May 1999, A1.

31. Alfred J. Tuchfarber, Stephen E. Bennett, Andrew E. Smith, and Eric W. Rademacher, "The Republican Tidal Wave of 1994," *PS: Political Science and Politics* 28 (December 1995): 689–96.

32. Earl Black, "The Newest Southern Politics," *Journal of Politics* 60 (August 1998): 611.

33. John R. Petrocik and Scott W. Desposato, "The Partisan Consequences of Majority-Minority Redistricting in the South, 1992 and 1994," *Journal of Politics* 60 (August 1998): 613–33.

34. Martin P. Wattenberg, *The Decline of American Political Parties* (Cambridge, Mass.: Harvard University Press, 1986).

35. Abramowitz, "End of the Democratic Era?"

36. Walter Dean Burnham, "Realignment Lives: The 1994 Earthquake and Its Implications," in *The Clinton Presidency,* ed. Colin Campbell and Bert A. Rockman (Chatham, N.J.: Chatham House, 1996), 363.

37. See Shanto Iyengar, Mark D. Peters, and Donald Kinder, "Experimental Demonstration of the 'Not-So-Minimal' Consequences of Television News Program," *American Political Science Review* 76 (1982): 848–58.

38. Maxwell E. McCombs and Donald L. Shaw, "The Agenda-Setting Function of the Press," in *Media Power in Politics,* ed. Doris Graber (Washington, D.C.: Congressional Quarterly Press, 1984).

39. But cf. Miller and Shanks, *New American Voter.*

40. Martin P. Wattenberg "The Hollow Realignment," paper presented at the annual meeting of the American Political Science Association, New Orleans, 1985, 14.

41. Frank J. Sorauf and Paul Allen Beck, *Party Politics in America,* 6th ed. (Boston: Little, Brown, 1984), 481–95.

42. John F. Bibby, *Politics, Parties, and Elections in America* (Chicago: Nelson-Hall, 1987), 94–116. See also John F. Bibby, "State Party Organizations: Coping and Adapting to Candidate-Centered Politics and Nationalization," in *The Parties Respond,* 3d ed., ed. L. Sandy Maisel (Boulder, Colo.: Westview Press, 1998), 23–49.

43. 450 U.S. 107.

44. Michael Margolis and Raymond E. Owen, "From Organization to Personalism," *Polity* 18 (Winter 1985): 313–28.

45. Joseph A. Schlesinger, "The New American Political Party," *American Political Science Review* 79 (December 1985): 1151–69.

46. John R. Frendreis, James L. Gibson, and Laura Vertz, "Local Party Organization in the 1984 Electorate," paper presented at the annual meeting of the American Political Science Association, New Orleans, 1985.

47. Steven J. Rosenstone and John Mark Hansen, *Mobilization, Participation, and Democracy in America* (New York: Macmillan, 1993). See also Robert Putnam, "Tuning In, Tuning Out," *PS: Political Science and Politics* 28 (December 1995): 664–83.

48. Barbara Sinclair, "The Emergence of Strong Leadership in the 1980s House," *Journal of Politics* 54 (August 1992): 657–84. See also David Rohde, *Parties and Leaders in the Postreform House* (Chicago: University of Chicago Press, 1991); Barbara Sinclair, "House Special Rules and the Institutional Design Controversy," *Legislative Studies Quarterly* 19 (November 1994): 477–94; Barbara Sinclair, *Unorthodox Lawmaking: New Legislative Processes in the U.S. Congress* (Washington, D.C.: Congressional Quarterly Press, 1997).

49. Ronald M. Peters Jr., "The Republican Speakership," *Extensions* (Fall 1995): 14–16.

50. John W. Kingdon, *Agendas, Alternatives, and Public Policies* (Boston: Little, Brown, 1984), 65–71.

51. Charles O. Jones, *An Introduction to the Study of Public Policy,* 3d ed. (Monterey, Calif.: Brooks/Cole, 1984), 115.

52. James A. Stimson, Michael B. MacKuen, and Robert S. Erickson, "Dynamic Representation," *American Political Science Review* 89 (September 1995): 543–65.

53. See, for instance, Benjamin R. Page and Robert Y. Shapiro, *The Rational Public* (Chicago: University of Chicago Press, 1992).

54. Stimson, MacKuen, and Erikson, "Dynamic Representation."

55. For a different analysis of operative values at work shaping elite decision making, see Dennis Coyle and Aaron Wildavsky, "Requisites of Radical Reform," *Journal of Policy Analysis and Management* 7 (Fall 1987): 1–6.

56. James E. Anderson, *Public Policymaking,* 3d ed. (Boston: Houghton Mifflin, 1997), 292–301.

57. Jones, *Introduction to the Study of Public Policy,* 18.

CHAPTER 6 POLICY ANALYSIS AND THE POLITICAL ARENA

1. Theodore J. Lowi, *The End of Liberalism,* 2d ed. (New York: Norton, 1979); Mancur Olson, *The Rise and Decline of Nations* (New Haven, Conn.: Yale University Press, 1982); Samuel P. Huntington, *American Politics* (Cambridge, Mass.: Harvard University Press, 1981).

2. Bert A. Rockman, *The Leadership Question* (New York: Praeger, 1985), 40–41.

3. Charles E. Lindblom, "The Science of 'Muddling Through,'" *Public Administration Review* 19 (Spring 1959): 88.

4. Gloria Borger, "The Land of Lost Opportunity," *U.S. News & World Report*, 22 August 1994, 43. See also Elizabeth Drew, *On the Edge: The Clinton Presidency* (New York: Simon and Schuster, 1994), 305; Robert Pear, "For Mrs. Clinton, Health Plan Left Lessons and Questions," *New York Times*, 21 October 2000, A1.

5. "Gurus in Government," *Economist*, 20 May 1995, 22.

6. Corydon Ireland, "Health Reform: How It Died," *Rochester Democrat and Chronicle*, 2 April 1995, 1B.

7. Paul R. Schulman, "Nonincremental Policy Making: Notes toward an Alternative Paradigm," *American Political Science Review* 69 (December 1975): 1355.

8. Ibid., 1364.

9. Ibid., 1366.

10. Seventy-five-year-old John Glenn's much publicized, and criticized, return to space travel in 1998 seemed to signal a continued effort by NASA to remain in the public eye.

11. "Rogers Commission Recommendations," *Congressional Quarterly Weekly Report* 44 (14 June 1986): 1326.

12. "The Super Collider's Final Crash," *1993 Congressional Quarterly Almanac*, 592.

13. Theodore J. Lowi, *The Personal President* (Ithaca, N.Y.: Cornell University Press, 1985), 25.

14. James L. Sundquist, *The Decline and Resurgence of Congress* (Washington, D.C.: Brookings Institution, 1981), 441.

15. Randall B. Ripley and Grace A. Franklin, *Congress, the Bureaucracy, and Public Policy*, rev. ed. (Homewood, Ill.: Dorsey Press, 1980), 96.

16. Cited in Morris P. Fiorina, *Congress* (New Haven, Conn.: Yale University Press, 1977), 49.

17. Sundquist, *Decline and Resurgence*, 446.

18. Lawrence C. Dodd and Bruce I. Oppenheimer, "The House in Transition: Change and Consolidation," in *Congress Reconsidered*, 2d ed., ed. Lawrence C. Dodd and Bruce I. Oppenheimer (Washington, D.C.: Congressional Quarterly Press, 1981), 41, 44.

19. Ibid., 45–46.

20. Sundquist, *Decline and Resurgence*, 432.

21. Roger H. Davidson, "Two Avenues of Change: House and Senate Committee Reorganization," in *Congress Reconsidered*, 2d ed., ed. Lawrence C. Dodd and Bruce I. Oppenheimer (Washington, D.C.: Congressional Quarterly Press, 1981), 116–17.

22. Everett Carll Ladd, "How to Tame the Special-Interest Groups," *Fortune* (20 October 1980): 66–80.

23. Mark Green, "Political PAC-Man," *New Republic*, 13 December 1982, 24.

24. David Adamany, "Political Parties in the 1980's," in *Money and Politics in the United States*, ed. Michael J. Malbin (Chatham, N.J.: Chatham House, 1984), 102.

25. Ibid., 101.

26. Barbara Sinclair, *Majority Leadership in the House* (Baltimore: Johns Hopkins University Press, 1983), 235.

27. Ibid., 233.

28. David S. Cloud, "GOP, to Its Own Great Delight, Enacts House Rules Changes," *Congressional Quarterly* 53 (7 January 1995): 13–15.

29. Melinda Henneberger, "Tom DeLay Holds No Gavel, but a Firm Grip on the Reins," *New York Times*, 21 June 1999, A1.

30. "House Managers Chafe at Senate's Dictates," *New York Times*, 30 January 1999, A9.

31. Quoted in Dan Carney, "GOP's Case for Rule of Law Came to a Political End," *Congressional Quarterly* 57 (13 February 1999): 375.

32. Edward N. Kearny, "Presidential Nominations and Representative Democracy: Proposal for Change," *Presidential Studies Quarterly* (Summer 1984): 350–51.

33. Herbert Stein, *Presidential Economics* (New York: Simon and Schuster, 1984), 272–73.

34. Robert E. DiClerico, *The American President*, 2d ed. (Englewood Cliffs, N.J.: Prentice Hall, 1983), 111.

35. Ibid., 114.

36. Ibid.

37. Ibid., 115.

38. B. Guy Peters, *American Public Policy*, 2d ed. (Chatham, N.J.: Chatham House, 1986), 125.

39. Richard P. Nathan, *The Administrative Presidency* (New York: Wiley, 1983), 40–41.

40. Ibid., 51–52.

41. Ibid., 74–76.

42. DiClerico, *American President*, 84.

43. Harold Wolman and Fred Teitelbaum, "Interest Groups and the Reagan Presidency," in *The Reagan Presidency and the Governing of America*, ed. Lester M. Salamon and Michael S. Lund (Washington, D.C.: Urban Institute Press, 1984), 307.

44. Dick Kirschten, "If It Needs Fixin'," *National Journal*, 9 July 1983, 1460.

45. Barbara Sinclair, *Unorthodox Lawmaking* (Washington, D.C.: Congressional Quarterly Press, 1997), 217. Sinclair concludes that "unorthodox lawmaking has become standard operating procedure in the U.S. Congress. Not only does the textbook model no longer describe how most major legislation becomes—or fails to become—law, no single model has replaced it."

46. *Washington Post National Weekly Edition*, 23 December 1985, 12.

47. *Bowsher* v. *Synar*, 478 U.S. 714.

48. Colin Campbell and Bert Rockman, eds., *The Bush Presidency: First Appraisals* (Chatham, N.J.: Chatham House, 1991), 174–80.

CHAPTER 7   POLICY DEVOLUTION AND POLICY ANALYSIS

1. William D. Eggers and John O'Leary, *Revolution at the Roots* (New York: Free Press, 1995), 320, 322.

2. William H. Young, *Ogg and Ray's Introduction to American Government*, 13th ed. (New York: Appleton-Century-Crofts, 1966), 65, quoted in Michael D. Reagan, *The New Federalism* (New York: Oxford University Press, 1972), 16.

3. Robert S. McNamara, *In Retrospect: Tragedy and Lessons of Vietnam* (New York: Times Books, 1995); see also Robert S. McNamara, James G. Blight, and Robert K. Brigham, *Argument without End: In Search of Answers to the Vietnam Tragedy* (New York: Public Affairs, 1999).

4. See John Kenneth White, *Still Seeing Red: How the Cold War Shapes the New American Politics* (Boulder, Colo.: Westview Press, 1998), 315–29.

5. William K. Stevens, "Governors Emerging as a New Political Elite," *New York Times*, 22 March 1988, A16.

6. Quoted in Richard L. Berke, "Florida Poll Gives Hope to Several Candidates," *New York Times*, 20 November 1995, B9.

7. John W. Kingdon, *Agendas, Alternatives, and Public Policies*, 2d ed. (New York: HarperCollins, 1995); David M. Ricci, *The Transformation of American Politics* (New Haven, Conn.: Yale University Press, 1993).

8. Jeffrey M. Berry, *The New Liberalism: The Rising Power of Citizen Groups* (Washington, D.C.: Brookings Institution Press, 1999), 56–57, 70.

9. 505 U.S. 833.

10. 410 U.S. 113.

11. 505 U.S. 144.

12. 514 U.S. 549.

13. 144 L.Ed.2d 636.

14. Norman J. Ornstein and Amy L. Schenkenberg, "The 1995 Congress: The First Hundred Days and Beyond," *Political Science Quarterly* 110 (Summer 1995): 184.

15. Walter Dean Burnham, "Realignment Lives: The 1994 Earthquake and Its Implications" in *The Clinton Presidency,* ed. Colin Campbell and Bert A. Rockman (Chatham, N.J.: Chatham House, 1996), 363.

16. Katharine Q. Seelye, "Democrats Fleeing to G.O.P. Remake Political Landscape," *New York Times,* 7 October 1995, A1.

17. Burnham, "Realignment," 383.

18. Noted in Ornstein and Schenkenberg, "1995 Congress," 185.

19. Quoted in R.W. Apple Jr., "A Blow for Democrats," *New York Times,* 17 August 1995, B10.

20. Ornstein and Schenkenberg, "1995 Congress," 189.

21. Ed Gillespie and Bob Schellhas, eds., *Contract with America* (New York: Random House, 1994).

22. John J. DiIulio Jr. and Donald F. Kettl, *Fine Print* (Washington, D.C.: Brookings Institution, 1995).

23. Reflecting the recent emergence of their impact on the policy process, Kingdon makes little mention of think tanks. Presumably he would include them within the policy communities that he so ably discusses in chapter 6. This discussion is remarkable, however, for its heavy focus on governmental sources of ideas. See Kingdon, *Agendas,* 116–44.

24. For a reasonably balanced view of the influence and activities of think tanks, see Berry, *New Liberalism,* 137–142.

25. Ricci, *Transformation,* 21.

26. Lewis M. Andrews, "These Think Tanks Think Small," *Christian Science Monitor,* 27 June 1995; Joyce Price, "Conservative Think Tanks Gain in Number, Respect Nationwide," *Washington Times,* 2 February 1995.

27. David Callahan, "State Think Tanks on the Move," *Nation,* 12 October 1998, 15, 17–19.

28. Ibid.

29. Matthew Cooper, "Run DLC," *New Republic,* 4 December 1995, 10.

30. Tamar Lewin, "Liberal Urging Has Given Way to Eerie Hush," *New York Times,* 24 November 1995, B20.

31. The typology offered here meshes closely with that of Winand Gellner, "The Politics of Policy 'Political Think Tanks' and Their Markets in the U.S.-Institutional Environment," *Presidential Studies Quarterly* 25 (Summer 1995): 499–500. See also the classifications suggested by R. Kent Weaver, "The Changing World of Think Tanks," *PS: Political Science and Politics* 22 (September 1989): 563.

32. James A. Smith, *The Idea Brokers* (New York: Free Press, 1991), 153.

33. Sanford F. Schram, *Words of Welfare* (Minneapolis: University of Minnesota Press, 1995), xxvii–xxviii.

34. Susan George and Fabrizio Sabelli, *Faith and Credit* (Boulder, Colo.: Westview Press, 1994), 197.

35. Ken Miller, "Study: Poisons Imperil Millions," *Rochester Democrat and Chronicle,* 16 August 1995, 4A.

36. Dirk Johnson, "Weed Killers in Tap Water in Corn Belt," *New York Times,* 18 August 1995, A10.
37. Stephen J. Breyer, *Breaking the Vicious Circle* (Cambridge, Mass.: Harvard University Press, 1993), 50.
38. Berry, *New Liberalism,* 138.
39. Barry Glassner, *The Culture of Fear* (New York: Basic Books, 1999), xxiii.
40. The following are some representative examples of Michael Fumento at work: "A Church Arson Epidemic? It's Smoke and Mirrors," *Wall Street Journal* 8 July 1996, A8; "'Road Rage' versus Reality," *Atlantic Monthly,* August 1998, 12–17; "A Silicone Meltdown," *Investor's Business Daily,* 17 December 1998, A20; "How Media Made Parkinson's a 'Man-Made' Disease," *Investor's Business Daily,* 17 February 1999, A24.
41. John Stossel, "Overcoming Junk Science," *Wall Street Journal,* 9 January 1997, A12.
42. Glassner, *Culture of Fear,* xviii.
43. In a creative response to the public's increasingly cynical view of media exposés, President Clinton and Vice President Albert Gore attempted to enlist the nation's weather forecasters in their efforts to arouse concern about the dangers of global warming. In October 1997, they invited more than one hundred forecasters from eighty of the largest television markets to the White House to tell them of their concern about the issue. The president and vice president understood very well that Americans may take their nightly news with a grain of salt, but few expect their weather reports to be advancing public policy agendas.
44. Ricci, *Transformation,* 196.
45. Berry, *New Liberalism,* 133–134.
46. For example, see Kingdon, *Agendas,* 56.
47. Peter Huber, *Galileo's Revenge* (New York: Basic Books, 1991); Walter Olson, *The Litigation Explosion* (New York: Dutton, 1991); Elizabeth McCaughey, "No Exit," *New Republic,* 7 February 1994, 21–25.
48. Gellner, "Politics of Policy Think Tanks," 501–2.
49. Weaver, "Changing World," 566, notes the dilemma posed by academics' attachment to lengthy, detailed research and think tanks' need to provide analyses brief enough that policymakers will read them.
50. Charles Murray, *Losing Ground* (New York: Basic Books, 1984).
51. George Hager, "Bush Shops for Advice at Calif. Think Tank," *Washington Post,* 8 June 1999.
52. Karen W. Arenson, "Legislation Would Expand Restrictions on Political Advocacy by Charities," *New York Times,* 7 August 1995, A10.
53. Ricci, *Transformation,* 235.
54. Ibid., 196.
55. Smith, *Idea Brokers,* 239.

CHAPTER 8 POLICY ANALYSIS IN THE JUDICIAL PROCESS

1. Serge Taylor, *Making Bureaucracies Think* (Stanford, Calif.: Stanford University Press, 1984), 239.
2. Ibid., 317.
3. Quoted in Edward McNall Burns, *Ideas in Conflict* (New York: Norton, 1960), 129.
4. Roscoe Pound, *An Introduction to the Philosophy of Law* (New Haven, Conn.: Yale University Press, 1922), 99. See also Roscoe Pound, *Interpretations of Legal History* (New York: Macmillan, 1923), 152–59.
5. G. Edward White, *Tort Law in America* (New York: Oxford University Press, 1980), 73.

6. Ibid., 63.

7. Bruce A. Ackerman, *Reconstructing American Law* (Cambridge, Mass.: Harvard University Press, 1984), 5, 39–41.

8. 347 U.S. 483.

9. Ibid., at 49.

10. 349 U.S. 294 (1955).

11. Charles A. Reich, "The New Property," *Yale Law Journal* 73 (April 1964): 771.

12. Ibid., 765.

13. Ibid., 784.

14. 397 U.S. 254.

15. Karen Orren, "Standing to Sue: Interest Group Conflict in the Federal Courts," *American Political Science Review* 70 (September 1976): 723–41.

16. Philip J. Cooper, *Hard Judicial Choices* (New York: Oxford University Press, 1988), 330–31. Based on his study of judicial intervention in social problems, Cooper argues that groups often become involved in judicial suits as the result of specific conditions that "trigger" a reaction rather than as the result of strategic planning.

17. *McCleskey* v. *Kemp*, 481 U.S. 279 (1987).

18. *Kumho Tire Company* v. *Carmichael*, 143 L.Ed. 2d 238 (1999).

19. 391 U.S. 430.

20. Bernard Schwartz, *Swann's Way* (New York: Oxford University Press, 1986), 61.

21. This discussion draws heavily on Schwartz, ibid.

22. 402 U.S. 1.

23. J. Anthony Lukas, *Common Ground* (New York: Knopf, 1985), 231–51. See also George R. Metcalf, *From Little Rock to Boston* (Westport, Conn.: Greenwood Press, 1983), 197–220.

24. 379 F. Supp. 410 (1974).

25. Lukas, *Common Ground*, 250.

26. Thomas R. Dye, *Understanding Public Policy*, 6th ed. (Englewood Cliffs, N.J.: Prentice Hall, 1987), 14. Dye notes that of the 57,000 students still in Boston's public schools when Judge Garrity removed himself from the case in 1985, 27 percent were white.

27. Tinsley E. Yarbrough, *Judge Frank Johnson and Human Rights in Alabama* (University, Ala.: University of Alabama, 1981). In his editorial eulogy upon Judge Johnson's death, Howell Raines notes that at one time Johnson was called "the real governor of Alabama"; see "Judge Johnson Goes Home to the Hills," *New York Times*, 26 July 1999, A18.

28. 325 F. Supp. 781 (1971).

29. For a discussion of the legal and scholarly sources that supported Judge Johnson's opinion, see Cooper, *Hard Judicial Choices*, 140–43, 174–75, 329.

30. James's efforts, however, fell short, and in 1983, Wallace again became governor, leading to another round of negotiations. See ibid., 198–200.

31. Robert A. Burt, "*Pennhurst*: A Parable," in *In the Interest of Children*, ed. Robert H. Mnookin (New York: Freeman, 1985), 350.

32. Material on Willowbrook is based on Mary Sue Rose, "Implementation of the Pennhurst Decision" (1984) and Maureen A. Lindberg, "The Willowbrook Consent Decree" (1984), Alfred University Graduate School, Alfred, N.Y.

33. Celia W. Dugger, "Big Day for Ex-Residents of Center for the Retarded," *New York Times*, 12 March 1993, A1, B3.

34. Burt, "*Pennhurst*," 272.

35. Yarbrough, *Judge Frank Johnson*, 72.

36. Donald L. Horowitz, *The Courts and Social Policy* (Washington, D.C.: Brookings Institution, 1977); Gerald N. Rosenberg, *The Hollow Hope* (Chicago: University of Chicago Press, 1991).

37. Cooper, *Hard Judicial Choices,* 334.
38. Horowitz, *Courts and Social Policy,* 33–56, 264, 273.
39. Yarbrough, *Judge Frank Johnson,* 208.
40. Burt, *"Pennhurst,"* 273.
41. Taylor, *Making Bureaucracies,* 203.
42. Ibid., 241.
43. Ackerman, *Reconstructing,* 35.
44. *Clinton* v. *City of New York,* 141 L. Ed. 2d 393 (1998).
45. *Department of Commerce* v. *House of Representatives,* 142 L.Ed. 2d 797 (1999). Here, the Court did not reach a constitutional issue, relying instead on a strict construction of the Census Act.
46. *U.S. Term Limits, Inc.* v. *Thornton,* 519 U.S. 779 (1995).
47. Several decisions indicate a consistent pattern in the Court's reorientation of the federal system. These include *New York* v. *U.S.,* 505 U.S. 144 (1992); *Seminole Tribe of Florida* v. *Florida,* 517 U.S. 44 (1996); *Alden* v. *Maine,* 144 L.Ed. 2d 636 (1999); *College Savings Bank* v. *Florida Prepaid Postsecondary Education Expense Board,* 144 L.Ed. 2d 605 (1999); and *Florida Prepaid Postsecondary Education Expense Board* v. *College Savings Bank,* 144 L. Ed. 2d 575 (1999). The last three decisions were handed down on the same day, 23 June 1999.
48. R. Shep Melnick, *Between the Lines* (Washington, D.C.: Brookings Institution, 1994), 40.
49. Ibid., 237.
50. Tony Mauro, "Court's Inaction Allows Confusion," *USA Today,* 23 December 1998, 2A.
51. Rosenberg, *Hollow Hope,* 280, argues that this lack of expertise causes the courts to give heightened deference to agency decisions.
52. Taylor, *Making Bureaucracies,* 193.
53. Important sources for this case study are Robert V. Bartlett, *The Reserve Mining Controversy* (Bloomington: Indiana University Press, 1980); and Frank D. Schaumburg, *Judgment Reserved* (Reston, Va.: Reston Publishing, 1976). Bartlett notes that Schaumburg's book was supported by a public relations firm representing Reserve Mining; see *Reserve Mining,* 225–26.
54. Quoted in Schaumburg, *Judgment,* 241–42.
55. *New York Times,* 5 May 1977, 35; 29 October 1977, 16.
56. Quoted in Jason Zengerle, "Water over the Dam," *New Republic,* 24 November 1997, 21.
57. Ibid., 20.
58. For two differing views on this issue, see ibid., 20-22, and Bruce Barcott, "Beyond the Valley of the Dammed," *Utne Reader* (June 1999), 51–57.
59. Taylor, *Making Bureaucracies,* 187, 193, 232, 236. Focus on proper procedure was to characterize the Burger Court's treatment of agencies generally. See Alan B. Morrison, "Close Reins on the Bureaucracy: Overseeing the Administrative Agencies," in *The Burger Years,* ed. Herman Schwartz (New York: Penguin, 1988), 198–99.
60. William W. Lowrance, *Modern Science and Human Values* (New York: Oxford University Press, 1985), 137.
61. Hugh Heclo, "Issue Networks and the Executive Establishment," in *The New American Political System,* ed. Anthony King (Washington, D.C.: American Enterprise Institute, 1978), 118–21, 124.
62. Lowrance, *Modern Science,* 120.
63. Ackerman, *Reconstructing,* 74.
64. Taylor, *Making Bureaucracies,* 235.
65. Rosenberg, *Hollow Hope,* 338–43.

66. Melnick, *Between the Lines,* 236–237. Melnick stresses the importance of litigation in lower federal courts in conjunction with the use of coalitions among groups and congressmen to achieve change. More recently, the tobacco industry has experienced the effects of coalitions of state attorneys general and other groups utilizing the courts.
67. Cooper, *Hard Judicial Choices,* 350.
68. Guido Calabresi, *A Common Law for the Age of Statutes* (Cambridge, Mass.: Harvard University Press, 1982), 172–73.
69. Bartlett, *Reserve Mining,* 212.
70. 410 U.S. 113.
71. 462 U.S. 416, at 452, 458.
72. 505 U.S. 833.
73. For a good study of the problems attendant on the implementation of deinstitutionalization of the mentally ill, see Steven M. Gillon, *"That's Not What We Meant to Do"* (New York: Norton, 2000).
74. Burt, *Pennhurst,* 350.
75. Rosenberg concludes that with regard to reform movements in particular, this expectation is seriously misplaced. See Rosenberg, *Hollow Hope,* 342–43.

CONCLUSION

1. Robert E. DiClerico and Eric Uslaner, *Few Are Chosen: Problems in Presidential Selection* (New York: McGraw-Hill, 1984), 194.
2. James MacGregor Burns, *The Power to Lead: The Crisis of the American Presidency* (New York: Simon and Schuster, 1984), 198.
3. Ibid.
4. William D. Coplin and Michael K. O'Leary, *Everyman's Prince: A Guide to Understanding Your Political Problems,* rev. ed. (North Scituate, Mass.: Duxbury Press, 1976).
5. Peter J. May, "Politics and Policy Analysis," *Political Science Quarterly* 101 (Spring 1986): 114, 122–25.
6. Charles E. Lindblom, *The Policy-Making Process,* 2d ed. (Englewood Cliffs, N.J.: Prentice Hall, 1980), 28–32, 48.
7. Charles Anderson, "Political Philosophy, Practical Reason, and Policy Analysis," paper presented at the annual meeting of the American Political Science Association, Washington, D.C., 1984, 10.
8. John Dewey, *The Public and Its Problems* (Chicago: Swallow Press, 1946), 27.
9. The approach suggested here is similar to that of Julius Kovesi, *Moral Notions* (New York: Humanities Press, 1967).
10. Anderson, "Political Philosophy," 15.
11. Ibid.

Index